ALSO BY HEALTH FOR LIFE

Amino Acids and Other Ergogenic Aids

Explosive Power — *Plyometrics for Bodybuilders, Martial Artists & Other Athletes*

Fast on Your Feet — *Building Athletic Footspeed and Agility*

The Health For Life Training Advisor

The Human Fuel Cookbook — *Recipes for Peak Athletic Performance*

The Human Fuel Handbook — *Nutrition for Peak Athletic Performance*

Legendary Abs Gold Edition — *6-Minute Synergistic Program for Abdominal Development*

Maximum Calves

Max O_2 — *The Complete Guide to Synergistic Aerobic Training*

Mind Gains — *A Synergistic Mental Focus Program for Peak Physical Performance*

Minimizing Reflex and Reaction Time

Power Forearms!

The 7-Minute Rotator Cuff Solution — *A Complete Program to Prevent & Rehabilitate Rotator Cuff Injuries*

Secrets of Advanced Bodybuilders

Secrets Supplement #1

Secrets Update

SynerShape — *A Scientific Weight-Loss Guide*

SynerStretch — *For Total-Body Flexibility*

T.N.T. — *Total Neck & Traps*

Transfigure I — *9 Minutes to the Ultimate Buttocks and Thighs*

Transfigure II — *For the Ultimate Upper Body*

The Weightless Workout — *For the Ultimate High-Intensity Bodyweight Workout Anywhere!*

ISBN 0-944831-41-9

Library of Congress Catalog Card Number: 97-078124

HEALTH FOR LIFE

8033 Sunset Blvd., Suite 483–Los Angeles, CA 90046–5622 (800) 874-5339

1 2 3 4 5 6 7 8 9

THE BACK RELIEF BOOK

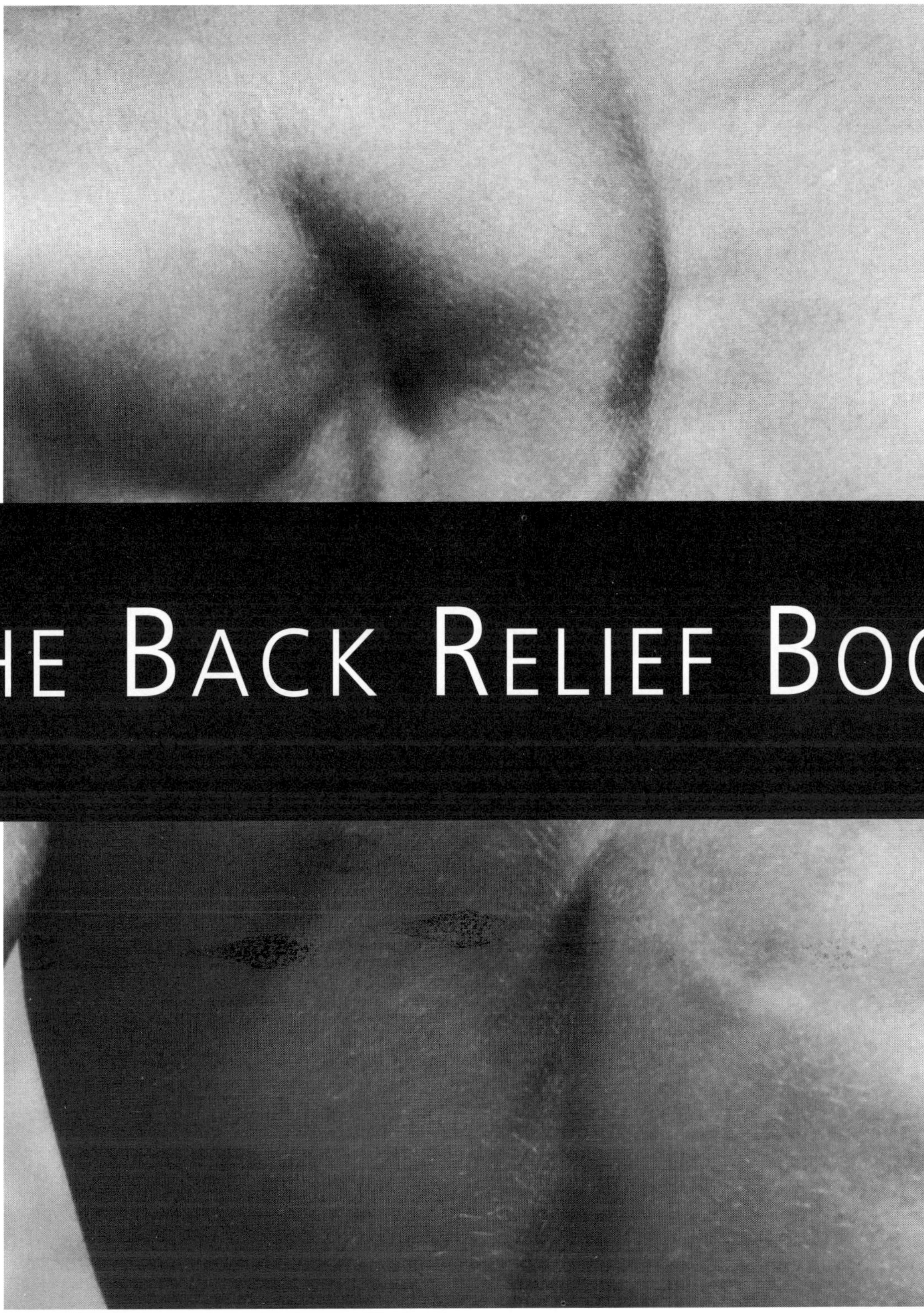

SYNERGISTIC TRAINING SERIES

THE BACK RELIEF BOOK

BY BEN WEITZ, D.C., C.C.S.P.

A SYNERGISTIC WORKOUT FOR THE PREVENTION AND RELIEF OF LOW BACK PAIN

HFL
HEALTH FOR LIFE

CREDITS AND ACKNOWLEDGMENTS

PROJECT EDITOR
Robert Miller

EDITED BY RICK RHOADS & ASSOCIATES
Lynne Kostman
Rick Rhoads

TECHNICAL ADVISORS
Jerry Robinson
Mark Hoffman

BOOK DESIGN
Jerry Graves Design

ILLUSTRATIONS
John Quinn III
Maritta Tapanainen

PHOTOGRAPHY
Ken Chen

PRODUCTION
Maritta Tapanainen

Thanks to Eliza Lewin and Ruth Silverman for additional production support.

WARNING

THIS PROGRAM CONTAINS EXERCISES THAT, DEPENDING ON YOUR PHYSICAL CONDITION, MAY BE HAZARDOUS TO YOUR HEALTH. CONSULT WITH YOUR DOCTOR BEFORE ATTEMPTING THESE EXERCISES. IT IS ALSO IMPORTANT THAT YOU USE CARE IN PERFORMING THE EXERCISES IN THIS BOOK, SINCE IMPROPER PERFORMANCE COULD RESULT IN INJURY. USER ASSUMES ALL RISK FOR PERFORMING THE EXERCISES DESCRIBED IN THIS COURSE. USE OF THIS COURSE CONSTITUTES A COVENANT NOT TO BRING ANY LAWSUIT OR ACTION FOR INJURY CAUSED BY PERFORMING EXERCISES ILLUSTRATED IN THIS COURSE.

This book is dedicated to my wife Karen and my daughter Madison, for putting up with my spending endless hours reading articles and working at the computer. I also want to give special thanks to my friend Paul Chek, whose seminars and videotapes on abdominal and back training provided me with new insights on the topic. Seminars by Stuart McGill, Vladimir Janda, Robin McKenzie, Gary Jacobs, Craig Liebenson and Jerry Hyman were also very helpful and inspirational. Thanks also go to Ms. Nehmat Saab, the librarian at LACC.

Contents

CONTENTS

Introduction

Back pain is often shrouded in mystery. Doctors frequently can't diagnose it. It can appear out of nowhere following an activity as innocent as tying your shoe. Often it disappears completely, only to return when you least expect it. But there is a scientific solution to this mystery, a way to catch the culprit and to relieve your pain. It lies in getting to know how your back functions and putting that knowledge to work in the synergistic exercise program described in this book.

INTRODUCTION

If you've ever experienced low back pain, you know how suddenly it can strike and how mysterious and puzzling it is. Perhaps you can identify with one of the following scenarios:

- *Steve is a freelance photographer, but if you ask him what he does, he'll tell you he's a triathlete. Steve lives to train and spends every available minute at the gym. He does sit-ups, crunches, and leg raises to strengthen his stomach for at least 15 minutes every day. One afternoon while doing overhead presses, Steve feels a brief twinge of pain in his low back. The next day during a run he feels his back go into severe spasms and finds that he can barely move. Steve hobbles home in pain, surprised and upset that this could have happened to someone with his level of physical conditioning. How could someone with Steve's level of conditioning have injured his back?*

- *Sara has been loading bags of mail into a truck nearly all day for several months. One day she picks up a bag, and as she twists to stand up, her back goes into spasm, and she finds herself frozen with severe pain. The doctor prescribes muscle relaxants, pain relievers, and bed rest. After a month Sara feels fine and returns to work. Several months later her back goes out again. Why did Sara experience a recurrence of her back pain when she seemed to have recovered?*

- *Barbara plays competitive tennis three times a week and walks on her treadmill for an hour five times a week. She also does sit-ups and light weight lifting three times a week. Barbara, who skis in the winter and plays volleyball in the summer, feels that she is in great shape; but one day when she twists and reaches for a volley in tennis, her back gives out. She applies ice, takes an over-the-counter pain medication, and rests. After a few weeks, her back seems fine, and she returns to her exercise regimen. About a year later Barbara's back goes out again, and the same pattern occurs six months later. Barbara's problem can't be related to lack of exercise. How can she prevent another recurrence?*

- *David sits in his favorite chair, glued to the big game for several hours. Afterward he has a little difficulty getting up but manages to make his way to bed. The next morning David experiences intense pain when he tries to get up. His doctor prescribes pain relievers, anti–inflammatory medication, and physical therapy. With this regimen, David feels better for part of each day, but by nighttime the pain has returned, and the next morning he is stiff as a board. What does David need to do to break this cycle?*

Steve, Sara, Barbara, and David are unlikely to find a solution for the mystery of their back pain by following a conventional treatment program. And, perplexing as their cases are, they are not the least bit unusual.

In modern industrialized societies like our own, back pain has reached epidemic proportions. This modern plague will affect more than 80% of us during our lifetimes. More money is spent in an often fruitless search for relief from back pain than on any other musculoskeletal disorder (with the lion's share going to often unsuccessful surgeries).

Low back pain is the leading cause of disability among those 45 and under and therefore poses a serious threat to our economy. It can turn activities as simple and pleasurable as taking a walk, lifting a child, or making love into sheer agony. Worse yet, back pain tends to be cyclical. Its initial onset is more often than not a prelude to one recurrence after another, a vicious roller coaster ride that can erode the quality of your life.

Given the widespread nature of back disorders and their serious consequences—personal and societal—why hasn't modern medicine produced a cure? Much remains unknown about the workings of the back, but one thing we *have* discovered over the past 20 years is that the approaches used by doctors have proven largely ineffective. These include prolonged bed rest, pills to relieve pain and relax muscles, and some surgical approaches (for example, lumbar fusions). Multiple surgeries in particular have in most cases proven a dismal failure.

Part of the inability of modern medicine to produce a cure lies in the fact that the pills, the surgeries, and the bed rest are aimed at alleviating your symptoms rather than addressing the factors that cause them—in particular, our sedentary lifestyle. Think about the daily routine of many of us: we sit in the car while we drive to work, sit at a desk for eight hours or more, sit in the car again on the way home, sit down to dinner, and wind up the day with a few hours sitting in front of the television. Even if you substitute one or two hours of working out for the television, you're still sitting about three-fourths of the time you're awake.

This prolonged sitting and the muscular deconditioning that develops as a consequence contribute to low back disorders. Tight hamstrings and hip flexors coupled with weak abdominal and back muscles render the low back vulnerable to injury. Given this combination of factors, back injury and reinjury are virtually inevitable. Random bouts of exertion or exercise, or even a regular regimen of exercise not based on an understanding of the workings of the low back, often cause further injury. That's the bad news.

The good news is that you can break the cycle of low back pain or prevent it from occurring in the first place. The key lies in taking a synergistic, or wholistic, approach to the prevention and rehabilitation of back injuries.

Research shows that doing the following is essential to a healthy back:

- Strengthen the back muscles
- Increase the size of the back muscles
- Increase the endurance of the back muscles
- Increase the density and strength of the vertebrae
- Strengthen the abdominal and other trunk muscles
- Improve aerobic capacity
- Improve overall fitness
- Improve the flexibility of the hip muscles
- Improve balance and coordination

A healthy back is not the result of conditioning a few isolated back muscles, but of a complex interaction. The program described in *The Back Relief Book* is based on the most up-to-date biomechanical research, and it incorporates exercises addressed to each of the above goals. More important, it combines these exercises in a sequence that is synergistic—one designed to maximize the effectiveness of each exercise to create a whole that is greater than the individual parts. This synergistic approach makes this program a revolutionary means of achieving and maintaining a healthy low back.

The program is also unique in its recognition that all backs are not created equal. Steve the triathlete, Sara the postal worker, Barbara the amateur athlete, and David the sports enthusiast all suffer from low back pain, but they are unique individuals with different abilities, lifestyles, and levels of fitness. The Back Relief Program is designed so that you can select the routine that meets your needs. Whether you need rehabilitation for an injury, relief from chronic low back pain, or you just want to ensure a healthy back, you'll find a routine that's right for you, one that takes into account your level of conditioning and the history of your back.

The first few chapters of this book describe the low back, how it works, and disorders common to it. The back is a complex system of nerves, bone, ligaments, and muscles. We've tried to keep the technical discussions as clear and simple as possible without sacrificing important details. Numerous illustrations help clarify the text.

Each exercise in the program is illustrated and discussed at length, followed by exercise routines for each lifestyle and level of fitness. A bibliography suggests additional sources of information.

Despite the alarming statistics and the threats that our vulnerable backs are exposed to on a daily basis, there is hope. Whether you spend your days in the gym or chained to your desk, the information and the exercise programs in *The Back Relief Book* will help you attain a healthier back and an increased overall level of fitness.

INTRODUCTION

Your Lower Back

How would you design a spinal column to handle the stresses and strains placed on it every day? Think about it. The spine must be *strong* enough to support your body in activities as diverse as walking or bending to lift a heavy weight. At the same time, it must be *flexible* enough to permit maneuvers as complicated as the twisting and arching of a pole vault. It must provide *protection* for the body's main nerve conduit, while allowing nerve signals to enter and exit all along its length. As a feat of engineering, the human spine makes just about everything, from the Roman aqueducts to the space shuttle, seem simple by comparison.

1

YOUR LOWER BACK

Our spinal column's miraculous design is achieved by a series of strong, interlocking bones wrapped with ligaments and muscles that facilitate both *motion* and dynamic *stability.* But this incredibly complex structure—as versatile as it is—leaves your spine vulnerable to injury. If it's not strong enough, your spine will fracture under too great a load. If it's too flexible, it won't be able to resist the stressful forces imposed on it in the course of your everyday activities. In addition, any number of factors can result in painful pressure on your spinal nerves or the spinal cord itself.

Your spine is an accident waiting to happen. If you have recently suffered a back injury or experience chronic back pain, you know you need a way to restore your back to health. If you are lucky enough to enjoy a healthy, pain-free back, now is the time to take measures to ensure you have it for life. Either way, this program is for you.

As you read on, you will learn more about your back's components and how they work together. You'll learn why increasing your muscular conditioning and building stronger bones—two of the most important goals of this program—are keys to attaining and safeguarding a healthy back for life. You'll be able to visualize the bones, ligaments, and muscles working together in each exercise you perform, helping you to build a strong and pain-free low back.

A Few Key Terms

Before we launch into a discussion of the spinal cord, we're going to present a few key terms that will be used throughout this book to describe the motions of the low back and some of the forces, or stresses, that act upon it.

LOW BACK MOVEMENTS

Your low back can move in many directions, but most movements can be expressed using four terms: **flexion**, **extension**, **lateral flexion**, and **rotation.** *Flexion* means bending forward (Fig. 1–1); *extension,* bending backward (Fig. 1–2); *lateral flexion,* bending to the side (Fig. 1–3); and *rotation,* turning around the axis of the spine (Fig. 1–4). The term **hyperextension** is used to refer to backward bending beyond the normal range (Fig. 1–5). Motion in each of these directions exerts its own unique type of force on your spine.

Fig. 1–1 Flexion

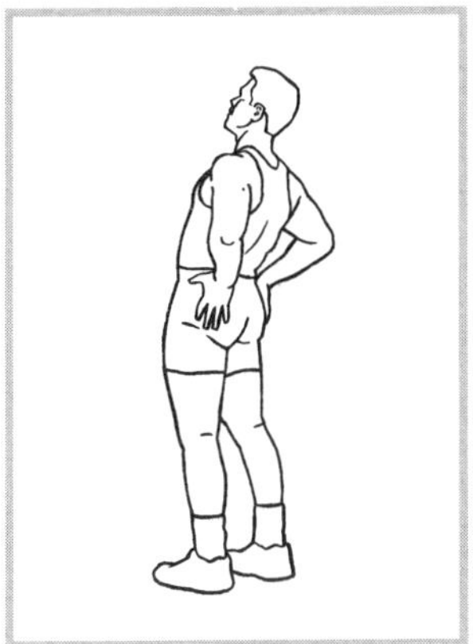

Fig. 1–2 Extension

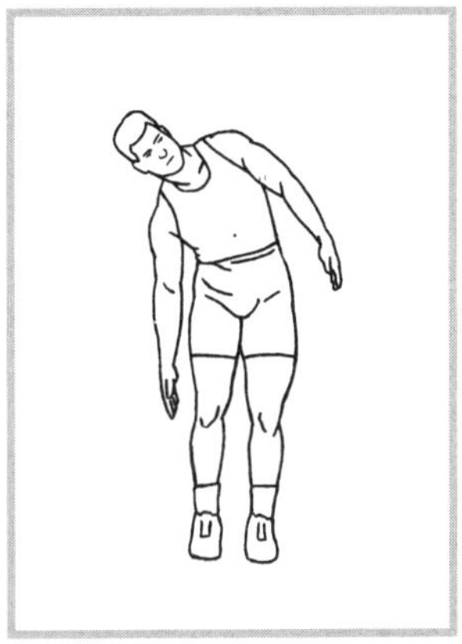

Fig. 1–3 Lateral Flexion

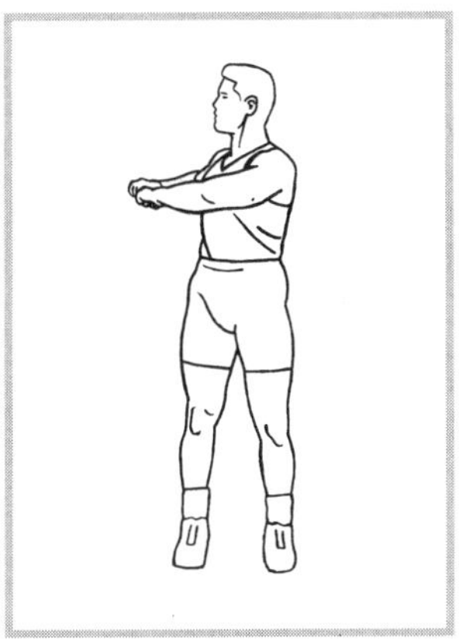

Fig. 1–4 Rotation

Fig. 1–5 Hyperextension

LOW BACK STRESSES

Two kinds of forces act on your spine: **shear loading**, also known as **shear stress**, and **compressive loading**. *Shear loading* occurs when a stress causes one of your vertebrae (the individual bones of the spine) to slide forward or backward on the one below it. This typically happens when you bend over or lift a heavy weight (Fig. 1–6). *Compressive loading* refers to pressure placed on your vertebrae and the discs between them; this force pushes your discs and vertebrae together. Just standing places a compressive load on your spine, as does lifting or holding heavy weights (Fig. 1–7).

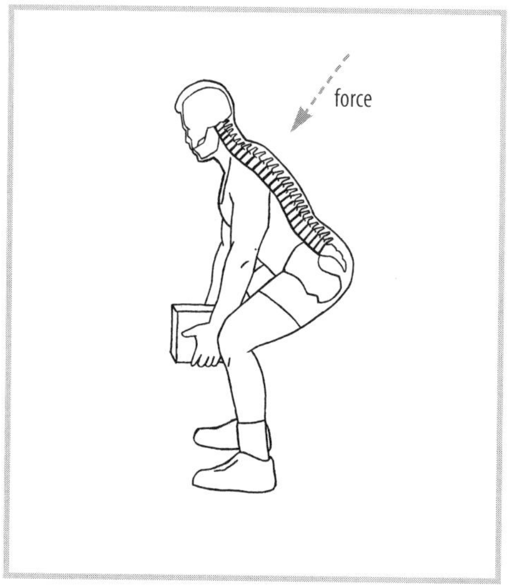

Fig. 1–6 Shear Loading

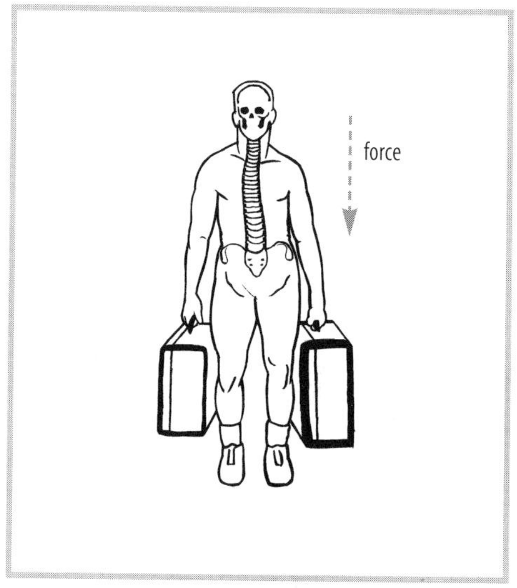

Fig. 1–7 Compressive Loading

Keeping these terms in mind will help you to better grasp the discussions that follow. Being familiar with them will also help in implementing the exercise routines in Chapter 6.

Now it's time to say hello to your back—the spinal cord, joint structure, intervertebral discs, ligaments, and muscles and fascia. As we've said, the back is a complex structure. We've used numerous illustrations, so you will be able to see exactly how each part of the back contributes to its overall structure and function. We've divided each of our main headings into three categories: *Description*, *Function*, and *Most Important Points.* There's no need to memorize this information, but visualizing what goes on when you bend, lift, stand, sit, or twist is the first step toward attaining a healthy back for life.

The Spinal Cord

Description

The **spinal cord** is an extension of your brain. It is the central nerve that runs through your body from your head down to your tailbone (Fig. 1–8a). Located inside a tunnel called the **spinal canal**, it is protected by bony vertebrae that surround it like beads on a string (Fig. 1–8b). Smaller nerves branch off the spinal cord and exit through openings between vertebrae (Fig. 1–8c).

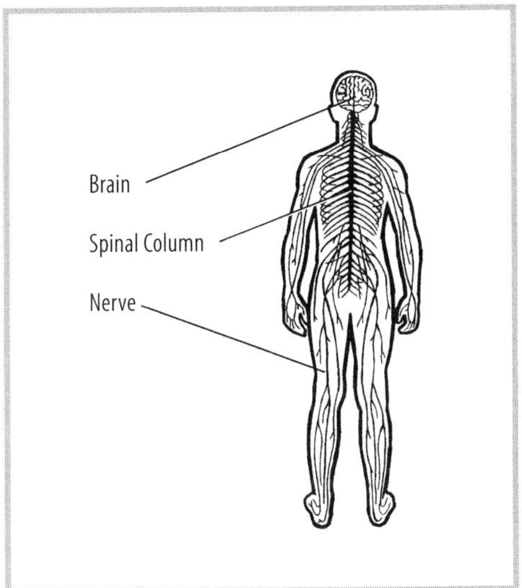

Fig. 1-8a

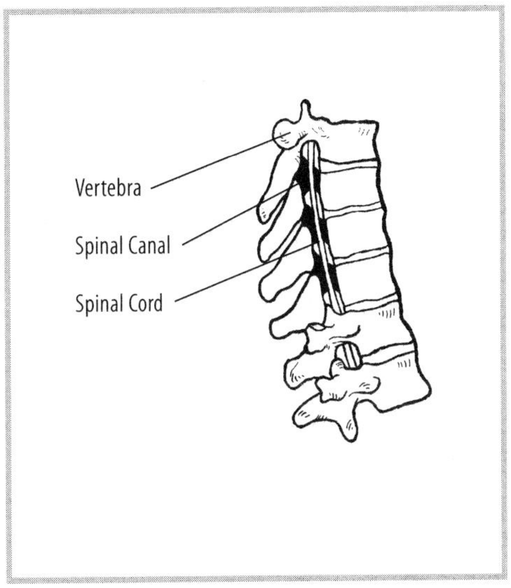

Fig. 1-8b

Function

The brain can be thought of as the command center of your body's communications network. It supplies the information needed to accomplish nearly all of your bodily functions. The spinal cord is the main line coming off this command center. The smaller spinal nerves that branch off the spinal cord are the secondary lines that communicate to the muscles and other organs of your body. Damage to the spinal cord can result in a communications shutdown—paralysis.

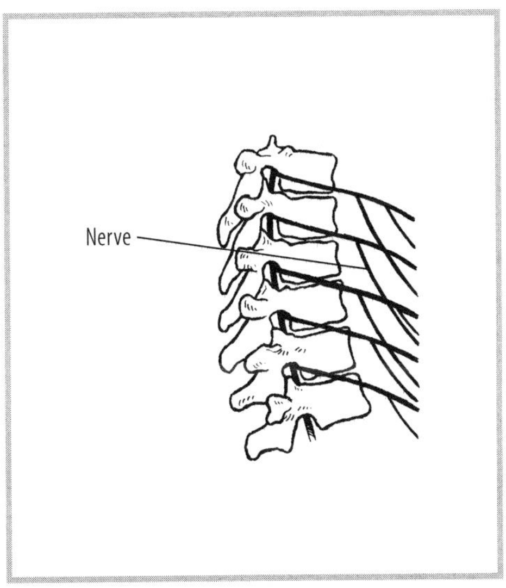

Fig. 1-8c

Most Important Points

Your spinal nerves are vulnerable to compression as they exit between the vertebrae, and pressure on these nerves in the low back can cause back pain that shoots down the leg. It can also produce tingling and numbness in the leg and foot, loss of strength, and sometimes bowel and bladder problems. Compression of the nerves can take many forms (Chapter 3 will discuss back pain and injuries in detail); it is often, however, caused by one of the fibrous cushions, or **discs**, situated between vertebrae, slipping out of its proper position. This condition is called a **bulging** or **herniated disc**. Certain exercises in the Back Relief Program are aimed specifically at keeping your discs healthy and in their proper position so that this kind of nerve root compression does not occur, or can gradually be relieved.

Joint Structure

LUMBAR VERTEBRAE

Description

Your spine, or vertebral column, has five different segments (Fig. 1-9). Moving from your head downward, the segments are…

- the **cervical spine** (neck) containing seven vertebrae
- the **thoracic spine** (midback) with twelve vertebrae
- the **lumbar spine** (low back) with five vertebrae
- the **sacrum** with five fused vertebrae
- the **coccyx** (tailbone) with four fused vertebrae.

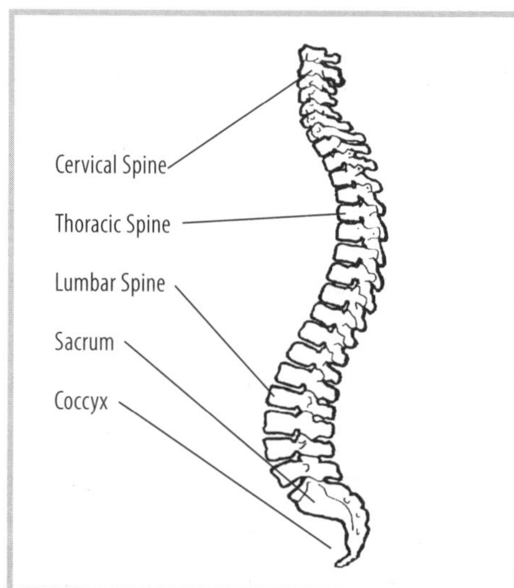

Fig. 1-9

The five vertebrae in your low back (Fig. 1–10) are traditionally numbered from the top down, with the topmost referred to as L1 (the first lumbar vertebra), and the bottommost as L5 (the fifth lumbar vertebra). This system is commonly used for the neck, or cervical, vertebrae (C1–C7) and the mid-back, or thoracic, vertebrae (T1–T12) as well. Although the five vertebrae in the sacrum are fused, the first of these is often referred to as S1.

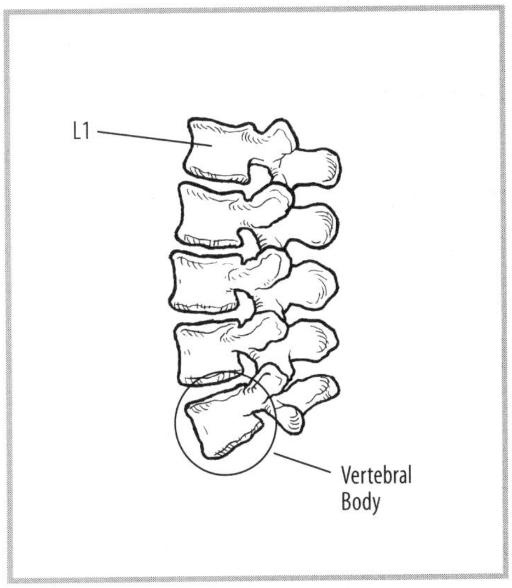

Fig. 1-10 Lumbar Vertebrae

Function

Your vertebrae form a protective covering for your spinal cord and allow you to maintain an upright posture. Because the spine is segmented, it is flexible as well as extremely strong. The vertebral bodies (Fig. 1–10) handle approximately 84% of the compressive forces sustained by your spine when you stand. (The facet joints, described in the next section, handle the remaining 16%.)

Most Important Points

Vertebrae are composed of strong, dense bone, but bone density varies from individual to individual. That doesn't mean you have no control over this important component of your health. You can increase your bone density. Bone reacts to regular stresses—such as the stress of lifting weights—by becoming stronger and denser, much as muscles do. If you consistently do the right kind of exercise, you most likely will increase the density of your vertebrae. This is especially good news for women because their bones tend to become thinner after menopause, a condition known as osteoporosis.

FACET JOINTS

Description

A pair of **facet joints**—interlocking pads of bone that slide on each other—are connected to the back of each vertebra, one pair on either side (Fig. 1–11 a,b). Each facet joint is surrounded by a ligamentous structure known as the **facet joint capsule**.

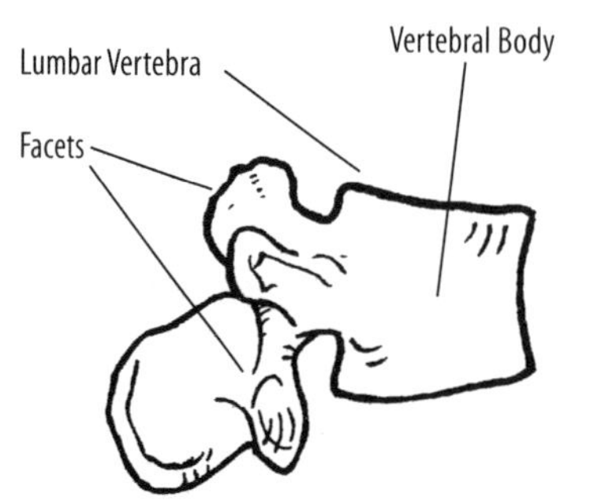

Fig. 1–11a

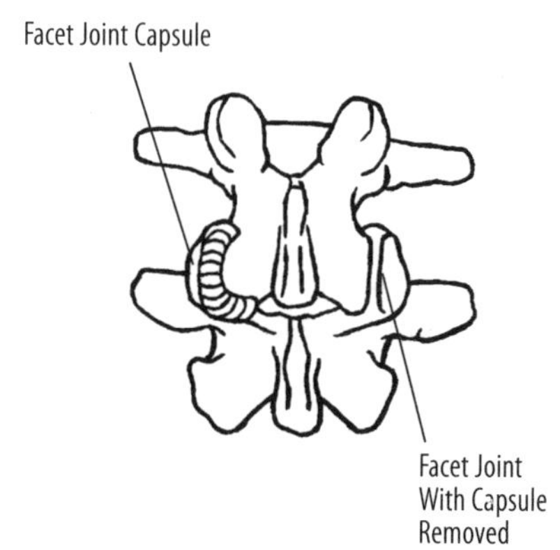

Fig. 1–11b

Function

The facet joints, which interlock like gears, guide spinal motion. They help to combat shear loading (Fig. 1–6), a force that can cause one vertebra to slide forward on the one below it. Your lumbar vertebrae typically undergo shear loading when you bend or lift. The facet joints also prevent excessive rotation of your spine, which could cause the intervertebral discs to tear, and they may help to limit excessive flexion and hyperextension of your spine as well.

Most Important Points

Any of the forces just mentioned—shear loading, rotation, flexion, or hyperextension—has the potential to injure your facet joints. In Chapter 2 you will learn more about each of these forces and how they can damage the facet joints and other spinal tissues. This knowledge can help you avoid potential injury at home, at work, and at the gym.

INTERVERTEBRAL DISCS

Description

The **intervertebral discs** are located between your vertebrae. They are composed of an outer ring, a gel-like center, and cartilage endplates (Fig. 1–12). The outer ring is made up of layers arranged in alternating directions. The gel-like center contains a high percentage of water and resembles the filling in a jelly donut. It is sometimes described as having the consistency of toothpaste.

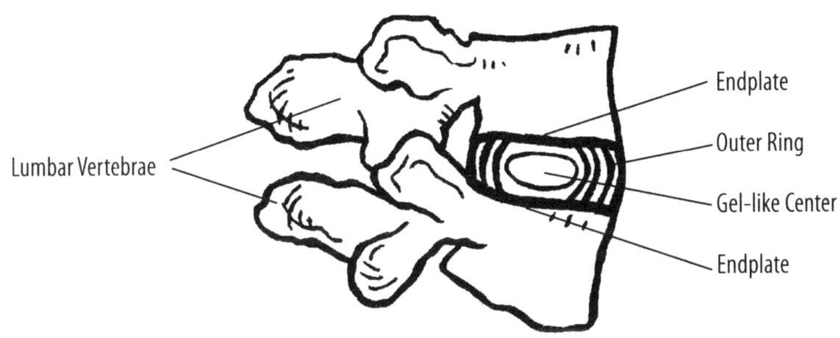

Fig. 1-12 Intervertebral Disc

Function

The discs absorb shock and cushion your vertebrae against compressive loading. They also serve as ligaments to resist rotational and shear forces and otherwise help stabilize the spine.

Most Important Points

There is no direct blood supply to your intervertebral discs. They receive nutrients via diffusion through their cartilage endplates. The lack of a direct blood supply means that if you suffer a disc injury, it can take a long time to heal. Compounding this problem is the fact that the outer third of the disc fibers are extremely pain sensitive. Moving your spine—especially flexing and extending, as well as loading and unloading it through activities such as weight training—promotes the flow of nutrients to your discs. Regular exercise will enhance the health of your intervertebral discs by keeping them properly nourished. The condition known as a **slipped,** or **herniated, disc** occurs when the gel-like center bulges through tears in the outer fibers of the disc. The exercises in this program will help to keep your discs healthy and less likely to become herniated. They may also gradually help a herniated disc to recede, though certainly not in all cases.

LUMBAR SPINE LIGAMENTS

Description

Ligaments are strong fibrous bands that connect bone to bone.

Function

Your ligaments act to stabilize your joints by limiting excessive motion. The spinal ligaments (Fig. 1–13) provide stability between your vertebrae and between your spine and your pelvis.

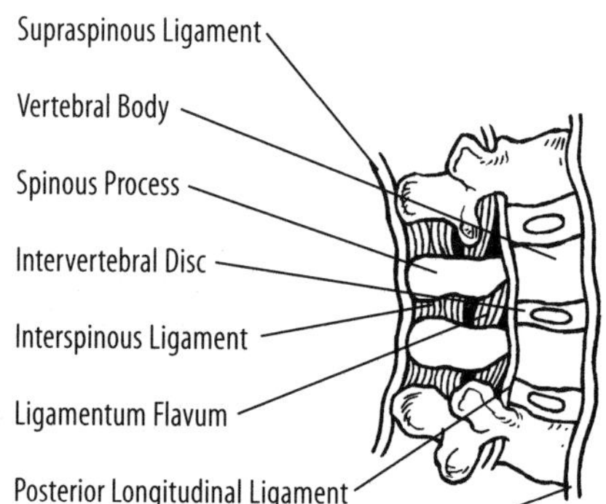

Fig. 1–13

Most Important Points

While your ligaments are extremely strong, they are vulnerable to injury because they cannot shorten or lengthen as muscles do when they react to forces placed on the spine. When you bend or lift improperly, your ligaments can suddenly receive a load that exceeds their tolerance. They can then develop microtears or sprains. If you place your ligaments under prolonged stress—through poor posture, for instance—they can slowly creep, or lengthen. Additional stress can result in partial or complete rupture of a ligament. Lax or torn ligaments can in turn lead to spinal instability.

You can avoid putting your ligaments at risk by maintaining the correct posture while lifting and bending. We'll discuss the mechanics of the low back in Chapter 2 and of sitting- and lifting-related injuries in Chapter 3 with an eye toward helping you protect your ligaments from damage. If you have already damaged a ligament, however, all is not lost. You can compensate, at least in part, by improving your muscular conditioning. The exercises to come are designed to increase your muscle strength, size, and endurance.

Muscles and Fasciae

Description

Muscle tissue is remarkable for its ability to lengthen or shorten when stimulated by your nervous system. Muscle fibers can shorten to about two-thirds of their relaxed length.

Function

Unlike ligaments, which mainly limit spinal motion, muscles actively move your spine. Their arrangement enables humans to do everything from climbing mountains to playing the violin.

Most Important Points

Because your muscles can contract, you can increase their strength, their size, and their endurance. This means that you will be able to lift heavier loads and perform your routine activities—whether they be weight lifting, vacuuming, or data entry—with less fatigue and reduced chance of injury. Even if you do sustain an injury, keeping your muscles in top form can reduce its severity. Because muscular conditioning is such an essential factor in keeping your back healthy and helping to relieve back pain, we will individually describe the muscles of the back and the abdomen.

A GLOSSARY OF BACK MUSCLES

The following section will acquaint you with the muscles of the back and abdomen. Taking a few minutes to learn about them will help you better appreciate how the back works and how it can get injured.

Erector Spinae Muscles

The four sets of erector spinae—or **spinal erectors**—run up the back along the sides of your spine (Fig. 1-14). They extend your trunk and extend and stabilize the lumbar vertebrae. They also work to counter shear loading that occurs when you flex your spine.

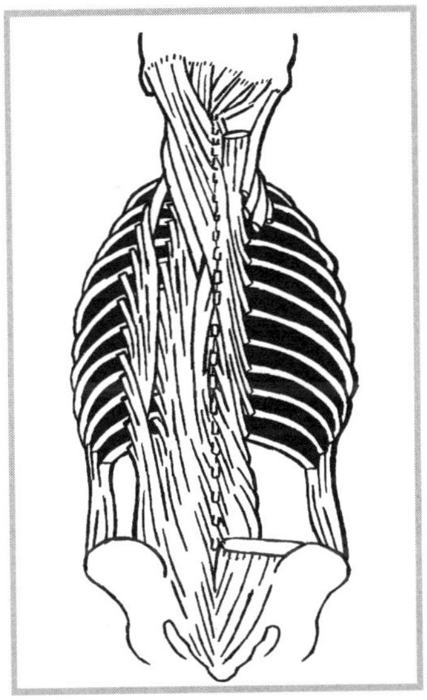

Fig. 1–14 Spinal Erectors

Short Intersegmental Muscles (Transversospinales)

The short muscles that run from one vertebra to the next along your spine are sometimes referred to by the tongue-twisting name **transversospinales** (Fig. 1–15). These muscles may play an important role in stabilizing your individual spinal segments and contributing to overall spine stiffness when you lift. They are believed to signal your brain when you make subtle changes in vertebral joint position and thus to help maintain neuromotor control over your spine.

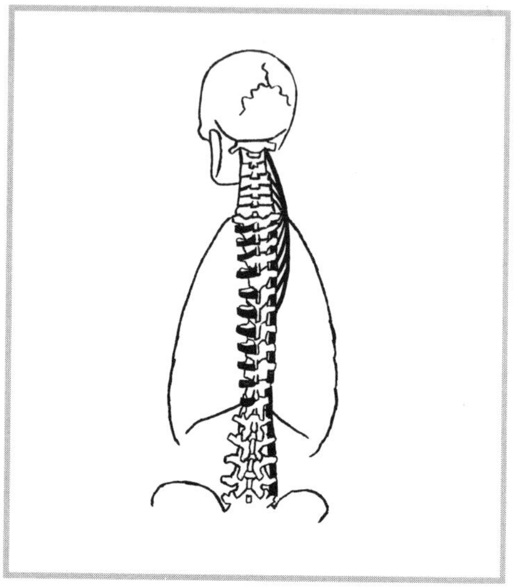

Fig. 1–15 Transversospinales

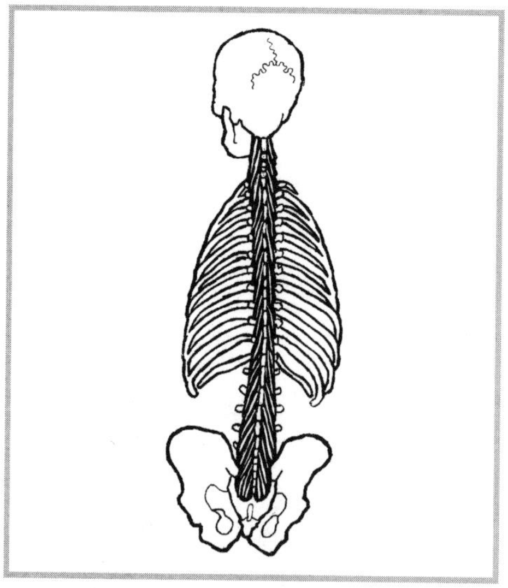

Fig. 1–16 Multifidus

Multifidus Muscles

Your **multifidus muscles** are relatively short, spanning two to five vertebral segments (Fig. 1–16). They extend your individual lumbar vertebrae and the lumbar spine as a whole, but their primary role is believed to be stabilization. They counter rotational forces on your spine, prevent excessive flexion, and prevent the shear loading that occurs when you flex your spine.

Quadratus Lumborum

The **quadratus lumborum** (Fig. 1–17) is a flat, triangular muscle that lies on either side of your spine and contains several sets of fibers. It acts to flex your spine laterally and is also active in lumbar extension. Its main role is that of a lateral stabilizer, but it also assists as a stabilizer during virtually all motions of your spine. The heavier the load you carry, the more active the quadratus lumborum becomes, indicating that it plays an important role in stabilization. Nevertheless, it is frequently ignored in low back rehabilitation programs—a big mistake given the importance of stability to a healthy back.

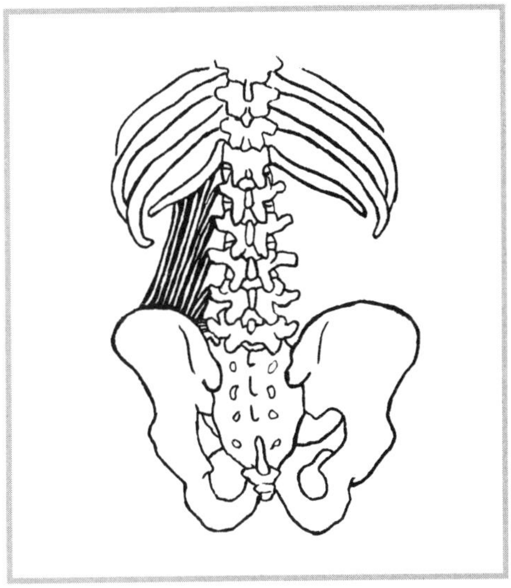

Fig. 1–17 Quadratus Lumborum

Psoas

The **psoas** muscle (Fig. 1–18) attaches to the fronts and sides of the vertebral bodies and discs and continues down to the top of the femur (the long bone in the upper leg). It primarily bends the hip, though it also helps to control the natural curvature of your lumbar spine, known as **lordosis.**

Unfortunately, the psoas is attached to your lumbar spine; when it flexes your hip, it pulls on your spine, producing shear and compressive forces. That's why you should avoid abdominal exercises that over involve the psoas—such as full sit-ups, straight leg raises, and exercises where the feet are hooked in place—if you want to prevent back pain.

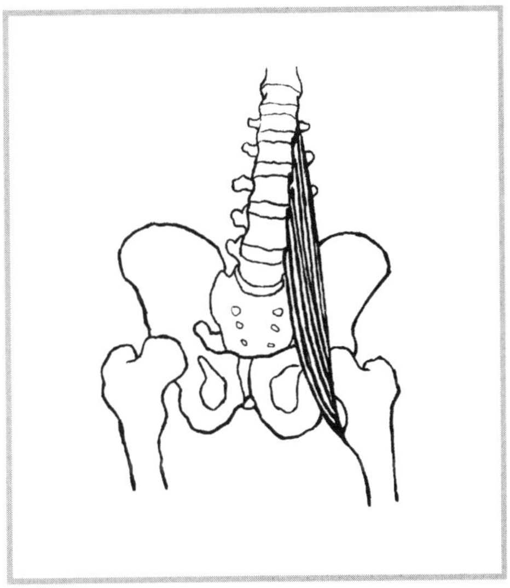

Fig. 1–18 Psoas

In fact, the psoas can exert such a strong pull on your spine that forceful contraction can fracture the portion of the vertebra where the psoas attaches. In most individuals the psoas is a powerful muscle that does not require additional strengthening.* Frequently, however, this muscle needs to be lengthened through stretching. It's also a good idea to perform isolated abdominal exercises to balance out the psoas' strength. We'll cover stretching and isolated abdominal exercises in Chapter 5.

A GLOSSARY OF ABDOMINAL MUSCLES

Now that we've examined the muscles that support and motivate your lower back, let's move around to the other side of your body. You have four layers of **abdominal muscles** on the front and sides of your trunk. They flex, laterally flex, and rotate your body. They also help to support your spine and provide protection for your abdominal organs. Let's explore the layers, starting with the deepest and working toward the surface.

Transverse Abdominis

The **transverse abdominis** is the deepest layer of your abdominal wall (Fig. 1–19); its fibers run horizontally around the abdomen. Until recently, it was thought only to assist with autonomic functions such as forced expiration (coughing or sneezing), digestion, and defecation. But it turns out that it plays an important role in the stability of your spine.

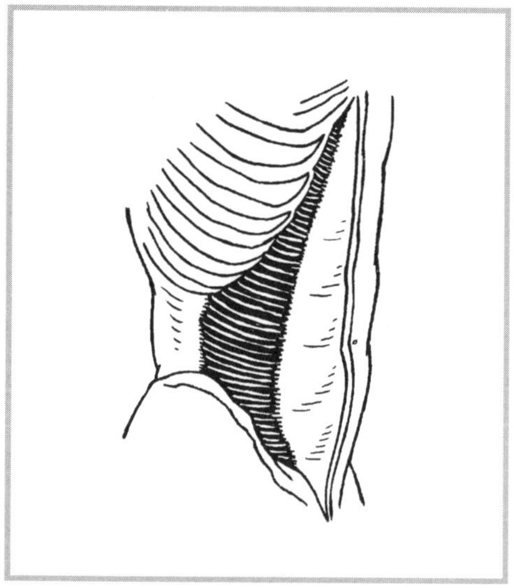

Fig. 1–19 Transverse Abdominis

The transverse abdominis functions as a girdle, holding in your abdominal organs and thus increasing intra-abdominal pressure. This results in stiffening the spine and thus helps to prevent spinal injuries. Despite popular misconception, your transverse abdominis does not contract to rotate your trunk, and doing trunk twists will not strengthen this muscle.

*Some athletes do need to train the psoas to improve performance; more on this later.

Although there is no exercise that can work this muscle in isolation, it is involved in most of the trunk stabilizing exercises described in Chapter 5.

Internal Oblique

The **internal oblique** is the next layer of your abdominal muscles; its fibers run diagonally across the side and front of your abdominal wall (Fig. 1–20). Through its attachment to your thoracolumbar fascia, the internal oblique is believed to play an important role in supporting your lumbar spine during lifting. It also assists the transverse abdominis in compressing your abdomen and plays a role in autonomic functions such as defecation and forced expiration.

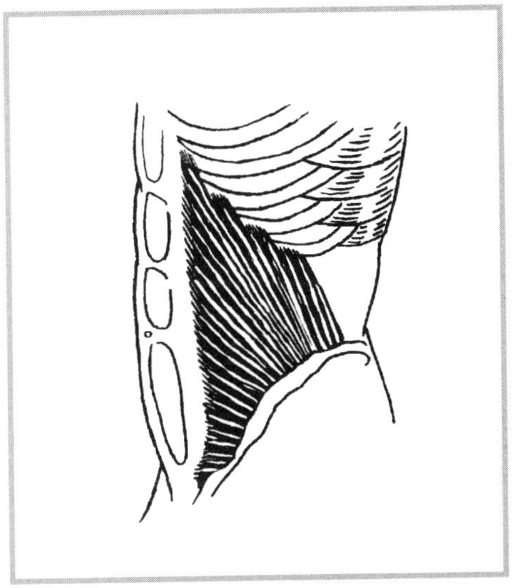

Fig. 1–20 Internal Oblique

If...

- both sides of this muscle contract, it assists another abdominal muscle, the rectus abdominis, in bending your spine.
- one side contracts and the pelvis is fixed, it flexes and rotates the trunk to the same side and brings the opposite shoulder forward.
- one side contracts and the torso is fixed, it pulls the same side hip up.

Although we've described it in isolation, in reality your internal oblique never acts alone. It works with your external oblique to produce diagonal, lateral, and rotational motions of your trunk.

External Oblique

The fibers of your external oblique muscle run from your lower five ribs diagonally down and across the abdomen to the iliac crest (Fig. 1–21). Research shows that this muscle also frequently attaches to the thoracolumbar fascia, thus helping to support your spine.

Fig. 1–21 External Oblique

If...

- both sides contract, the external oblique pulls the pubis toward the rib cage, tilting the pelvis to the rear. Reverse crunches, hip thrusts, and pelvic tilting exercises strongly stress your external obliques.
- one side contracts and the feet are fixed, the external oblique produces lateral flexion of the same side of the trunk and forward rotation of the opposite side.
- one side contracts and the trunk is fixed, it causes the same side of the pelvis to tilt.

Once again, although we've described it in isolation, in reality your external oblique never acts alone. It works with your internal oblique to produce diagonal, lateral, and rotational motions of your trunk.

Rectus Abdominis

The **rectus abdominis** is the topmost layer of your abdominal muscles (Fig. 1–22). It is a long flat muscle that runs from the top of the pubic bone and attaches to the bottommost tip of the sternum, or breastbone, and to the fifth, sixth, and seventh ribs.

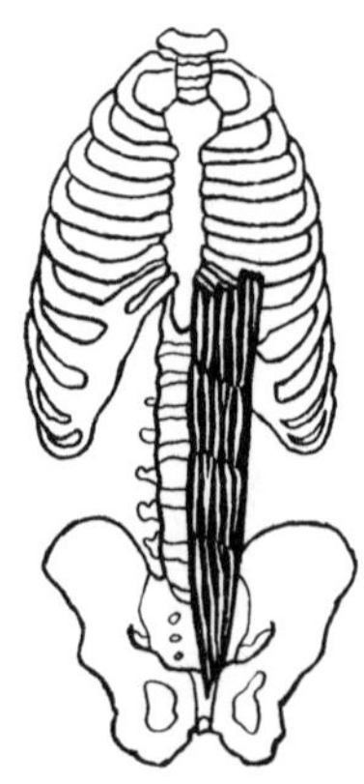

Fig. 1–22 Rectus Abdominis

The rectus abdominis is a longitudinal muscle that appears to be horizontally divided into small squares by the fibrous bands (known as the **tendinous insertions**) that cross it. It is also divided down the center by the **linea alba**, a tendinous median line. The much sought after "washboard" is created by this muscle bulging out between its tendinous insertions, much the same way, when sitting your skin bulges out between the straps of a lawn chair.

Some exercises, such as crunches, emphasize your upper rectus abdominis (or *upper abs*) while others, such as reverse crunches, emphasize your lower rectus abdominis (*lower abs*).

A SPECIAL STRUCTURE: THORACOLUMBAR FASCIA

One more structure deserves special mention. The **thoracolumbar fascia** is a key stabilizing force on your lumbar spine (Fig. 1–23). It consists not of muscular tissue but of fascia, a connective tissue that cannot contract and typically covers muscles or groups of muscles. Your thoracolumbar fascia consists of three layers of connective tissue that cover your back muscles.

Various muscles attached to the thoracolumbar fascia pull on it, like wires on a tent, and add stability to your lower spine. These muscles include the transverse abdominis; the internal and external obliques, which pull from the side; the latissimus dorsi (a broad muscle in the upper back), which pulls from above; and the gluteus maximus (a muscle in the buttocks) and hamstrings, which pull from below.

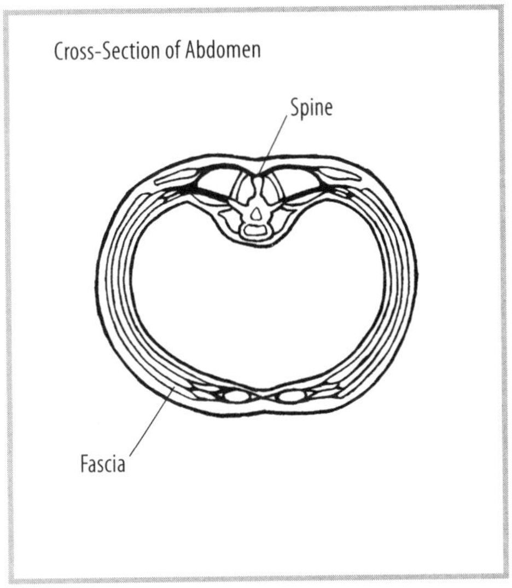

Fig. 1–23 Thoracolumbar Fascia

Several theoretical mechanisms have been suggested to describe how the thoracolumbar fascia helps support your spine. These have colorful names, such as the **gain mechanism** and the **hydraulic amplifier mechanism**. We'll explore these in detail in the next chapter.

How Your Low Back Works

If you're like most people, your day includes a lot of activities like these: getting out of bed, stretching, brushing your teeth, checking under the hood of your car, driving, vacuuming, sitting at a desk, swimming, running to an appointment, retrieving your glasses from the floor, waiting in line at the bank, working out at the gym. Like most people, you probably tend to take your activities for granted...until back pain strikes. Nevertheless, every activity places its own set of stresses on your back. In this chapter, we'll explore how the back works *in motion.* Learning about the dynamic abilities—and limitations—of your spine will bring you one step closer to a strong, healthy, pain-free lower back.

2

How Your Low Back Works

Even the smallest movement of the low back involves one or a combination of the four movements described in Chapter 1:

- Flexion
- Extension
- Lateral Flexion
- Rotation

In this chapter, we'll see how the parts of the back contribute to each of these motions. We'll also cover three major theories that have been advanced to explain how the abdominal and back muscles, together with the thoracolumbar fascia, work to support the lumbar spine. Strengthening these two muscle groups is a primary goal of the exercise routines to come.

Being able to picture how the bones, ligaments, and muscles work together in moving the back can help you to avoid injury. It also brings with it another significant benefit. The ability to visualize how the exercises involve and affect the spinal structures will make your performance of the routines in Chapter 6 more exact and more effective. Now let's take a closer look at the four main back movements.

Functional Ranges of Motion

FLEXION

Although your spinal flexibility is typically considered normal if you can bend forward and touch your toes, this is really a measure of not only spinal flexion, but also hip flexion. The combination of the two is often called *trunk flexion.* Trunk flexion involves bending forward at your hips as well as rounding your lumbar and thoracic spine. Some very flexible individuals can bend over completely at their

Fig. 2–1 Flexion

hips and touch their toes without bending their spines at all. A range of 40 to 60 degrees of pure lumbar spine flexion is considered normal (Fig. 2–1).

Your range of spinal flexion is limited by your ligaments, intervertebral discs, facet joint capsules, thoracolumbar fascia, and passive tension in your spinal erector muscles. When you stand and bend forward, trunk flexion occurs simply from the pull of gravity. To actively flex your spine (such as during a crunch), you mainly use your abdominal muscles.

The Flexion-Relaxation Response

During spinal flexion a bizarre phenomenon occurs that is known as the **flexion-relaxation response of the spinal erector muscles.** It explains why bending over to pick something up is the single most common cause of back injury.

Here's what happens: As you bend forward, your back muscles work harder and harder to support your trunk until you reach a certain critical point. At this point, just shy of full spinal flexion, your back muscles relax, and the stress of supporting the spine is shifted to the ligaments along the back of the spine. *This is like having your brakes fail when you're driving along at top speed—precisely when you need them most.*

Placing the stress of supporting the spine on the ligaments is not a good idea. Ligaments are efficient at *passively* limiting excessive motion, just as your dog's leash does. But they can't lengthen and shorten as muscles can to adjust to a given situation. As a result, ligaments are unable to respond to sudden changes in load, and this makes them vulnerable to injury.

Flexing your spine when bending down to pick something up, especially a heavy weight, is dangerous due to this transferring of the load to the spinal ligaments. It's better in such situations to try to maintain the normal backward curvature of your spine. In the gym, you should be especially careful to avoid rounding your back while rowing or performing similar exercises. (We'll go into more detail about correct lifting and rowing techniques in Chapters 3 and 5.)

EXTENSION

Your ability to extend is usually assessed by having you place your hands on your hips and lean backward as far as possible. A range of about 30 degrees is considered normal (Fig. 2-2). Dancers and gymnasts often have a considerably greater range. (Fig. 2-3).

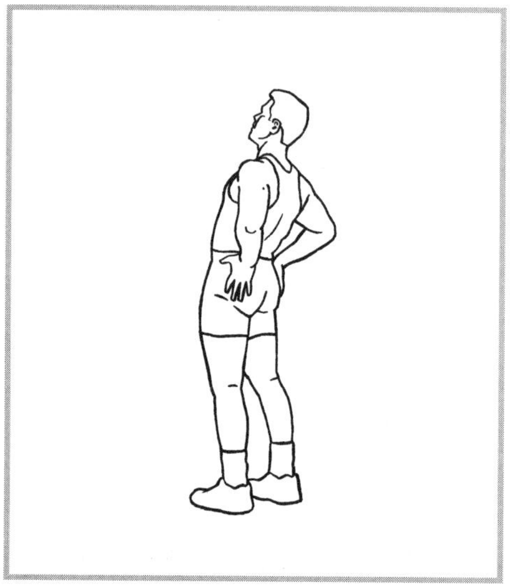

Fig. 2-2 Extension

Fig. 2-3 Hyperextension

Your ability to extend your back is limited by...

- your spinous processes (bony protrusions at the back of the vertebrae)
- your facet joints
- tension in the ligaments at the front of your spine
- your facet joint capsules
- the outer rings of your discs.

Your erector spinae and multifidus muscles extend your spine, and your hip extensors—the gluteals and the hamstrings—extend your trunk. Your psoas muscle may also assist in trunk extension if your feet are in a fixed position.

LATERAL FLEXION

If you can bend about 40 degrees to each side, your range of lateral flexion is considered normal (Fig. 2-4). *This motion is limited by...*

- your facet joints coming into contact with each other
- simultaneous compression and stretching of your discs
- your spinal ligaments
- your thoracolumbar fascia.

The primary muscles involved in lateral flexion are your quadratus lumborum, which pulls your rib cage sideways toward your pelvis, and your psoas, which pull sideways on each lumbar vertebra. Your abdominal oblique muscles also assist.

The thoracolumbar fascia is believed to play a significant role in supporting the spine during lateral flexion, while the muscles on the sides of your hips add stability.

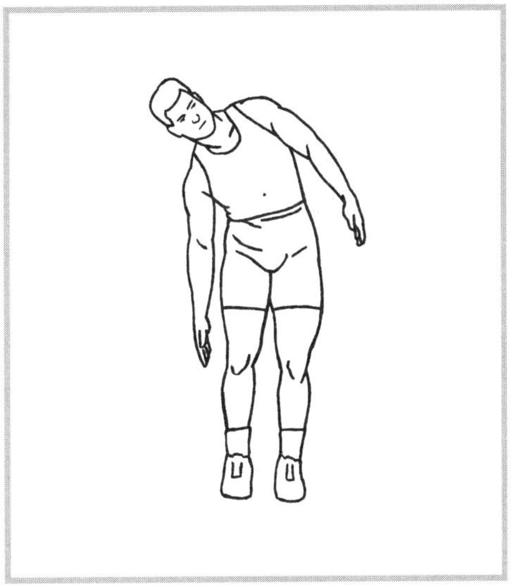

Fig. 2–4 Lateral Flexion

ROTATION

Rotation of approximately 30 degrees in each direction is considered normal (Fig. 2–5). This motion is limited by your facet joints and their capsules and the outer fibers of your discs. Rotation occurs through the combined action of your internal and external obliques, your erector spinae and multifidus muscles, and your latissimus dorsi muscles in your upper back.

Like flexion, rotation is a frequent source of injury, often to the facet joints and the discs. This is why you should avoid exercises such as broomstick twists and barbell twists. (In Chapter 3 you'll learn more about the type of damage that can occur when your spine is subjected to rotational forces, and in Chapter 5 we will explain in greater detail why you should avoid the twisting exercises mentioned above.)

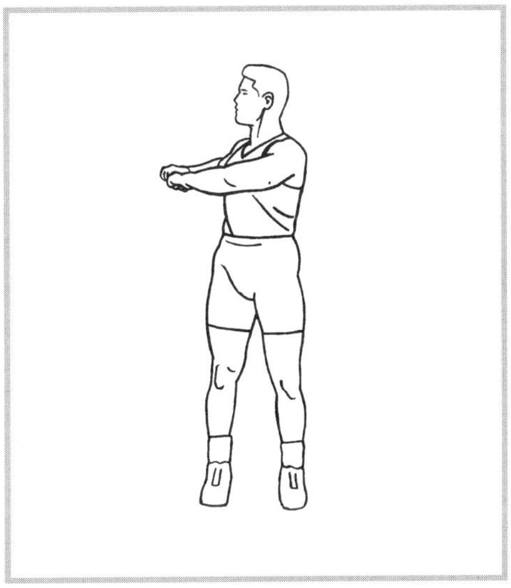

Fig. 2–5 Rotation

Normal Posture

Your lumbar spine has a natural curvature that is known as **lordosis** (Fig. 2–6). This, along with other curves in your thoracic and cervical regions, allows your spine to function like an elastic rod and to resist compressive forces. During compression your lumbar lordosis is increased; this tenses the ligament at the front of your spine and allows it to absorb some of the force so that all the stress isn't placed on the vertebrae and discs.

Maintaining normal posture, especially while you are sitting and lifting, is crucial to preventing low back pain. Prolonged sitting tends to flatten or even reverse your normal lordosis. In addition to back pain, this can sometimes produce disc herniation.

Too great a lumbar curvature can also result in injury. Excessive arching of the spine can occur, for example, when you lift overhead. Individuals with very tight hip flexor muscles may stand with an exaggerated arch in their back (Fig. 2–7). This can lead to abnormal weight bearing, with additional load being placed on the facet joints. Back pain and early degenerative changes in the facets can result.

Gymnasts and other athletes who have very strong hip flexors and need to hyperextend frequently tend to assume this posture. A protruding belly can contribute to this stance as well—a good reason to consider a sensible weight reduction program.

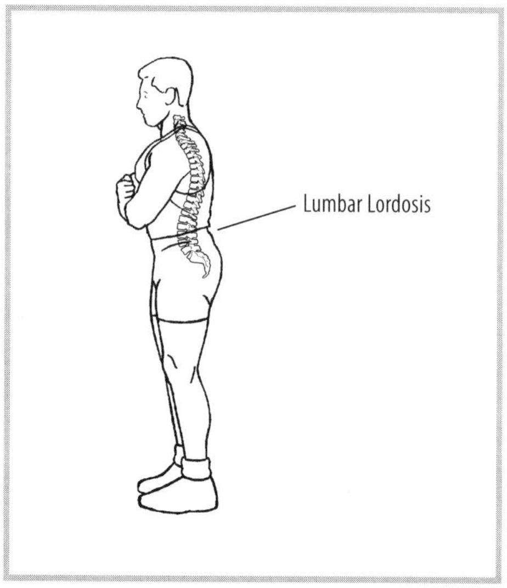

Fig. 2–6 Normal Curvature

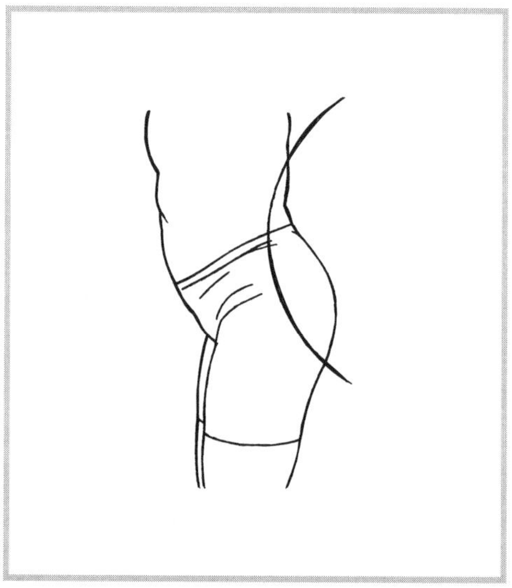

Fig. 2–7 Excessive Curvature

Lumbar Support Mechanisms

There is a lot of controversy about just how the abdominal and back muscles and the thoracolumbar fascia that connects them work together to support your lumbar spine. By looking at three of the prevailing theories, you will gain more insight into this biomechanical process and begin to develop a better sense of how you can increase the stability of your own back. One thing you'll notice is that each mechanism relies on the strength of certain muscles—either the abs or spinal erectors—giving further support to the idea of performing strengthening exercises for spinal health.

THE INTRA-ABDOMINAL BALLOON MECHANISM

The **intra-abdominal balloon mechanism** is one of the oldest and most widely discussed theories about how the abdominal muscles help to support the spine.

When you lift heavy weights, you instinctively hold your breath and contract your stomach muscles—the internal and external obliques and transverse abdominis muscles (Fig. 2–8). Your abdominal cavity then becomes a closed chamber, and the resulting pressure pushes the viscera upward against your diaphragm. This pumped-up balloon prevents your spine from flexing forward while you're holding a weight in front of you. Since part of your diaphragm is attached to the first three lumbar vertebrae, when it is pushed up, it also exerts a decompressive (pulling up) force on your lower lumbar

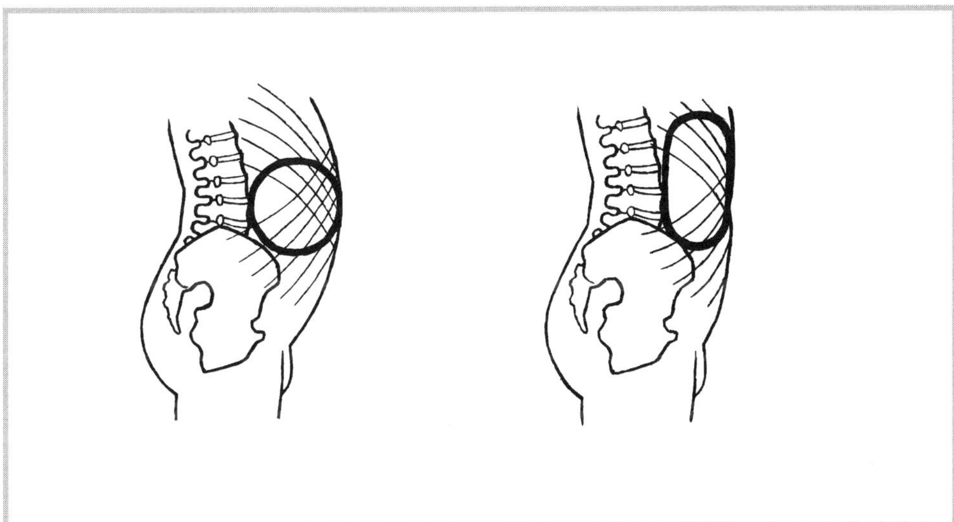

Fig. 2–8 Intra-Abdominal Balloon Mechanism

spine (L4 to S1). This mechanism unloads the spine and decreases the amount of work your back muscles must do to prevent you from falling forward.

The validity and significance of this intra-abdominal balloon mechanism has been challenged by a number of researchers. Nevertheless, when you lift heavy objects, you do bear down and contract your abdominal muscles. This makes your trunk more rigid and helps to support your spine.

Although this abdominal support mechanism may provide only a modest amount of support for your spine, it is probably significant, especially in conjunction with other lumbar support mechanisms. Even if researchers eventually conclude that the abdominal support mechanism does not reduce compression of your spine, it does make it stiffer—and that can prevent potential injury created by shear and other forces. A stiffer spine is more resistant to a heavy load. *Recommendation:* Ab exercises to increase abdominal support.

THE GAIN OF THE THORACOLUMBAR FASCIA

The **gain of the thoracolumbar fascia** is another theory how the abdominal muscles support your spine, in this case through their attachment to the thoracolumbar fascia.

Research has shown that the transverse abdominis, the internal oblique, and the external oblique muscles are attached to the sides of your thoracolumbar fascia. The sides of your fascia are pulled when these abdominal muscles act, as they do when you lift. The fibers of the topmost layer of the thoracolumbar fascia are crisscrossed, and tension created by the pull of your abdominal muscles causes these fibers to pull the spinous processes of L2 and L3 down and pull the spinous processes of L4 and 5 up. This creates an extension force across your lumbar spine (Fig. 2-9). It's almost as though you were wearing a corset that helps to straighten your spine.

In addition, since fibers of your transverse abdominis are attached to the diaphragm, this reduces some of the load on your lower spine by transferring it to your thoracic spine and shoulders.

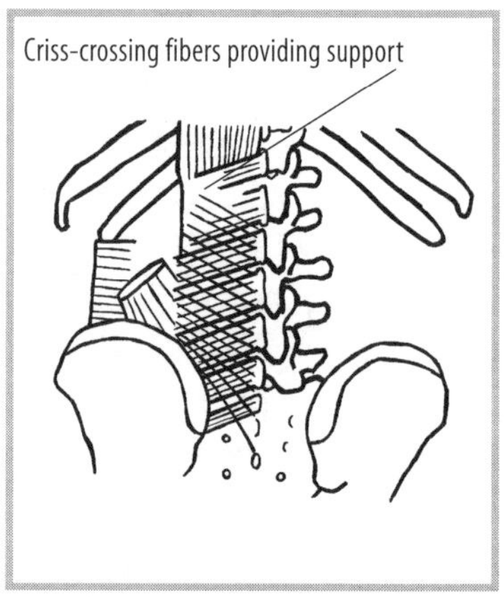

Fig. 2-9 Rear View of Fascia

As with the abdominal balloon mechanism, the gain of the thoracolumbar fascia theory has its critics, who note that its contribution to support of the spine is likely to be small. In combination with the other mechanisms described here, however, it is significant. *Recommendation:* Strengthen your oblique and transverse abdominis muscles to take advantage of whatever spinal support can be derived from this mechanism. (More on this in the Exercises and Routines Chapters.)

THE HYDRAULIC AMPLIFIER MECHANISM

A third theory, the **hydraulic amplifier mechanism**, suggests that when the erector muscles of your back contract, they expand, putting pressure on the surrounding thoracolumbar fascia, the deep layer of which opposes the expansion. This opposition tends to straighten your spine from a flexed position, much like pumping air into a deflated bicycle tire restores its original shape.

A corollary of this hydraulic amplifier mechanism is that performing strengthening exercises for the erector spinae muscles would help to stabilize your lumbar spine. Thicker back muscles would tend to fill up this fascial sheath, creating more support for the spine. Conversely, overstretching the thoracolumbar fascia by doing standing forward-bending stretches or by doing deadlift or row exercises with the back rounded may reduce the effectiveness of this mechanism and destabilize your spine.

A number of experts are interested in this theory partly because if it is true, your thoracolumbar fascia has the potential to increase the strength of your erector spinae muscles by 30%. There have been no serious criticisms of the theory, but more research needs to be done to support it. *Recommendation:* It makes sense to work to increase the bulk of your back muscles to take advantage of the potential spinal support provided by this hydraulic amplifier mechanism. A number of the exercises in Chapter 5 target that goal.

In this chapter, we've covered how the back works when all goes well and touched on the most credible theories of how the trunk musculature supports the spine. In the next chapter, we'll pick up another piece of the puzzle and move a step closer to a healthy, pain-free back as we explore what can go wrong and how to most effectively analyze back pain and injuries.

What Goes Wrong

When you're in pain, the last thing you want is a mystery; you want a solution. Unfortunately, doctors can give a specific diagnosis in only a small percentage of cases—such as a fracture or some instances of herniated disc. If you don't suffer from a condition of this type, chances are that you'll get lumped into that vague category known as "mechanical back pain of indeterminable origin." In other words, your doctor says your back hurts (which you already knew) but doesn't know why.

3

What Goes Wrong

There are many pain-sensitive structures in your low back—discs, facet joints, nerve roots, ligaments, muscles, sacroiliac joints—and it is often difficult to tell which of them is the source of your low back pain. Often several structures contribute.

The inability of the medical profession to give a diagnosis for most cases of low back pain doesn't mean that your back pain is unavoidable or that you have to learn to live with it. The more in tune you become with your back's movements and the forces that cause it to hurt, the more you can take steps to relieve or prevent the pain.

Recognizing common mechanisms of injury can help you avoid placing dangerous stresses on your spine at home, at work, and at the gym. In addition, when you finish this chapter, you'll have the knowledge—the ability to visualize how your back works and to analyze causes of injury—that you need to perform the routines in Chapter 6 to maximum effect. Doing the right exercise routine on a consistent basis will provide relief from pain or prevent back problems from occurring in the first place.

One important point: The inability of medical and chiropractic doctors to diagnose many cases of low back pain doesn't mean that you should avoid doctors or attempt self-diagnosis. **You should definitely consult a qualified chiropractic or medical doctor initially if you have an injury or back pain.** In the majority of cases, the right kind of exercise program is crucial to your rehabilitation. But initially you may need other measures, such as pain killers, chiropractic manipulation, or muscle relaxants to ease your pain during the transition to exercise.

Mechanisms of Low Back Injuries

FLEXION INJURY

The majority of low back injuries occur when you bend over to pick something up. Your discs, ligaments, thoracolumbar fascia, and back muscles are susceptible to flexion injuries. They occur chiefly because at a certain point in flexing, your back muscles lose their ability to contract and can no longer compensate for any sudden change in position or weight. (This is the flexion-relaxation response described in Chapter 2.)

Flexion also causes the front of your discs to narrow and the back to widen (Fig. 3–1), and widening can produce tears in the fibers at the back of the disc. Once these fibers are torn, further flexion can result in bulging or herniation of the disc. Studies show that when you lift frequently while keeping your legs straight and your spine flexed, you increase your risk of disc herniation (Fig. 3–2).

Fig. 3–1 Flexion causes discs to compress in front and widen in back.

Fig. 3–2 Straight-legged lifting increases the risk of disc herniation.

Anyone who stands with straight legs and repeatedly bends to lift heavy parcels—like the postal worker in the Introduction—would be a good candidate for a flexion injury.

Chapter 5 goes into more detail about exercises you should avoid because they place excessive flexion forces on your spine. These include such old standards as Standing Toe Touches and Windmills.

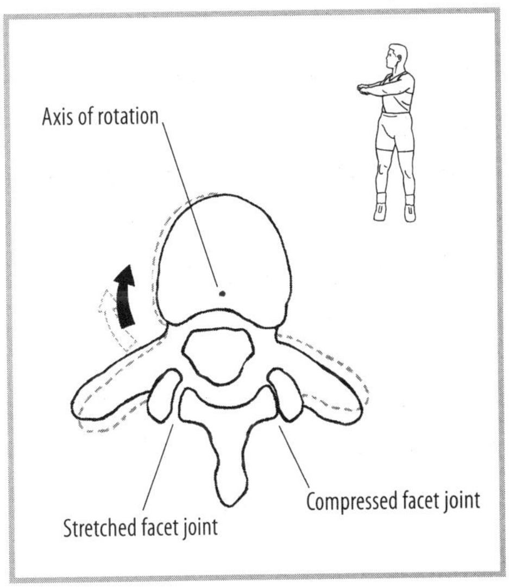

Fig. 3–3 Rotation stresses facet joints.

ROTATION INJURY

Rotation injuries are common and most frequently involve the facet joints and discs. When you rotate to the left, you compress the facet joints on the right and stretch your left facet joint capsules (Fig. 3–3); the opposite is true when you rotate to the right. Your facet joints act to block excessive rotation, but they perform effectively only if they are correctly aligned. Some individuals are born with variations in facet orientation that can lead to rotation injuries.

Rotation can also place shear forces on your discs and lead to tearing or herniation. The potential for injury to the discs is heightened if you combine rotation with flexion, which unlocks your facet joints somewhat and prevents them from blocking excessive rotation. Add compression (as when holding a heavy object) to the combination of flexion and rotation, and you have the perfect combination of forces to rupture a disc.

Twisting while flexing forward to reach for a volley in tennis—as Barbara did in the Introduction—could produce a rotation injury.

The section called *Avoid Ballistic, or Uncontrolled, Rotation* in Chapter 5 describes a number of exercises to avoid because they place excessive rotational stresses on your spine. These include broomstick twists and barbell twists.

HYPEREXTENSION INJURY

You rarely hyperextend, or lean backward beyond the normal limit, while performing daily activities. Hyperextension injuries occur primarily among athletes, particularly those engaged in sports such as Olympic weight lifting, gymnastics, and football.

Hyperextension compresses and may injure your facet joints. Flexion or rotation is more likely to injure your discs, but hyperextension forces, which stretch the front of a disc and compress the back, can also damage them. Stretching can tear the fibers in the front of the disc.

Your spinous processes impact each other—or the back of the vertebra below—to limit hyperextension, and pain can also result from irritation to these bones when they come in contact (Fig. 3–4). Furthermore, since hyperextension compresses the back of your vertebrae, it can result in a fracture. This fracture can in turn cause one vertebra, which is normally held in place by the one below, to slip forward, a condition known as **spondylolisthesis**.

You should avoid hyperextended postures while performing back strengthening exercises because of the potential for injury. Such exercises are performed more effectively in an *extended,* not a hyperextended, position.

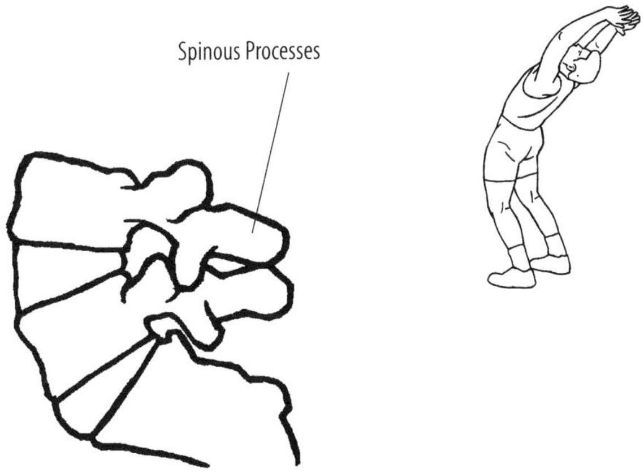

Fig. 3–4 Hyperextension may cause spinous processes to press together.

Steve, the triathlete, whom you met in the Introduction, probably suffered a hyperextension injury while doing overhead presses. Running the next day with tight hip flexors—the result of his imbalanced abdominal strengthening program—would have made this injury worse.

COMPRESSIVE INJURY

Compression is frequently a factor in back injuries, but it is less significant than flexion and rotation. If your spine is healthy, it can withstand considerable amounts of pure compressive loading. Excessive, repeated, or traumatic compressive forces can, however, result in injury—usually to your vertebrae. Because the cartilage endplates of your vertebrae are often damaged in compressive injuries, a portion of one of your discs may be forced through the endplate into the vertebra above it.

Compression contributes most to back injury when combined with flexion, rotation, or hyperextension. This is why you need to exercise special care when you bend or, worse still, bend and twist to lift a heavy object. This combination of forces can spell disaster for your back.

BLUNT TRAUMA

Many forms of trauma, such as automobile accidents, falls, or sudden shifts in load while lifting, can result in injury to your back. Anything from minor sprains and strains to a fracture with spinal cord damage and paralysis may result. The exact mechanism—the angles and the forces involved—determines the nature and extent of such injuries.

CUMULATIVE MICROTRAUMA

Cumulative microtrauma refers to a slow accumulation of stresses and strains on your spine that may lead to an episode of acute low back pain. Such stresses progressively weaken the supportive tissues of your spine and lower their ability to handle additional stresses. The result is a slow process of spinal degeneration. Cumulative microtrauma is probably a factor in the majority of cases of low back pain.

Often back pain arises after a seemingly innocent event, such as bending over to tie your shoelaces. It is unlikely that such a low-stress activity alone—one that you've performed hundreds of times in the past without ill effect—could be the single cause of your low back pain. But repeated loading of your discs and other tissues can progressively weaken them to the point where even a small amount of stress can trigger tissue failure and pain—the straw that breaks the camel's back!

To avoid cumulative microtrauma, you should try to maintain a neutral or optimal spinal posture whenever possible, especially when lifting or sitting for a prolonged period. This neutral posture is a mid-range position that avoids all the tissue-loading forces that occur when you engage in flexion, rotation, and hyperextension. For the average person, this neutral posture is the normal lordosis that occurs when standing erect.

SITTING

Consider the modern office worker who slouches in a car while commuting, slouches at a desk for eight hours or more, sits slouched at the dinner table and in front of the television, and may even sleep in a fetal position. Assuming a seated posture for a prolonged period of time tends to round or flatten your back and can lead to deformation of spinal tissues (Fig. 3–5). Slouching in a chair for as little as twenty minutes can result in increased laxity of the ligaments at the back of your spine, and it may take thirty minutes or more for these ligaments to recover and regain their normal shape. Prior to recovery, there is an increased risk of a flexion injury to your ligaments and discs. This danger is compounded by the fact that your lumbar muscles also become fatigued when you sit for long periods and are less able to help stabilize your spine.

Fig. 3–5 Prolonged sitting, especially in a bent-over posture, causes a gradual weakening of discs.

Recent research has confirmed that the mechanical stresses associated with prolonged sitting in the typical bent-over position can result in lumbar disc herniation. The combination of sitting and bending produces the greatest pressure on the disc. When you sit in a car, you also experience vibrational forces, which repetitively load your spine and have been shown to lead to tissue weakening and breakdown over time.

If you perform standing toe touches or similar flexion-type stretches for your tight back muscles, you can actually contribute to the ill effects of prolonged sitting. Chapter 5 shows exactly which of these exercises to avoid.

David, the sports enthusiast in our Introduction, has experienced firsthand the ill effects of prolonged sitting. Regularly spending a couple of hours sitting in front of the television—bent forward to better give advice to his team—he is a good candidate for a herniated disc.

LIFTING

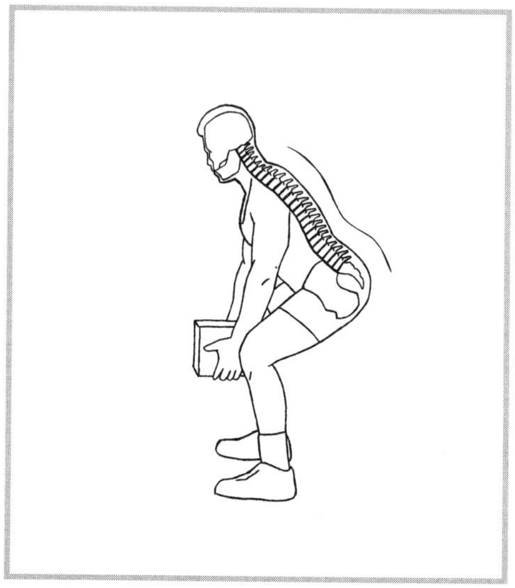

Fig. 3–6 When lifting, it is best to maintain the back's normal curvature.

If you learned that the best way to lift is to try to keep a flat back or maintain your normal lordosis, it may come as a surprise to you to find out that there are some researchers who believe that rounding the back is safer. They argue that when we lift "naturally"—that is, without being instructed how to lift—we round our backs and rely on the ligaments to support our spines. They claim that these ligaments are better designed to support the spine than the muscles. Further, they point out that if you lift while maintaining the back's normal lordosis, this primarily engages the muscles and increases the compression on the spine.

We strongly disagree with this theory, however, and contend that it's best to try to maintain your back's normal curvature—as opposed to a flexed back—when you lift (Fig. 3–6). Your back muscles can then remain active and generate greater force to protect your spine. When you use a flexed spine to lift, your back muscles stop working at a certain point, and the stress is transferred to your ligaments. (This is the flexion-relaxation response that we discussed in Chapter 2.) Your muscles can shorten or lengthen to react to various stresses and forces at joints, but your ligaments cannot. In fact, if your ligaments are placed under stress for any length of time, they creep, or stretch out, and may not be able to return to their original shape.

Your muscles also have a plentiful blood supply and heal fairly rapidly after injury, whereas your ligaments are poorly supplied and have limited capacity for healing. Your muscles are clearly, therefore, more suited to performing the work of lifting. Maintaining the normal curve of your lumbar spine while lifting allows your muscles to take on this job and spares your ligaments from serious injury.

In lifting it's also important to hold objects as close to your body as possible. Holding a weight with arms extended increases disc pressure. One final piece of advice concerning lifting: Studies have shown that during sleep your discs swell with fluid due to decreased loading of your spine. During the first several hours after you rise, the fluid content of your discs remains high. This results in increased pressure on your discs when you bend forward and the increased possibility of disc injury in the morning. If you are going to lift heavy objects or engage in repeated lifting, therefore, it is better to do so later in the day. Mark this page to show your spouse when you're asked to start the garage clean-up first thing Sunday morning!

Common Diagnoses

As we mentioned at the beginning of this chapter, most cases of low back pain or injury can't be diagnosed. A small percentage can, though, and in some cases a diagnosis may affect the way you perform the exercise program you select in Chapter 6. The following brief discussions will familiarize you with some of the more common diagnoses for back pain. But keep in mind that many of these conditions can exist without symptoms. So even if you meet the criteria for one of the diagnoses, it may not be the source of your low back pain.

We will not discuss the rarer causes of low back pain, such as fractures, dislocations, spinal cord tumors, and infections. These conditions usually require emergency medical care and can be ruled out only by a competent medical professional. Fortunately, they account for less than 1% of the instances of low back pain.

BULGING, OR HERNIATED, DISC

A **herniated disc** (also known as a **slipped disc**) involves a bulging, or leaking, of the gel-like center of the disc through tears in the disc's outer fibers (Fig. 3–7). This gel-like material can press on the ligament at the back of the spine, a spinal nerve, or the spinal cord, causing pain in the back, the buttocks, the groin, or the leg. Symptoms such as tingling, numbness, or weakness in the legs or feet, or even bowel and bladder problems, can result from pressure on a spinal nerve or the spinal cord.

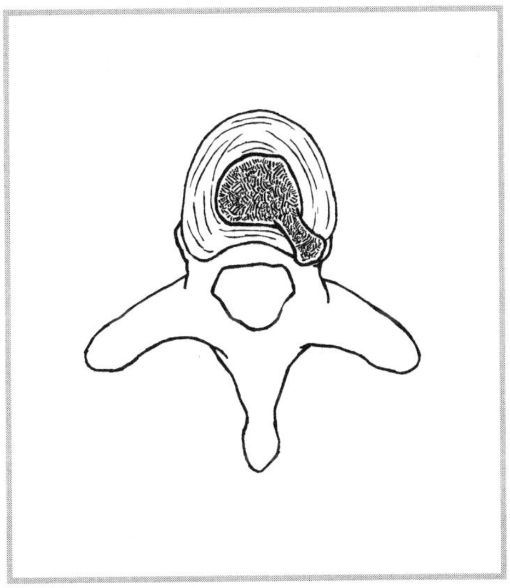

Fig. 3–7 Herniated Disc: Seepage of gel-like center *outside* the boundary of the disc.

INTERNAL DISC DERANGEMENT

Internal disc derangement (also known as **inflammation of the disc**) is an injury to the outer fibers of the disc. It may result in a seepage of the gel-like center through these fibers but within the boundaries of the disc (Fig. 3–8).

We now know that at least the outer third of the fibers of the disc are pain sensitive, and tears in this area can produce severe back pain and muscle spasms. Sometimes internal disc derangement produces pain that radiates down the leg, which can lead to its being mistaken for a herniated disc.

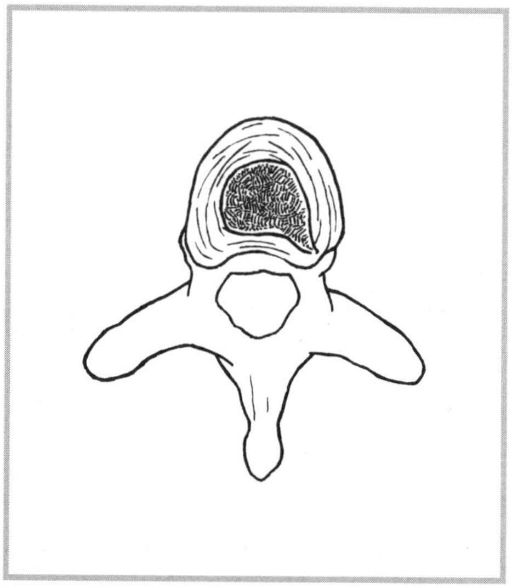

Fig. 3–8 Internal Disc Derangement: Seepage of gel-like center *within* the boundary of the disc.

SPONDYLOLISTHESIS

Spondylolisthesis is usually related to a defect or fracture (known as **spondylolysis**) at the back of a vertebra. This allows the vertebra above it to slide forward (Fig. 3–9,10).

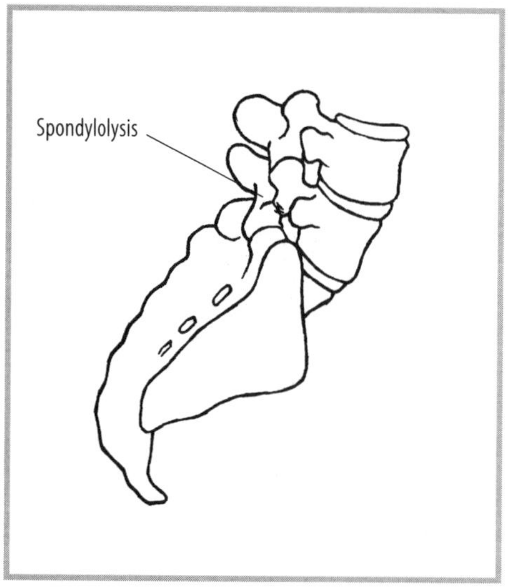

Fig. 3–9 Spondyloysis: a small defect or fracture in a vertebra.

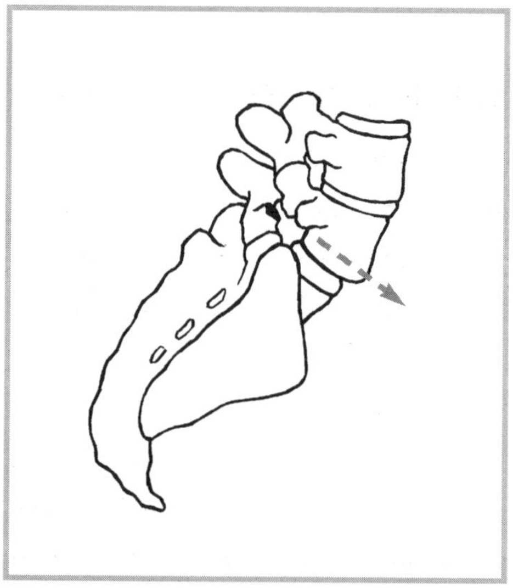

Fig. 3–10 Spondylolisthesis: weakened vertebra allows vertebra above to slide, compressing disc and causing pain.

The disc between the two affected vertebrae is likely to become injured in the process, and degenerative changes may result. The greater the amount of slippage, the more likely that the spondylolisthesis will result in pain. A large amount of slippage may result in pressure on the nerve roots or the spinal cord.

Those who perform activities that require significant amounts of hyperextension or rotation, such as diving, gymnastics, Olympic weight lifting, wrestling, and ballet, have a high incidence of spondylolisthesis.

Individuals with spondylolisthesis often experience pain when performing extension exercises. If you feel pain while doing these exercises, discontinue them.

SPINAL STENOSIS

Spinal stenosis involves narrowing of the spinal canal, narrowing of the passages between the vertebrae where the nerve roots exit, or both, with resultant pressure on the spinal cord and nerve roots. This narrowing may be present from birth. More commonly it results from degenerative changes in the discs and the facet joints. Spinal stenosis most often occurs in those over sixty. It is frequently accompanied by radiating pain, numbness, and weakness in the lower extremities. This pain is typically made worse by walking or standing and is relieved by sitting. In general, movements involving flexion typically relieve the symptoms, while those involving extension aggravate them.

SPRAINS

A **sprain** is an injury to a ligament, and lumbar sprain is one of the most common diagnoses for the sudden onset of low back pain. Approximately 20% of patients who undergo back surgery for disc herniation are found to have a torn interspinous ligament. (Interspinous ligaments span the entire length of the spine and run from one spinous process at the back of a vertebra to the next.)

Most of these tears occur at the level of L4-L5 and L5-S1, where the majority of back pain syndromes arise. The combination of a torn interspinous ligament and a herniated disc appears most commonly in the thirty-to-forty age group, the group that experiences the highest incidence of back pain. In a certain number of cases, injury to the interspinous ligament may lead to an unstable spinal segment and eventually to disc herniation.

SACROILIAC JOINT SPRAINS

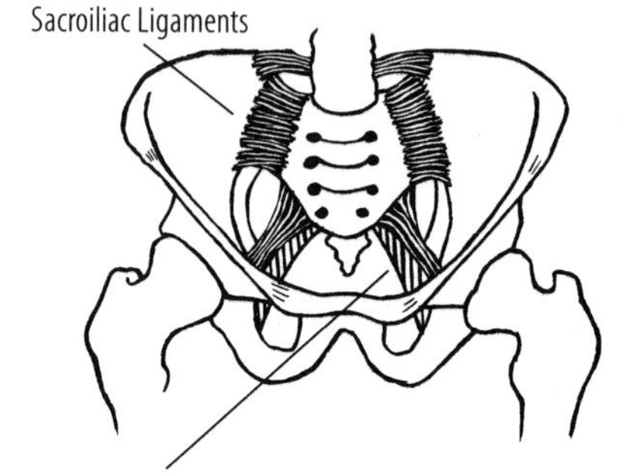

Fig. 3–11 Ligaments of the sacroiliac joint

The sacroiliac joint connects the sacrum to the ilium, or hip bone. Some researchers believe that this joint is not very mobile. They note that it is stabilized by ligaments so strong that they permit only small amounts of motion (Fig. 3–11). These researchers conclude, therefore, that the sacroiliac joints are not likely to be injured, except during pregnancy when the hormone **relaxin** causes these and other ligaments to loosen.

Other researchers, however, have clearly shown that this joint does move and participates in motions such as walking, bending, and lifting. Therefore, the sacroiliac joint is a potential source of low back pain, though it accounts for only a small percentage of cases.

FACET JOINT SYNDROME

The facet joints can be injured through compression—as in sudden hyperextension or extension combined with rotation—or through overstretching—as may occur in flexion or rotation. A small percentage of older individuals may suffer from pain produced by severe degenerative changes of the facet joints.

THORACOLUMBAR FASCIA STRAIN OR TEAR

Most of the research has failed to find evidence of sensory nerves in the thoracolumbar fascia, suggesting that it is not pain sensitive. So injury to the fascia is not a likely cause of back pain. As we saw in Chapter 2, though, this structure plays a critical role in the stability of the lumbar spine, and injury to it could render the spine more vulnerable to future injury.

MUSCLE STRAIN

Muscle strain is a common diagnosis for low back pain, but it is probably not justified in many cases. Patients with acute low back pain frequently experience muscle spasms, but these may represent the body's attempt to immobilize the area to prevent further injury.

Although injured muscles are unlikely to be the primary cause of low back pain, after an injury these muscles are likely to be weak. Strengthening them will help to prevent future episodes of back pain.

DEGENERATIVE JOINT DISEASE

Degenerative joint disease refers to arthritic changes that occur in the spine and the other joints in the body. There are two forms of degeneration that typically occur in the spine. Degenerative changes associated with the discs are referred to as **spondylosis**, or **degenerative disc disease**. Degeneration of the facet joints is usually referred to as **osteoarthritis**.

Degenerative disc disease includes disc space narrowing and the formation of bone spurs (Fig. 3–12). These spurs are jagged extensions of the bone that typically occur along either the front or back edges of the vertebrae where they meet the discs. *Osteoarthritis* of the facet joints is typically marked by bone spurs growing on the margins of the facets.

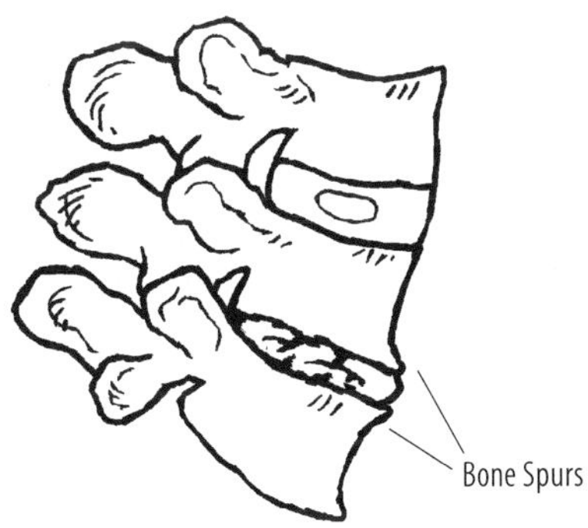

Fig. 3–12 Bone spurs forming along edges of vertebrae.

Degenerative changes are usually associated with aging and should not be viewed as a disease process but rather as an adaptation to various stresses and strains that the spine has been subjected to over the years. But they do tend to make the spine less able to tolerate the stress of various activities. Previous back injuries, trauma, and heavy physical work, have, however, been associated with cases of excessive degeneration.

SUBLUXATION

Chiropractors typically use the term **subluxation** to describe restricted or abnormal motion between vertebrae. Such subluxations (also known as **joint dysfunctions**) are believed to play a role in back pain. Manipulation, which has been shown to help relieve back pain, is believed to restore proper motion between vertebrae either by releasing adhesions around the spinal joints or by affecting the nerve receptors that are present either in these joints or in the surrounding muscles.

ACUTE LOCKED BACK SYNDROME

Walter Brennan in the television show *The Real McCoys* used to walk around bent over, complaining about his sacroiliac. His bent-over position, however, would suggest that he may have been suffering from **acute locked back syndrome** (also known as **lumbago**). Acute locked back syndrome involves severe pain and the inability to straighten up from a bent position (Fig. 3–13). A variety of causes have been proposed for this syndrome, including muscle spasm, ligament sprain, and disc derangement or herniation. Disc derangement and bulging, or herniation, appear to be the most likely explanations.

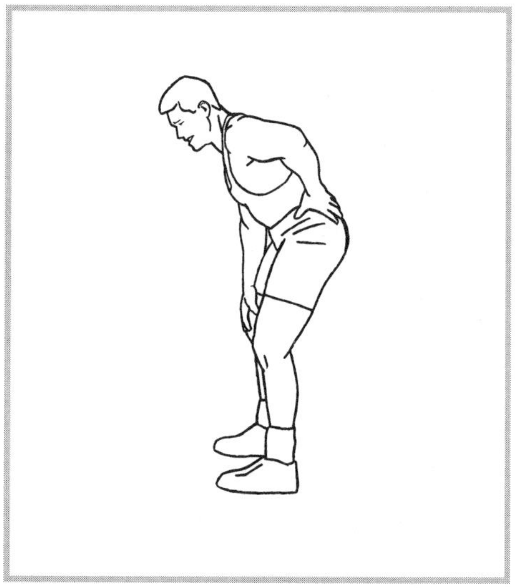

Fig. 3–13 Acute Locked-Back Syndrome

When tears occur in the outer fibers of the disk, all or part of its gel-like center can bulge through these tears and become wedged to the back or the side. An injury of this type typically occurs when you bend forward or sit in a flexed position. The gel-like material presses against the pain-sensitive fibers at the back of the disc, or the posterior longitudinal ligament. Attempting to stand up straight compresses the gel-like center, forcing it to press harder against the outer disc fibers. Remaining bent forward decreases pain because it takes pressure off the material in the disc's center.

Other Factors

Scoliosis, leg length inequality, facet tropism, obesity, pregnancy, emotional stress, cigarette smoking, and vibrational forces are frequently mentioned as possible causes of low back pain. Let's take a quick look at the current research on these potential contributors.

SCOLIOSIS

Scoliosis is a condition marked by sideways curvature of the spine (Fig. 3–14). As a consequence of this curvature, the muscles on one side of the spine protrude more than those on the other side. This condition may be present from birth, or it may develop from the tendency to overuse the muscles on one side of the back. This results in functionally created lateral curves in the spine. A bowler or a professional baseball pitcher would be a candidate for this type of scoliosis.

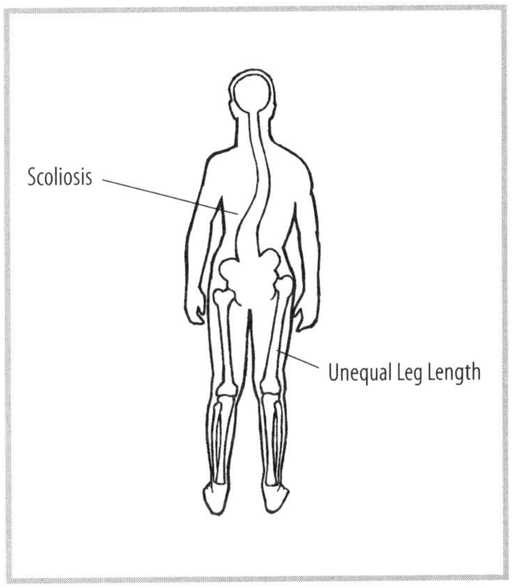

Fig. 3–14 Scoliosis

Scoliosis may or may not produce back pain in an individual. If back pain occurs, it can usually be relieved through conservative measures such as chiropractic manipulation, though such techniques will usually not correct the scoliosis. Specific exercises to address the muscle imbalance may be beneficial for a patient with scoliosis. These can be prescribed by a competent medical or chiropractic physician once the precise nature of the problem is determined.

LEG LENGTH INEQUALITY

Leg length inequality is common. Small degrees of inequality are usually benign; larger degrees, however, may result in a tilting of the sacrum and the pelvis with resulting distortion of the sacroiliac joints, the pelvis, and the lumbar spine. A lateral curvature of the spine, or scoliosis, may result. Asymmetrical weight bearing and the resulting uneven stresses on the spine may cause back pain and may produce structural and degenerative changes in the facet joints, the vertebral endplates, and the discs.

Fortunately, this condition can often be corrected by placing a heel lift in the shoe of the shorter leg. Exercise can then help to correct the pre-existing muscle imbalances.

FACET TROPISM

Facet tropism is an asymmetrical orientation of the facets that may be related to increased likelihood of back pain. This condition is fairly common and allows more rotation to occur in one direction than another. Since the facets protect the discs from injury by limiting the amount of rotation that can occur, facet tropism may result in increased incidence of disc injury.

OBESITY

Many researchers believe obesity increases likelihood of low back pain. The argument goes like this: Excess body fat, especially in the abdomen, places more loading on the spine and leads to more back problems. Overweight individuals frequently lean back to counterbalance the additional load that they carry, thereby increasing the normal curvature of the lumbar spine (Fig. 3–15). This posture places an increased load on the facet joints and jams them together; it also compresses the back of the discs.

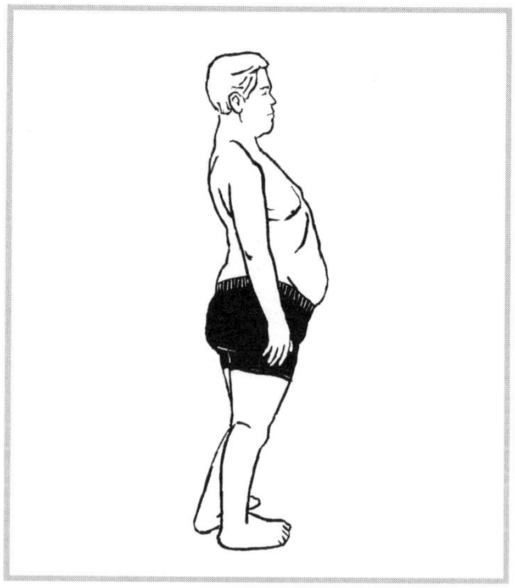

Fig. 3–15 Obesity can increase the curve of the lumbar spine, compressing discs.

Obesity is also linked to poor fitness levels, which have in turn been connected with low back pain. Overweight individuals should try to lose weight in a slow, safe manner with a low calorie diet (not less than 1200 calories per day) in conjunction with a synergistic exercise program selected from Chapter 6.

PREGNANCY

Pregnancy is clearly associated with an increased occurrence of low back pain. Shifts in the alignment of the spine combined with weight gain (typically 20 to 40 lbs) are responsible. Furthermore, the hormone **relaxin** causes the ligaments to loosen during pregnancy, resulting in misalignments of the spine and pelvis. In particular, shifts in the sacroiliac joints have been noted.

Manipulation and exercise are virtually the only two effective techniques for relieving this pain, until, of course, delivery. While it is often safe to perform exercise during pregnancy, you should consult your physician before doing so.

EMOTIONAL AND PSYCHOSOCIAL FACTORS

Factors such as depression and job dissatisfaction are recognized as playing a role in low back pain and disability. Because it is often difficult to find a specific cause for many cases of low back pain, it is easy to jump to the conclusion that the pain is psychological. But it is more likely that psychological problems arise after an individual experiences and tries to deal with back pain.

Many chronic back pain sufferers end up afraid to be active. This is part of a pattern known as **illness behavior**. The challenge for these patients is to focus on becoming more functional rather than on simply avoiding pain. Research shows that becoming fit and conditioning the muscles that support the spine may result in a decrease of pain. Exercise itself frequently has a pain-relieving effect through release of chemicals known as endorphins, which can produce a feeling of happiness and well being. Exercise can also bolster self-confidence and help overcome fear of activity.

SMOKING

A number of studies have found a positive correlation between cigarette smoking and low back pain, especially in cases of herniated discs and chronic back pain. Nicotine is thought to cause a reduction in blood flow to the vertebrae. This would adversely affect disc metabolism and nutrition and make the discs more vulnerable to mechanical strain. This is a good reason—in addition to the other well-known health risks—to stop smoking now.

VIBRATIONAL FORCES

Bus, truck, and tractor drivers, as well as operators of heavy equipment, suffer from increased instances of low back pain and disc herniation. Vibrational forces are believed to reduce the transport of nutrients into discs and to therefore increase the rate of disc degeneration.

Though vibrational forces are likely to play a role in the incidence of back injuries in drivers of motor vehicles, commercial and otherwise, prolonged sitting is also likely to play a substantial role.

❖ ❖ ❖

Preventing or relieving low back pain requires knowing how your back functions and putting that knowledge to work. In the previous three chapters, we've covered a good deal of theoretical material. Now it's time to discuss the synergistic exercise program itself. Chapter 4 will give you an overview of the program's goals, and in Chapter 5 you'll find complete descriptions of each of the exercises used in the routines in Chapter 6.

CHAPTER 3

WHAT GOES WRONG

9 Steps to Relief

Time for all the theory we've covered to pay off. In this chapter we'll outline the whys and wherefores of the HFL Back Relief Program. In the next, we'll cover the individual exercises used in the program and then, in the final chapter, we'll lay out how to select and implement the routine that's right for you. Your informed and consistent performance of that routine is the final piece of the puzzle. When you put it in place, the image you'll see is your own back—healthy, pain free, and strong.

4

The right exercise program can help you promote the health of your spinal tissues, increase your bone density, improve your posture, and reduce your risk of disc herniation. But it must be the *right* program. Every aspect of your program should function wholistically to reinforce, and amplify, all other parts of the program. This is **synergism**, and it's what makes HFL's Back Relief Program unique.

Take, for example, the issue of **exercise order**. For any group of exercises there is a particular sequence that affords maximum benefit to all the muscles involved. When you perform the routine in that sequence, each exercise becomes more powerful than when done in other sequences or alone.

The program is also unique in recognizing that your back history and lifestyle are not the same as those of other users. The needs of a bodybuilder differ from those of a beginning exerciser, an athlete recovering from injury, or a non-exercising office worker. So, in Chapter 6, you'll find a number of variations on the basic rehabilitative and preventative exercise routine. Choose the one that most closely matches your requirements and fitness level.

All of the routines in the Back Relief Program focus on the following nine objectives—goals that take into account the complex interactions of the muscles, nerves, bones, and ligaments that make your back so versatile.

Checklist: 9 Steps to Back Relief

1. STRENGTHEN THE BACK MUSCLES

Strengthening the back muscles is based on a simple equation: when your muscles are stronger, your back can handle greater loads. Research has shown that strengthening decreases the incidence and severity of back injury. The symptoms of chronic low back pain also tend to improve with increased back strength, even for patients with herniated discs.

We should take a minute here to mention the psychic boost that you get from the endorphins that are released into the bloodstream when you perform virtually any exercise. Endorphins are chemicals that promote a general sense of well being, and they may even contribute to reducing pain.

2. INCREASE THE SIZE OF THE BACK MUSCLES

Larger, thicker muscles—like stronger muscles—are better able to support your spine. The back muscles play an important role in lifting, and their size directly affects this ability. This is probably due to the hydraulic amplifier mechanism that we discussed in Chapter 2. As you'll remember, this theory suggests that when your back muscles contract, they expand and put pressure on the thoracolumbar fascia. An opposition, or tension, is created as a result, and this helps the spine to straighten out from a flexed position. Larger back muscles can better fill the thoracolumbar fascia and make your lifting more efficient.

Many sufferers of low back pain tend to experience atrophy, weakness, and decreased endurance of their back muscles. Part of the atrophy, or reduction in muscle size, results from inactivity following injury—an important reason for beginning a rehabilitative exercise program as soon as possible after you injure your back.

3. INCREASE THE ENDURANCE OF THE BACK MUSCLES

The endurance of your back muscles may be even more important than strength in preventing back injuries. Your low back's endurance is put to the test constantly throughout the day. Your back muscles must contract repeatedly without fatiguing during bending, and they must contract and hold a position during activities that involve leaning forward, such as brushing your teeth, washing the dishes, or pulling weeds. Increased back muscle endurance has also been shown to decrease depression and physical limitation associated with chronic back pain.

4. INCREASE THE DENSITY OF THE VERTEBRAE

Like your muscles, your bones adapt to stress. By placing regular stresses on your spine through exercise, you can actually increase the bone density of your vertebral bodies. This makes your vertebrae better able to resist compressive forces. Increasing bone density is important for everyone, but it is especially crucial for post-menopausal women, because their bones tend to become thin due to hormonal changes.

5. STRENGTHEN THE ABS AND OTHER TRUNK MUSCLES

Because the back and abdominal muscles must work together to support the lower spine, it's important to strengthen abdominal and other trunk muscles in concert with your back muscles. Research has shown that increasing abdominal strength may reduce low back pain.

6. IMPROVE AEROBIC CAPACITY

Increased aerobic capacity adds significantly to your overall fitness level, thereby lowering your chances of back injury. Regular aerobic training, such as walking or cycling, increases your endurance and stimulates blood and oxygen circulation.

Many low back pain sufferers have less stiffness and pain when walking or performing other low-intensity forms of aerobic training. This may be because the increased oxygen flow promotes the healing capacity of the muscles, discs, and other connective tissues in the back. Sitting and standing are often reported to increase stiffness and sometimes pain as well.

7. IMPROVE OVERALL STRENGTH AND ENDURANCE

A full-body weight-training program is essential to promoting a healthy back. More than any other activity, weight training helps you to strengthen your muscles, tendons, ligaments, and bones. Weight-training exercises involve pushing, pulling, and lifting, and they provide the best training for the stresses and strains you encounter in day-to-day living and athletic performance.

8. IMPROVE THE FLEXIBILITY OF THE HIP MUSCLES

In our sedentary society, shortened hip flexors and hamstrings are fairly common, and they can alter your movement patterns while lifting and bending. This can cause increased or asymmetrical stresses on your low back. Exercises to increase the flexibility of your hip muscles are essential to back health and can reduce your potential for injury.

9. IMPROVE BALANCE AND COORDINATION

Your eyes furnish your brain with information about the location of your body and its parts in space. This information also comes to your brain through various nerve receptors located in your ligaments, joints, and muscles. In order to balance and control your body in space, your brain must have constantly updated input. Following a back injury, this ability can be diminished and delay your recovery. By performing certain exercises, specifically those that involve balance and coordination, you can regain this lost sensory input. Increasing this input (known as proprioception) to your trunk muscles may help to improve your spinal stability and decrease your pain.

❖ ❖ ❖

These nine objectives form the basis for the Back Relief Program. Now, let's take the plunge and begin to explore the exercises themselves.

The Exercises

This chapter describes each exercise used in the routines in Chapter 6. Step-by-step instructions, tips on technique, and detailed illustrations will help you optimize your performance of these exercises. To minimize your risk of injury, please pay special attention to the tips on technique.

After you've selected the appropriate routine from Chapter 6, take *The Back Relief Book* along with you to the gym, where you can practice the right way to do the exercises and see firsthand the pitfalls to avoid.

5

THE EXERCISES

Key Terms

Isolation Exercises—Movements that aim to strengthen by targeting specific muscles; in this case, the back and abdominal muscles.

Stabilization Exercises—Also known as functional strength exercises, movements that aim to increase overall spinal stability by working the back, abdominal, and hip muscles in combination.

Isometric Exercises—Exercises that involve an intense muscular contraction that doesn't produce movement (e.g., pushing against a door jamb). We'll use isometric exercises to help build postural endurance.

Dynamic Exercises—Also known as isotonic exercises, these involve a muscular contraction that does result in movement (e.g., a barbell curl). Dynamic exercises can be used to achieve a number of goals—increasing muscular strength, tendon strength, endurance, and speed. We'll be using them to increase muscular strength, primarily of the lower back and abdominal muscles.

Finding Your Neutral Position

In a number of the exercises, you'll be asked to maintain a "neutral" position of your spine. This is—for most individuals—the normal, pain-free, moderately arched position you assume when you are standing upright.

Try the following exercise to get a better sense of this position: Get down on your hands and knees with your hands directly under your shoulders and your knees under your hips. Round your back up like an angry cat; then, arch it down as far as possible. Find a position between these two extremes that is comfortable for you. For most people, this is the neutral position.

If you have trouble attaining this neutral position or if you are uncomfortable or feel pain in this position, you should seek help from a competent medical or chiropractic doctor or physical therapist.

General Training Principles

IF YOU'RE INJURY-FREE

If you are currently injury-free, you should perform each exercise until you feel a burning sensation in the target muscles. This burning is caused by the body producing a waste product called lactic acid and is usually a sign that you are working a muscle hard enough to make it become stronger and larger.

Keep in mind, though, that there is a big difference between the soft burn of muscle being urged beyond its limits, and the sharp pain of muscle being injured by overzealous training. The first is a necessity; the second, a set-back.

IF YOU'RE INJURED

If healthy, non-injured tissue can be thought of as steel cable, injured tissue by comparison has the strength of slightly torn cardboard (yes, there really is that big a difference). So if you're recovering from a back injury or suffering from chronic back pain, forget the "Go for the burn!" approach.

To start off, exercise only to the point of fatigue, *not pain*. As you get stronger and your back condition improves, you can gradually increase intensity until, as is appropriate for someone who is injury-free, you feel the lactic acid burn at the end of each set.

One more note: Exercises at the beginning stages of a rehabilitation program emphasize lying on the back or face down. As you get stronger, your spinal tissues heal and the ability to stabilize the spine improves. At that point, you'll be ready for movements that make greater use of more weight-bearing positions.

Isometric Back Movements

The following exercises contract your back muscles and hold them in one position for a short period of time. They help to build your isometric strength, or postural endurance.

If you suffer from uncontrolled high blood pressure (diastolic pressure above 90 or systolic pressure above 140), you should consult your doctor before performing isometric exercises because they cause a short-term rise in blood pressure and could be harmful to your health.

1. PRONE HEAD AND SHOULDER LIFTS

Lie face down on an exercise mat or the floor (Fig. 5–1a). Place your arms by your sides; you may want to place your hands in the small of your back. Tuck your chin in, and lift your head and shoulders up (Fig. 5–1b). Feel the contraction in your low back muscles as you lift, but don't force your back to arch as much as it can. Hold this position for 1 to 10 seconds.

As you get stronger, hold each contraction longer. This exercise can also be made more challenging (and more comfortable) by placing one or more pillows under your stomach.

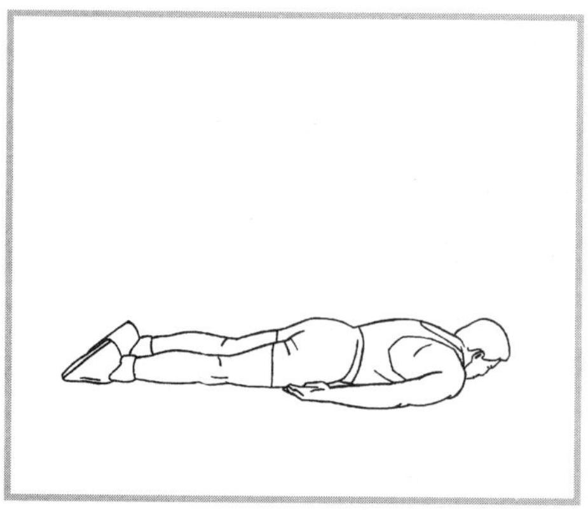

Fig. 5–1a

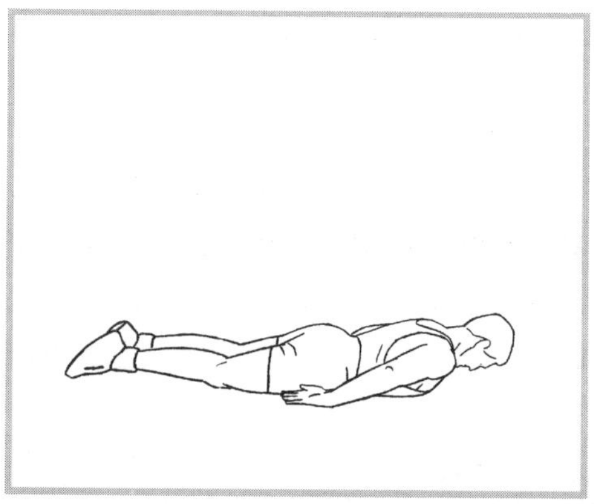

Fig. 5–1b

2. PRONE LEG LIFTS (ISOMETRIC)

This exercise is similar to the one above. Lie face down on an exercise mat or the floor (Fig. 5–2a). Place your arms by your sides; you may want to place your hands in the small of your back. Lift your legs (Fig. 5–2b). You will probably feel more contraction in your low back than you did while doing prone head and shoulder lifts. You will also feel a contraction in your buttocks and, to a lesser extent, your hamstrings; this exercise has the added benefit of conditioning your buttocks. Hold this position for 1 to 10 seconds. Gradually increase the time you hold the contraction. Again, this exercise can be made more challenging by placing one or more pillows under your stomach.

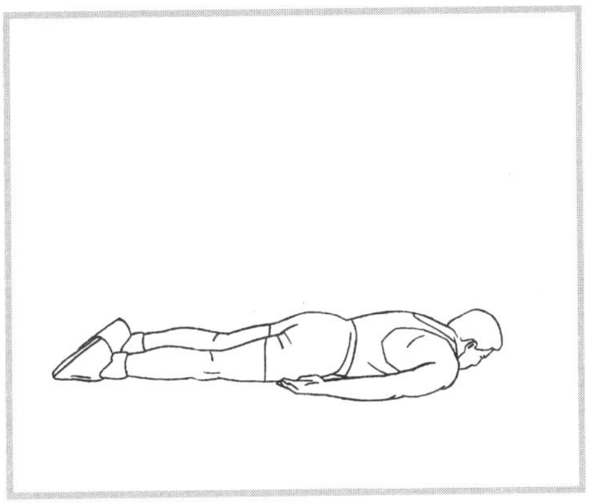

Fig. 5–2a

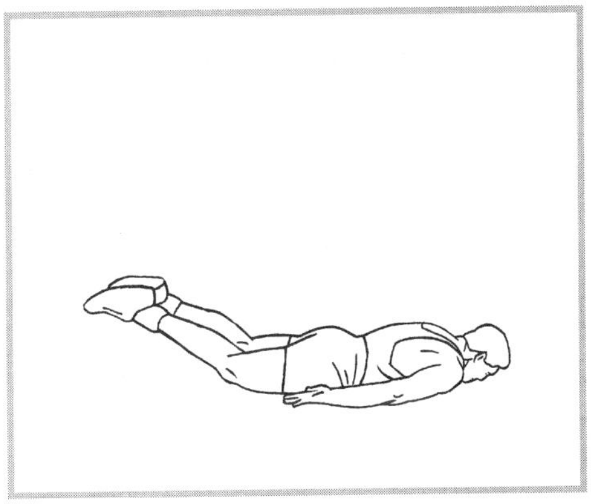

Fig. 5–2b

3. PRONE SHOULDER AND LEG LIFTS (ISOMETRIC)

This exercise combines Prone Head and Shoulder Lifts with Prone Leg Lifts. Lie face down on an exercise mat or the floor (Fig. 5–3a). Place your arms down by your sides; you may want to place your hands in the small of your back. Tuck in your chin and simultaneously lift your head and shoulders and your legs (Fig. 5–3b). Hold this position for 1 to 10 seconds. Gradually increase the time you hold the contraction. Again, this exercise can be made more challenging and more comfortable by placing one or more pillows under the stomach.

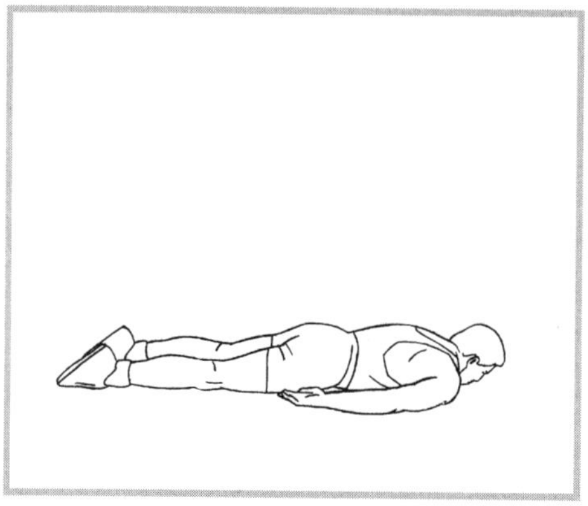

Fig. 5–3a

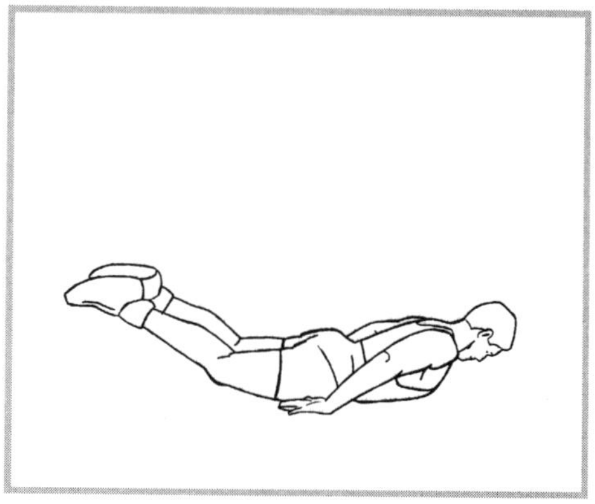

Fig. 5–3b

You can further increase the difficulty by placing your hands behind your head or extending them *over* your head, so you look as if you are flying like Superman.

4. STANDING OR KNEELING ISOMETRIC HOLDS

Stand and bend your knees slightly. Fold your arms across your chest (Fig. 5–4a). Tense your buttocks; then bend forward with your back slightly arched (Fig. 5–4b). Hold this position for 30 seconds or more. You should feel tension in your hamstrings, your buttocks, and your back muscles.

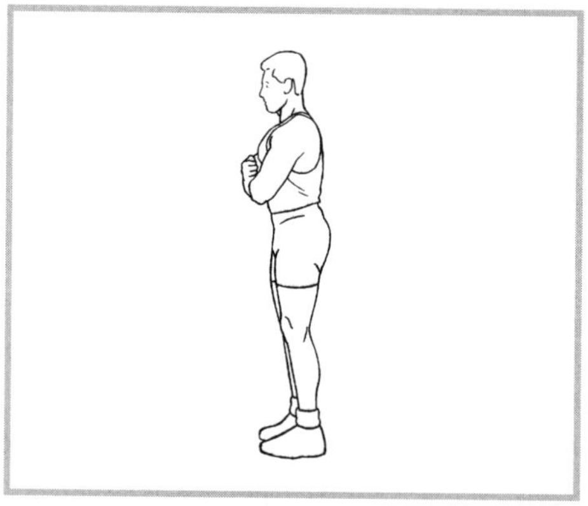

Fig. 5–4a

Fig. 5–4b

The kneeling version is essentially the same as the standing version. Kneel on several pillows, several exercise mats, or a step-class step (Fig. 5–4c). Hold your legs locked in one position. Bend only at your hips and keep your back arched in the neutral position (Fig. 5–4d).

Fig. 5–4c

Fig. 5–4d

If you are trying this exercise for the first time and have had a back injury, do not force yourself to bend too far forward. The farther you bend, the more difficult it becomes. Slowly increase the amount of bending, but try to exercise in the pain-free range of motion. Your goal should be to build up to at least a 2-minute hold.

5. HORIZONTAL ISOMETRIC HOLDS

Position yourself face down on a horizontal back extension bench with your hips over the edge. Contract your hamstrings, buttocks, and low back muscles and hold your body out straight for a count of 10 seconds or more. If you can keep your knees slightly bent, this is preferred because it keeps them from hyperextending and involves the buttocks more. This exercise can be done with your arms in the small of your back, folded over your chest, behind your head, or extended above your head. It is best to start with your arms in the small of your back. Folding your arms across your chest, as shown in Figure 5–5, increases the difficulty. Keeping your arms behind your head is even harder, and holding your arms extended above your head is the most difficult version. You should try to build up to a 3-minute hold.

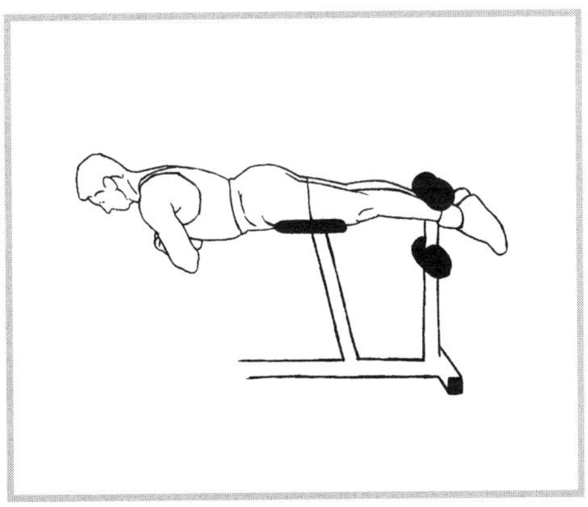

Fig. 5–5

6. BALL ISOMETRIC HOLDS W/FEET AGAINST WALL

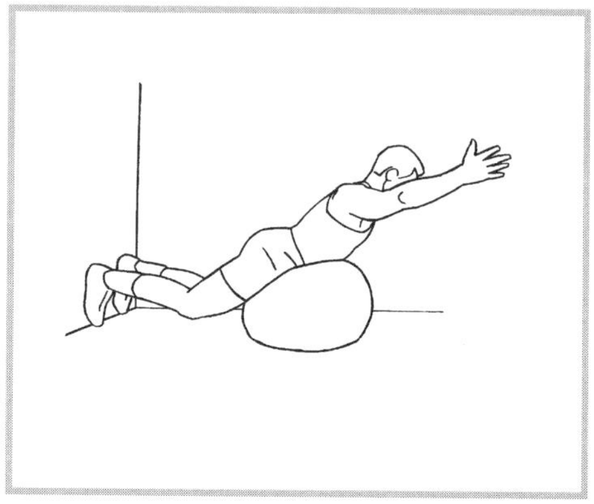

Fig. 5–6

Kneel and place the bottoms of your feet against the wall behind you. Wedge an appropriately sized exercise ball (the average size is 65 cm) against your thighs and lean over it. Then push yourself out over the ball until your knees are only slightly bent. Your body should now be suspended over the ball with the ball under your hips and stomach. Your back should be slightly arched and both arms should be extended above your head (Fig. 5–6). Hold this position for up to 2 minutes. Repeat if desired.

Dynamic Back Movements

To isolate your back muscles, you must eliminate pelvic rotation so you can prevent your buttocks and hamstrings from doing most of the work. Bending should occur at the center of your lumbar spine (roughly L3), which is approximately the same level as your navel.

7. PRONE HEAD AND SHOULDER LIFTS (DYNAMIC)

Lie face down on an exercise mat or the floor (Fig. 5–7a). Place one or more pillows under your stomach to increase your range of motion. Place your arms by your sides; you may want to place your hands in the small of your back. Tuck your chin in, and lift your head and shoulders up (Fig. 5–7b). Feel the contraction in your low back muscles as you lift, but do not force your back to arch as much as it possibly can. Hold this position for a second only and return to the starting point. Perform repetitions slowly and smoothly.

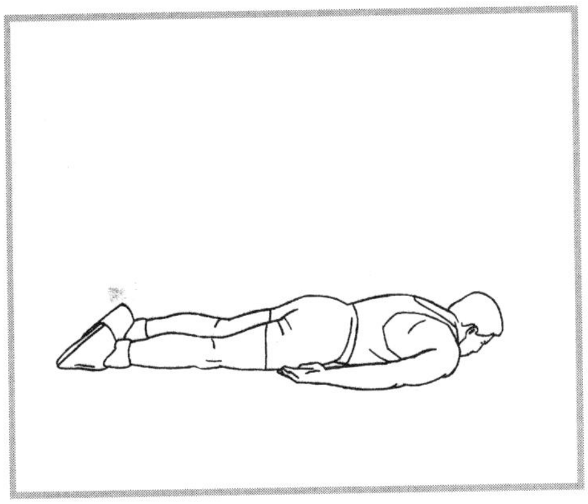

Fig. 5–7a

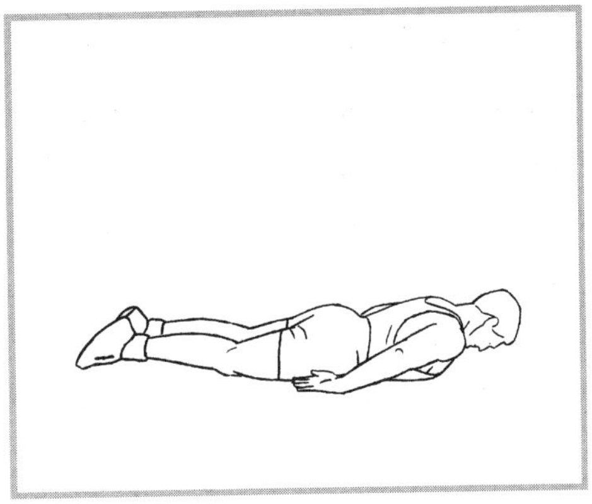

Fig. 5–7b

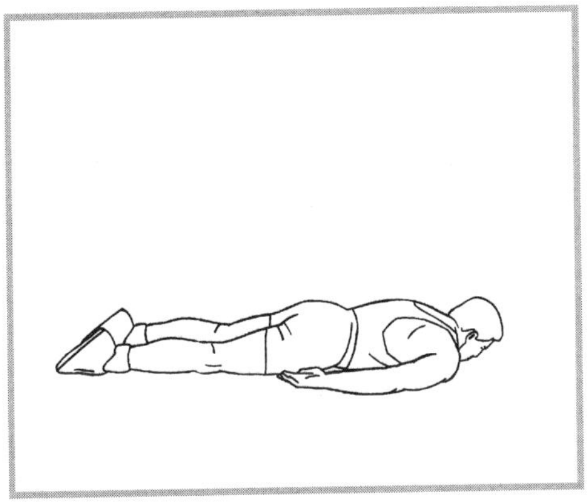

Fig. 5–8a

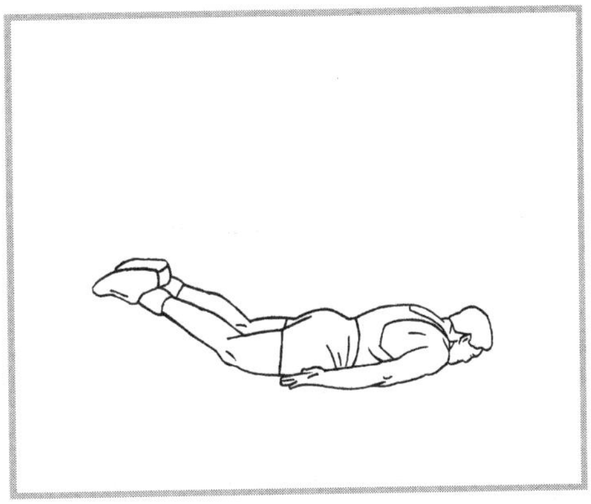

Fig. 5–8b

8. PRONE LEG LIFTS (DYNAMIC)

Lie face down on an exercise mat or the floor (Fig. 5–8a). Place one or more pillows under your stomach to increase your range of motion. Place your arms by your sides; you may want to place your hands in the small of your back. Lift your legs (Fig. 5–8b). You will probably feel more contraction in your low back than you did while doing the prone head and shoulder lifts. Hold this position for 1 second only and return to the starting point. Perform repetitions slowly and smoothly.

9. PRONE SHOULDER AND LEG LIFTS (DYNAMIC)

This exercise combines Prone Head and Shoulder Lifts with Prone Leg Lifts. Lie face down on an exercise mat or the floor (Fig. 5–9a). Place one or more pillows under your stomach to increase your range of motion. Place your arms by your sides; you may want to place your hands in the small of your back. Simultaneously lift your head and shoulders and your legs (Fig. 5–9b). Hold this position for 1 second only and return to the starting point. Perform repetitions slowly and smoothly.

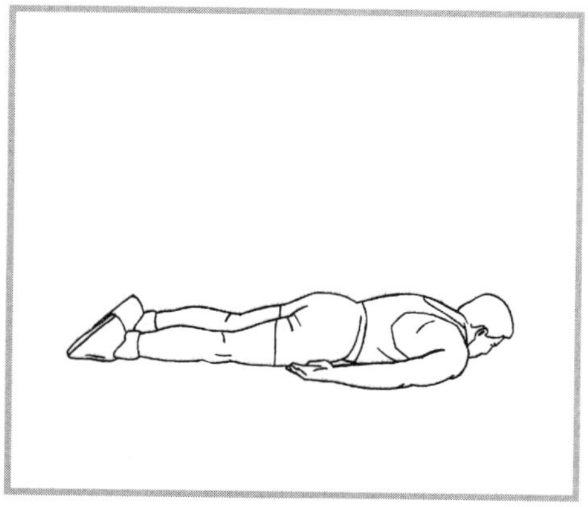

Fig. 5–9a

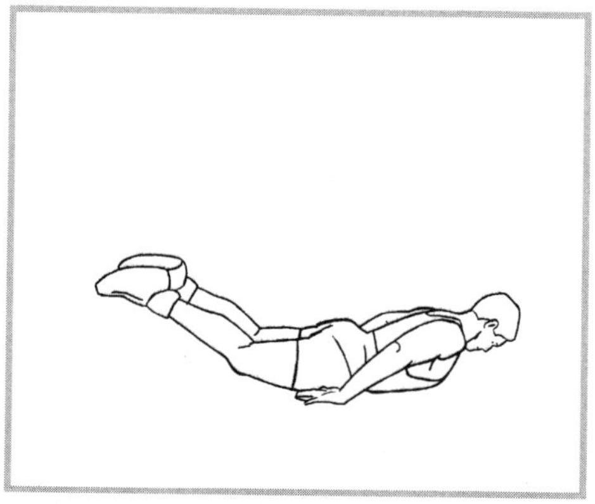

Fig. 5–9b

10. QUADRUPED (DYNAMIC)

Fig. 5–10a

Get on your hands and knees on an exercise mat. Make sure your hands are underneath your shoulders and your knees underneath your hips (Fig. 5–10a). Find your neutral position, and then lift and bend one arm, bringing the elbow toward your navel. At the same time, bend your opposite knee and bring it up toward the elbow (Fig. 5–10b). Feel your abdominals contract. Then simultaneously extend the arm over your head and the leg backward in one slow, smooth movement (Fig. 5–10c). Make sure that you point your thumb upward as you raise your arm over your head. Your back will round slightly during the crunch portion of the exercise and

Fig. 5–10b

Fig. 5–10c

will return to the neutral position at the completion. Both your back and abdominal muscles are active during this exercise. Repeat 5 to 15 times and then change to the opposite arm and leg. Ankle and wrist weights can be added to increase difficulty.

11. QUADRUPED W/ROTATION (DYNAMIC)

Get on your hands and knees on an exercise mat. Make sure your hands are underneath your shoulders and your knees underneath your hips (Fig. 5–11a). Find your neutral position, and then extend one arm straight out to the side. Lift your arm up in a circular fashion and turn your head, shoulders, and upper body along with it in the same direction (Fig. 5–11b). Repeat 5 to 15 times. Then perform the exercise on the other side. You may initially have difficulty with this motion because it requires your spine to rotate through the normally tight thoracolumbar region. Eventually the exercise will help to loosen this area. This exercise also calls into play some of the spinal muscles active in rotation.

Fig. 5–11a

Fig. 5–11b

12. 45° LUMBAR EXTENSIONS

Position yourself face down on a 45° back extension bench with the pad just slightly above your hips so that you can block them from moving (Fig. 5–12a). Try to keep your knees slightly bent and tighten your buttocks and hamstrings. The goal is to lock in your hips to keep your powerful hip muscles—the gluteus maximus and the hamstrings—from doing most of the work. Instead, you want to bend only at the spine so that the low back muscles are forced to do all the work.

Bend at the waist, letting your back round as you slowly and smoothly lower your upper body (Fig. 5–12b). Start with a narrow range of motion—say 20° of bending. This is enough to recruit the back muscles. As you feel more confident in this movement, slowly increase the range of motion. Do not pause in the bottom position; instead, come back up with a slow, controlled movement until your spine is parallel to the line of the bench. Avoid hyperextending the spine at the top. Repeat.

We consider the 45° bench superior to the horizontal bench for the back extension exercise. The resistance of the 45° bench better matches the force-generating capabilities of your back muscles. When your trunk is bent at 45° on this bench (parallel to the floor), the resistance supplied by gravity is greatest. This is the point at which the back muscles are approximately halfway through their range of motion and can generate the most force. Thus, there is an ideal match of force and resistance curves.

Fig. 5–12a

Fig. 5–12b

13. BALL EXTENSIONS

Drape yourself face down over an appropriately sized gym ball so that it supports your midsection (Fig. 5–13a). Place your hands behind your back or at your sides. Allow your back to round over the ball. Then slowly raise your upper body one segment at a time—head, then shoulders, then upper back—until your low back is moderately arched (Fig. 5–13b). Avoid the hyperextended position. Lower yourself and perform repetitions. Placing your hands behind your head increases the difficulty. Extending your arms over your head (as if you're flying like Superman) makes this exercise even more challenging.

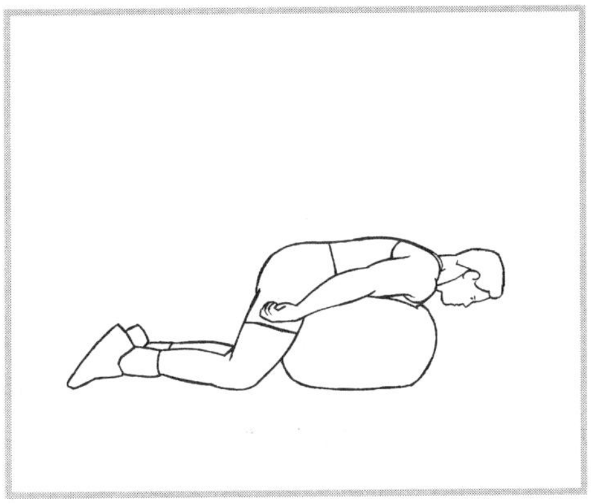

Fig. 5–13a

Fig. 5–13b

14. HORIZONTAL LUMBAR EXTENSIONS

This exercise is essentially the same as the 45° Lumbar Extension, but it is performed on the more popular horizontal bench. Position yourself face down on the bench with the pad just slightly above your hips so that you can block them from moving (Fig. 5–14a). Try to keep your knees slightly bent and tighten your buttocks and hamstrings. This will further lock in your pelvis and isolate the motion to the spine. Bend only at the waist, letting your back round as you slowly lower yourself (Fig. 5–14a). Do not pause at the bottom position; instead, come back up with a slow controlled movement. Start with a limited range of motion and increase it as you become comfortable with the movement.

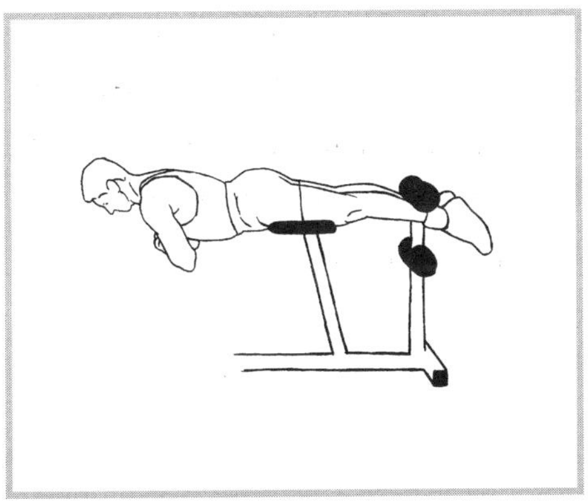

Fig. 5–14a

Fig. 5–14b

15. STANDING LUMBAR EXTENSIONS

This exercise can be performed without any special benches for those who are not avid gym-goers. Assume a comfortable stance, bend your knees slightly, and try to lock your hips by tensing your buttocks and hamstrings (Fig. 5–15a). Allow your spine to round as you bend slightly forward in a slow controlled manner (Fig. 5–15b). Then re-extend to the erect position. Start with a short range of motion and gradually increase it as your back becomes stronger.

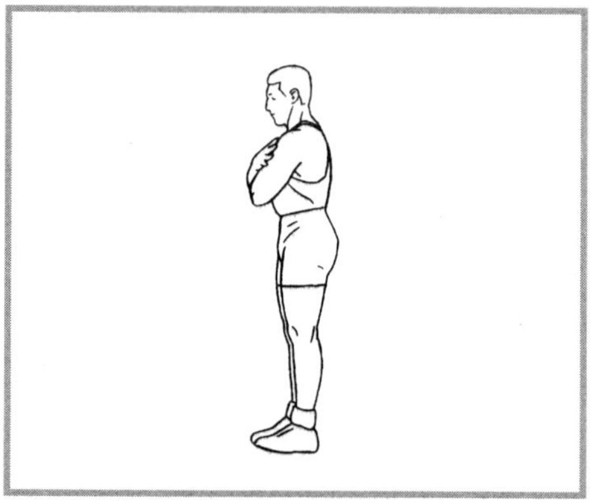

Fig. 5–15a

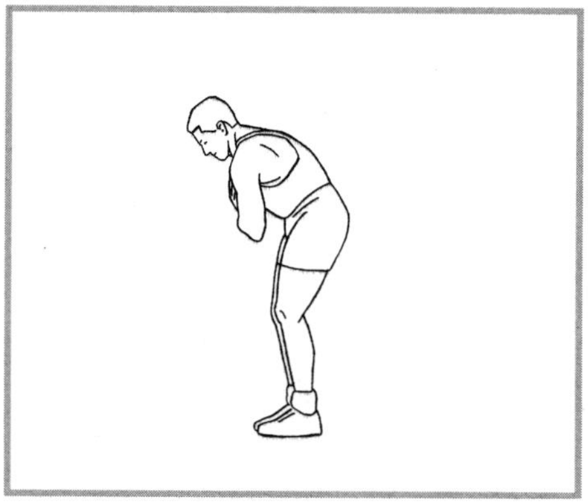

Fig. 5–15b

Fig. 5–15c

To perform the kneeling variation, kneel on several pillows, several mats, or a step-class step. Tense your buttocks and your hamstrings to lock your hip position, slowly allow your spine to round as you bend slightly forward (Fig. 5–15c), then smoothly and slowly return to the starting position. Start with a short range of motion and gradually increase it as you become comfortable with the exercise. A short range is sufficient to recruit the back muscles while avoiding the danger associated with the fully flexed position.

16. 45° LUMBAR EXTENSIONS W/ROTATION (ATHLETES ONLY)

Position yourself face down on the 45° bench with the pad just slightly above your hips so that you can block them from moving (Fig. 5–16a). Try to keep your knees slightly bent and tighten your gluteal muscles and hamstrings. This will further lock in your hips and isolate the motion to the spine. As you slowly lower yourself and round your back, simultaneously rotate your upper body in one direction (Fig. 5–16b). You can keep your hands crossed on your chest, or reach with your right hand toward the left. Then slowly reverse the motion, rotating back to center while extending back to the starting position. It is crucial that you keep a limited range of motion on this movement. Start with no more than 10° of rotation and 30° of bending. This is sufficient to recruit the small rotational muscles of the back. Repeat on the other side.

This exercise should only be performed in the advanced levels of the exercise routines and only by athletes. It carries a high degree of risk. Perform it in a very slow and controlled manner. Avoid excessive range of motion. If you have a known or suspected disc injury, skip this one.

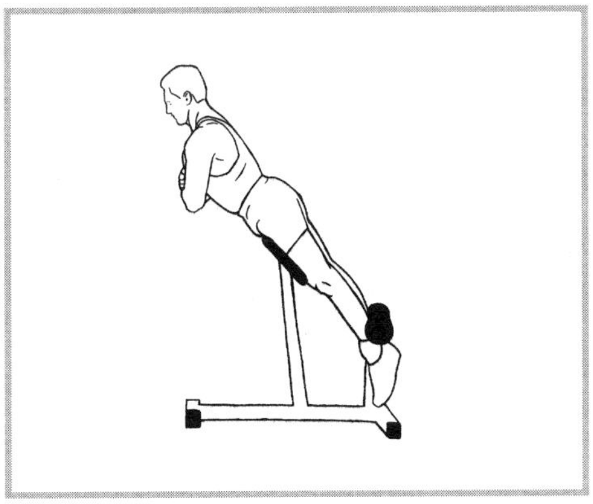

Fig. 5–16a

Fig. 5–16b

17. REVERSE RUSSIAN TWISTS (ATHLETES ONLY)

Hold yourself over the back extension bench, face down, with your hands in front of you, palms together, and fingers pointing straight ahead (Fig. 5–17a). Your back should be flat or slightly arched. Slowly rotate your body in one direction as far as you can while maintaining control (Fig. 5–17b), hold this position a second, and then return to the starting position. Repeat on the other side. **Caution: This exercise carries a high degree of risk and should only be performed by athletes involved in rotational sports.**

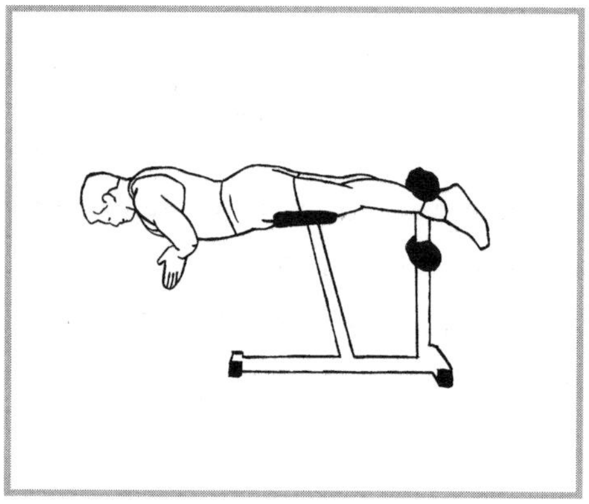

Fig. 5–17a

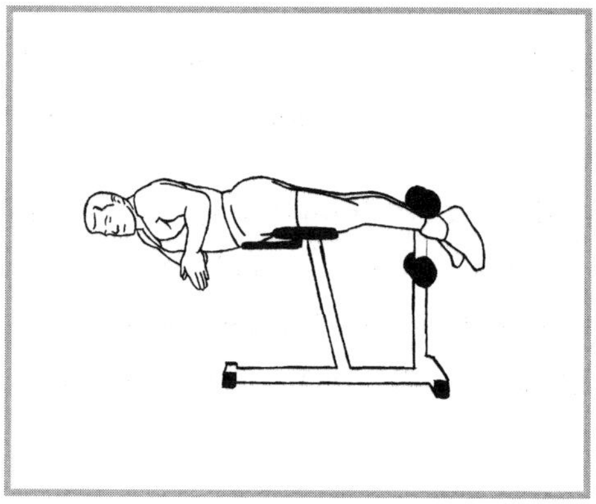

Fig. 5–17b

18. BACK EXTENSION BENCH TWISTS W/MED BALL (ATHLETES ONLY)

Place yourself over the horizontal back extension bench, face down, holding a medicine ball. Slowly rotate your body in one direction as far as you can while maintaining control (Fig. 5–18). You can release the medicine ball at the end of the rotation if a coach or partner is there to catch it and if you need to develop explosive power and speed. Hold onto the ball if you want to emphasize eccentric lumbar rotational strength. Repeat on the other side. **Caution: This exercise carries an even higher degree of risk than the Reverse Russian Twist and should only be performed by athletes involved in rotational sports.**

Fig. 5–18

Isometric Ab Movements

The exercises described below emphasize your lower abdominal, oblique, and transverse abdominis muscles. Your abdominal muscles are called upon to help stabilize your trunk and prevent trunk movements as much as or more than they are required to initiate them. Performing stabilization exercises will help your spine resist the stresses placed on it every day.

There are two main types of exercises included in this section: "pelvic tilting" and "bridging with pelvic tilting." These exercises are grouped into progressions, or series. Once you master one level in either progression, move on to the next level.

19. PELVIC TILTS – LEVEL 1

Lie on your back on the floor or a firm mat and bend your knees (Fig. 5–19a). Tilt your pelvis upward by drawing your lower abdominals toward your chest and pressing your back flat against the floor (Fig. 5–19b). When first learning this movement, place your hands palms down on the mat under the small of your back. This will allow you to feel the movement of your pelvis. Your abdominal contraction should put enough pressure on your hands that it would be difficult to slide one of them out from under your back. As you draw your lower abdominals toward your chest, try to pull your navel toward your back. This will maximally recruit the oblique and the transverse abdominis muscles, along with the lower abdominals.

Fig. 5–19a

Fig. 5–19b

Avoid pushing down with your feet during this movement, as this will transfer emphasis to the gluteal muscles. Also avoid tensing your neck; it should stay relaxed. After you get used to the feel of your back pressing against your hands, you can remove them and rest your arms alongside your head as illustrated. Make sure that you are lying on a firm mat or the floor so that you can feel your back pressing against the underlying surface.

Perform 5 repetitions of the pelvic tilt with a 5-second hold on each. Build up to 15 repetitions. When this is no longer challenging, increase to a 10-second hold for 5 repetitions. Build up to 15 repetitions.

20. PELVIC TILTS – LEVEL 2 (LEG SLIDE)

Lie flat on your back with both knees bent. Perform a posterior pelvic tilt (Fig. 5–20a) and then slowly slide one foot away from you. Extend your leg only as far as you can and still maintain the tilt. Attempt to lower until it is straight (Fig. 5–20b). The further your leg moves from your trunk, the more difficult it is to maintain your pelvic tilt. Make sure to keep firm pressure against your hands or the floor with your back. Then slide your leg back up to the bent-knee position. Perform 5 repetitions with each leg. Build up to 15 repetitions.

Fig. 5–20a

Fig. 5–20b

21. PELVIC TILTS – LEVEL 3

Lie flat on your back with both knees bent. Perform a posterior pelvic tilt (Fig. 5–21a) and then slowly raise one knee toward your chest (Fig. 5–21b); return your foot to the floor without losing your tilted position. Make sure to keep firm pressure against the floor with your back. Perform 5 repetitions with each leg. Build up to 15 repetitions.

Fig. 5–21a

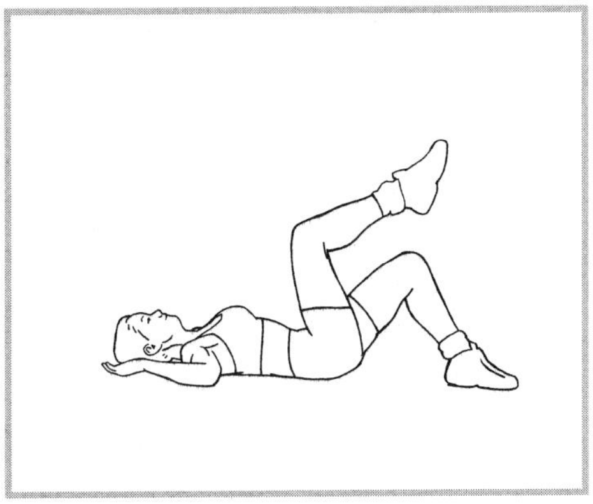

Fig. 5–21b

22. PELVIC TILTS – LEVEL 4

Lie flat on your back with both knees bent. Perform a posterior pelvic tilt and hold it (Fig. 5–22a). Straighten one knee (Fig. 5–22b) and then slowly lower the leg toward the floor, making sure to keep your back pressed against the floor (Fig. 5–22c). Reverse the motion and return to the starting position. Perform 5 repetitions with each leg. Build up to 15 repetitions with each leg.

Fig. 5–22a

Fig. 5–22b

Fig. 5–22c

23. PELVIC TILTS– LEVEL 5

Lie flat on your back with your knees bent and your arms bent and placed alongside your head on the floor. Raise both your knees up so both feet are off the floor (Fig. 5–23a). Perform a posterior pelvic tilt. Slowly lower one knee as far as you can, keeping your back flat (Fig. 5–23b)—ideally, until your foot touches the floor; then, slowly raise it back up. Because neither foot is on the ground initially, you are unable to use your gluteus maximus to push off. That makes this version of the pelvic tilt exercise difficult. Perform 5 repetitions on each side. Work up to 15 repetitions with each leg.

Fig. 5–23a

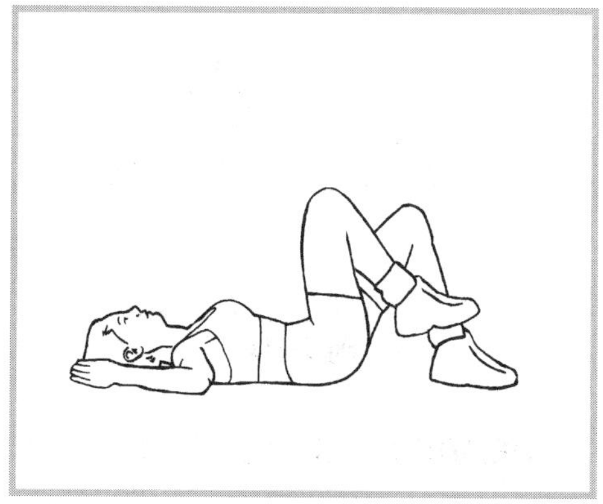

Fig. 5–23b

24. PELVIC TILTS – LEVEL 6

Lie flat on your back with your knees bent and your arms bent and alongside your head on the floor. Raise both knees so that your feet are off the floor (Fig. 5–24a). Perform a posterior pelvic tilt. Keeping one foot off the floor, straighten your other knee (Fig. 5–24b), slowly lower your straightened leg to the floor (Fig. 5–24c) and raise it back up. Start with 5 repetitions with each leg. Progress to 15 repetitions.

Fig. 5–24a

Fig. 5–24b

Fig. 5–24c

25. PELVIC TILTS – LEVEL 7

Lie flat on your back with your knees bent and your arms bent and alongside your head on the floor. Raise both knees so that your feet are off the floor (Fig. 5–25a). Perform a posterior pelvic tilt. Keeping one foot suspended off the floor, slowly extend the other leg straight out as though trying to kick the wall (Fig. 5–25b). Return your extended leg to the starting position. Perform 5 repetitions with each leg. Work up to 15 repetitions.

Fig. 5–25a

Fig. 5–25b

Fig. 5–26a

Fig. 5–26b

26. PELVIC TILTS – LEVEL 8

Lie flat on your back with your knees bent and your arms bent and alongside your head on the floor (Fig. 5–26a). Perform a posterior pelvic tilt and then slowly raise one knee toward your chest without losing your tilted position. Simultaneously, raise the opposite arm toward your knee (Fig. 5–26b). Slowly return your leg and your arm to the floor without losing the pelvic tilt. Repeat on the other side. Perform 5 repetitions and work up to 15 repetitions.

Fig. 5–27a

Fig. 5–27b

27. PELVIC TILTS – LEVEL 9

Lie flat on your back with both knees bent (Fig. 5–27a). Raise and lower both knees simultaneously while maintaining a posterior pelvic tilt (Fig. 5–27b). Slowly build up to 15 repetitions.

Fig. 5–28a

Fig. 5–28b

Fig. 5–28c

28. PELVIC TILTS – LEVEL 10

Lie on your back with knees bent. Perform a posterior pelvic tilt and hold it (Fig. 5–28a). Straighten both knees (Fig. 5–28b) and slowly lower your legs toward the floor (Fig. 5–28c), making sure to keep your back pressed flat. If your back starts to arch, return to the starting position. Don't attempt a wider range of motion than you can do and still keep your back flat. Work up to 15 repetitions.

29. PELVIC TILTS – LEVEL 11

You can perform all of the pelvic tilting exercises while lying lengthwise along a 6-inch foam roll cut in half with the flat side down (Fig. 5–29a,b). The foam roll increases the difficulty of these exercises by forcing you to balance on an uneven surface. This tends to increase the roles of the transverse abdominis and the abdominal oblique muscles.

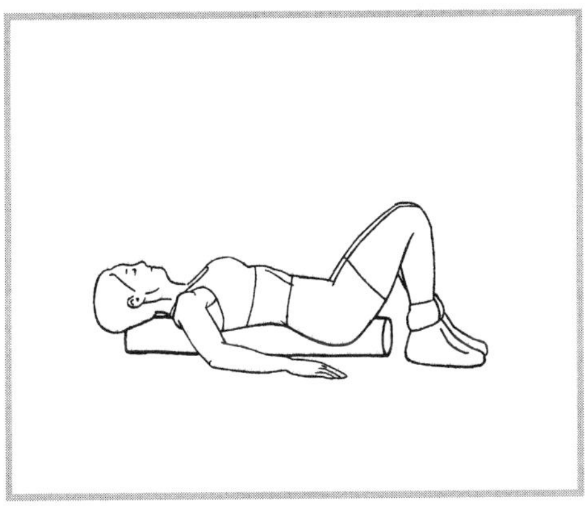

Fig. 5–29a

Fig. 5–29b

Fig. 5–30a

Fig. 5–30b

30. BRIDGING W/PELVIC TILTS – LEVEL 1

Bridging involves performing a pelvic tilt and then raising your hips, which engages the gluteal muscles along with the abdominals. Lie flat on your back with your knees bent and your arms bent and placed alongside your head (Fig. 5–30a). Perform a posterior pelvic tilt and then slowly lift your bottom off the floor (Fig. 5–30b). Hold for up to 5 seconds and then lower your hips back to the floor. Perform 5 repetitions. Build up to 15 repetitions. Then increase the hold for 10 seconds and perform 5 repetitions. Work back up to 15 repetitions.

31. BRIDGING W/PELVIC TILT – LEVEL 2

Lie flat on your back with your knees bent and your arms bent and alongside your head on the floor (Fig. 5–31a). Perform a posterior pelvic tilt and then slowly lift your bottom off the floor. Slowly raise one foot an inch or so off the floor (Fig. 5–31b). Hold this position for 5 seconds, and then lower the foot back to the floor. Perform 5 repetitions with each foot and progress to 15 repetitions. Then increase the hold for 10 seconds. Start with 5 repetitions again and work up to 15 repetitions.

Fig. 5–31a

Fig. 5–31b

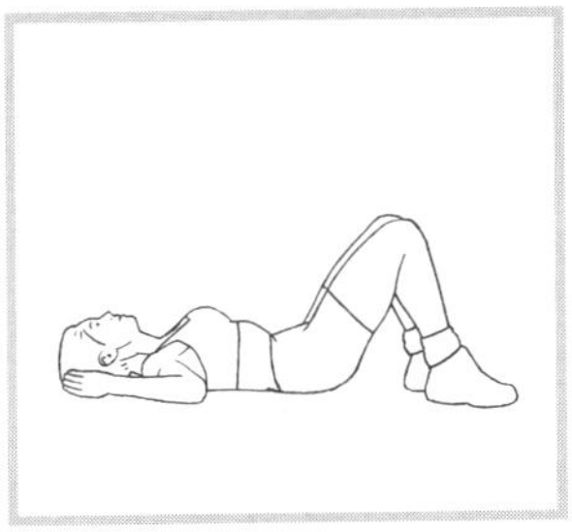

Fig. 5–32a

Fig. 5–32b

Fig. 5–32c

32. BRIDGING W/PELVIC TILTS – LEVEL 3

Lie flat on your back with your knees bent and your arms bent and alongside your head on the floor (Fig. 5–32a). Perform a posterior pelvic tilt and then slowly lift your bottom off the floor (Fig. 5–32b). Slowly extend one knee till your leg is straight out on a plane with your body (Fig. 5–32c). Hold for up to 10 seconds. Bring that leg down and change to the other leg. Perform up to 15 repetitions with each leg.

33. BRIDGING W/PELVIC TILTS – LEVEL 4

Lie with your head and upper back on a large gym ball (Fig. 5–33a). Perform a posterior pelvic tilt and then lift your hips up into the bridge position (Fig. 5–33b). Hold this tilted and bridged position throughout the exercise. Then, slowly raise one foot an inch or so off the floor (Fig. 5–33c). Hold this position for 5 seconds and then lower the foot back to the floor. Perform 5 repetitions with each foot and build up to 15 repetitions. Then increase the hold time to 10 seconds and perform 5 repetitions. Build back up to 15 repetitions.

Fig. 5–33a

Fig. 5–33b

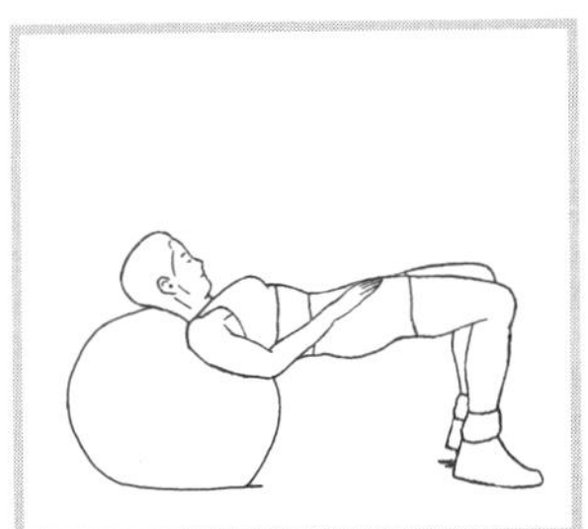

Fig. 5–33c

Fig. 5–34a

Fig. 5–34b

34. BRIDGING W/PELVIC TILTS – LEVEL 5

Lie with your head and upper back on the ball and perform a pelvic tilt and bridge (Fig. 5–34a). Extend one leg out straight (Fig. 5–34b). Hold this position for up to 10 seconds and then lower the foot back to the floor. Perform 5 repetitions with each leg and build up to 15 repetitions. Then increase the hold time to 10 seconds and perform 5 repetitions. Build back up to 15 repetitions.

35. STANDING POSTERIOR PELVIC TILTS

You can gradually work up to doing a pelvic tilt while standing with your back against a wall. Stand with your back and arms against a wall with your elbows at right angles alongside your head (Fig. 5–35a). Your heels should be several feet away from the wall. Perform the posterior pelvic tilt and hold (Fig. 5–35b).

Fig. 5–35a

Fig. 5–35b

Fig. 5–35c

As an alternative, you can start with your arms at your sides, slowly raise them over your head, and slowly return them to your sides. Perform multiple repetitions. You can also hold light dumbbells in your hands to increase the difficulty.

Once you feel comfortable with the pelvic tilt against the wall, try it while standing free of the wall: Assume a comfortable stance and perform a slight posterior pelvic tilt by drawing your pelvis up and your abdominals in. You can raise or lower weights in front of you with your arms. Three exercises that work well with this are the front raise with barbell, the barbell curl (Fig. 5–35c), and the stiff-arm pullover with cable.

36. ISOMETRIC CROSS-CABLE HOLDS

Fig. 5–36

Use a high or adjustable cable-pulley machine. If the pulley is adjustable, set it for chest level. Otherwise, use the high pulley. Start with a light weight, say, 10 lbs. Grasp the handle and stand sideways to the cable column, several feet away from it. Hold the handle with both hands directly out in front of you at approximately the level of the bottom of your rib cage (Fig. 5–36). Your elbows should be slightly bent. Tighten your abdominals by doing a slight posterior tilt and bearing down a little bit. Hold this position without letting your hips rotate for 10 to 30 seconds. Repeat on the other side. If no cable is available, secure an elastic band to the side of a door frame and use it in the same manner.

Dynamic Ab Movements

These exercises involve the abdominals in a range of motion starting with a posterior pelvic tilt and continuing through a flexed spinal position. Most of them can be performed on the floor, an exercise mat, or an abdominal slant board.

We recommend starting with the lower abdominal exercises—such as reverse crunches—first, since they involve both upper and lower abdominals. The upper abdominal exercises—such as crunches—on the other hand, involve primarily the upper abdominals. Starting with crunches fatigues the upper abdominals, and as a consequence the lower abdominals don't get a good workout.

37. REVERSE CRUNCHES

Lie flat on your back with your knees bent and your arms resting on the floor alongside your head (Fig. 5–37a). If possible, lie on a slant board that is placed flat and hold onto the handle above your head. This will help keep your body from wiggling around and inching along the floor. If no slantboard is available, you can hold onto the top of an exercise mat. In one smooth motion, perform a posterior pelvic tilt and roll your knees and hips toward your chest (Fig. 5–37b,c). Your hips should roll off the floor. Smoothly lower your hips back to the floor. Make sure that you use your abdominals to draw your hips up rather than pulling with your legs and hip flexors. The goal of this exercise is *not* to see how high you can roll your hips. It is the initial part of the motion that really emphasizes the lower abdominals.

To increase the difficulty, you can raise the head of the slant board. Start with a slight incline and increase it as you get stronger. Alternatively, you can squeeze a medicine ball between your knees for added resistance.

Fig. 5–37a

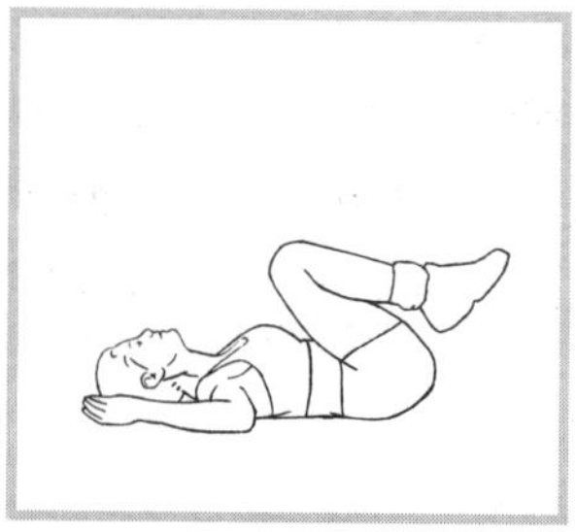

Fig. 5–37b

Fig. 5–37c

This exercise produces a dynamic stretch of your low back muscles. It is not unusual to feel a stretching-type pain across your low back during the first few repetitions; this should diminish as the set continues. To counter this, try stretching your back first by performing the Two-Knees-to-Chest Stretch described under Flexibility Exercises. If you continue to experience back pain, see your physician or physical therapist.

One modification that may decrease back pain is to pre-position your pelvis in a posterior tilt. Place your fists under your buttocks so that your pelvis is rocked backward, flattening your spine (Fig. 5-37d). Start and end from this position.

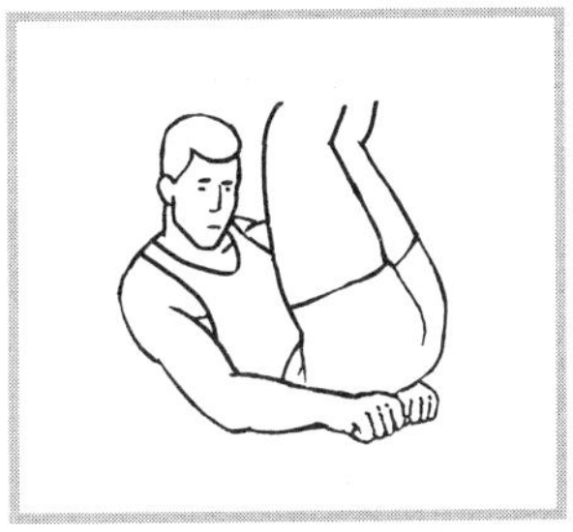

Fig. 5–37d

To increase difficulty, perform the reverse crunch starting from an arched-back position. Place a rolled towel in the small of your back (Fig. 5–37e); lie with your back over a gym ball; or position yourself so that your tailbone (sacrum) is just off the end of an exercise bench (holding onto the bench with both hands alongside your head) (Fig. 5–37f). Do a posterior pelvic tilt to bring your pelvis back to a flat position, and then roll your hips up into the reverse crunch (Fig. 5–37g).

Fig. 5–37e

Holding yourself off the end of an exercise bench is an extremely difficult exercise with a high risk of injury—this is a move for athletes only. Take care to maintain abdominal control while lowering your hips to avoid hyperextending your spine. (Holding yourself over a gym ball is also fairly risky because it's easy to fall off!)

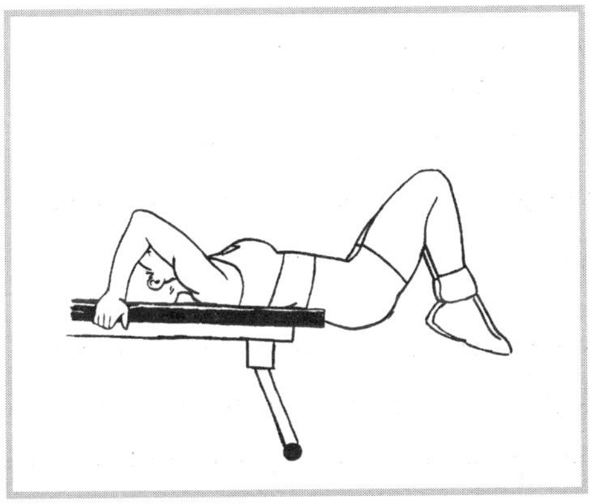

Fig. 5–37f

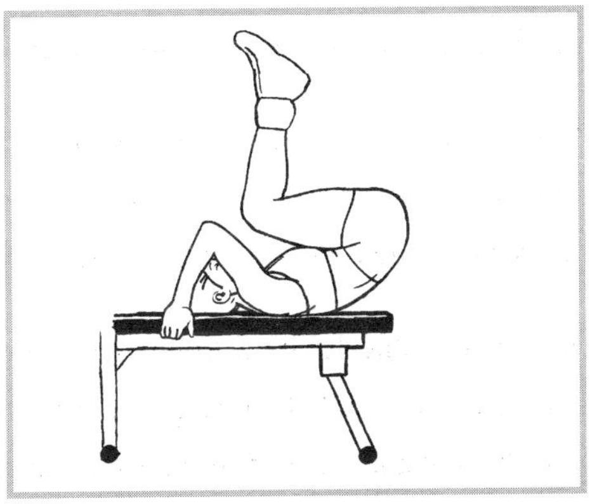

Fig. 5–37g

Fig. 5–38a

Fig. 5–38b

Fig. 5–38c

Fig. 5–38d

Fig. 5–38e

Fig. 5–38f

38. LYING HIP THRUSTS

Lie flat on your back with your arms resting on the floor either alongside your hips or alongside your head. You can perform this exercise on a slant board; make the board flat and grasp the handle over your head with both hands. For the straight-leg version, start with your legs extended up in the air but with a slight bend in the knees (Fig. 5–38a). Lower your legs somewhat to get a slight amount of momentum to assist you in this difficult exercise (Fig. 5–38b). Start from a slightly arched back position. Slowly rock back by performing a pelvic tilt to flatten the back and then thrust your hips straight up in the air (Fig. 5–38c). Make sure to lift your hips/pelvis with your lower abdominals rather than with your legs. A short motion is sufficient. Do not be overly concerned about gaining too much elevation or you will use your leg muscles to accomplish the motion.

If you experience back pain, you should try pre-positioning the pelvis in a posteriorly tipped position by placing your fists under your pelvis on either side of your tailbone. Keep your head down and your neck relaxed throughout the hip thrust.

To increase difficulty, lie on your back with your hips bent at 90°, your feet off the ground, and your knees fully bent (Fig. 5–38d). Your knees should point straight up. Start with your back slightly arched. In one smooth motion, perform a posterior pelvic tilt, flatten your back, and thrust your knees straight up in the air (Fig. 5–38e). Your hips may only raise an inch or less off the floor. This exercise does not require a large movement.

As with Reverse Crunches, you can also increase the difficulty by doing this exercise with a medicine ball between your knees (Fig. 5–38f).

39. LYING HIP ROTATIONS

Lie flat on your back with your arms resting on the floor alongside your head. Bend your knees and draw your legs up so that your knees are pointing straight up (Fig. 5–39a). Slowly rotate your knees to one side without allowing your back to come off the mat more than an inch or two (Fig. 5–39b). This movement should be controlled completely with your abdominal oblique muscles, not with your low back muscles. If you have a back injury, start with a very short range of motion and slowly increase it as you gain strength and confidence with this movement. Rotate 5 to 15 times to one side and then rotate to the other side (Fig. 5–39c). A medicine ball may be placed between your knees for added resistance (Fig. 5–39d).

Fig. 5–39a

Fig. 5–39b

Fig. 5–39c

Fig. 5–39d

Fig. 5–40a

Fig. 5–40b

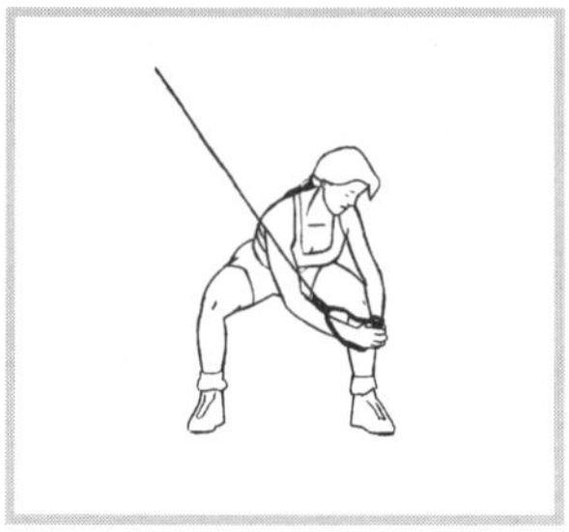

Fig. 5–40c

40. CROSS-CABLE PULLS

Using a high pulley station, grasp the handle with both hands and then position yourself several feet to the side of the cable column or in the center of a cable crossover machine. Assume a comfortable stance with your legs spread to increase stability (Fig. 5–40a). At the starting position, hold the handle up and out to your left side with both hands. Tighten your abdominals and keep your pelvis straight and aligned with your feet. Pull the handle down and across your body (Fig. 5–40b). As the handle crosses the midline, simultaneously begin to bend your knees, continuing to pull until your hands are on either side of your right knee (Fig. 5–40c). Imagine that you are chopping wood. Feel your abdominals contract as you pull the handle across your body and down toward the floor.

Slowly stand and allow the handle to return smoothly back across your body and up to your left. Keep the weight under control. Do not allow your hips to rotate or your back to arch as the weight returns to the top. This requires keeping your abdominal oblique muscles tight. Perform the designated number of repetitions. Repeat on the other side.

CRUNCH VARIATIONS

Straight Crunches work mostly the rectus abdominis, Twisting Crunches work the obliques and the rectus abdominis, and Side Crunches primarily work the obliques. Crunches are most easily and effectively performed when you are lying on the floor on a mat. You can place your feet over an exercise bench, against the wall, or flat on the floor, whichever is most comfortable. It is not clear that one variation is superior to another, though at least some bend in the hips helps to relax the psoas muscle.

Fig. 5–41a

Fig. 5–41b

41. STRAIGHT CRUNCHES

Lie on the floor with your knees bent (Fig. 5–41a). Cup your ears with your hands and slowly raise your head and shoulders off the ground as you contract your abdominals (Fig. 5–41b). Hold for a second or so and then return to the starting position. Perform the suggested number of repetitions.

During this exercise, use your hands to gently support the weight of your head. Make sure not to pull on your head or you will strain your neck. Keep your head in line with the rest of your body, with your chin slightly tucked in. Avoid jutting your chin out, as this results in tightening of the sternocleidomastoid muscles and promotes the development of a forward head posture that is linked to neck pain. Also avoid flexing your head to your chest, as this too may strain your neck. You can fold your arms across your chest during this exercise, but your neck muscles will then have to work harder to support the weight of your head. There is nothing wrong with this except that your neck muscles will get tired and a little sore until they become strong enough to handle the load.

If you are very heavy or have very weak abdominals, the crunch may be difficult for you initially. You can start by performing it at a slight incline on a slant board. Arrange the board so your head is higher than your feet and you are crunching downhill.

Avoid performing crunches with your feet anchored. Anchoring the feet tends to recruit the psoas muscle and places more strain on the back.

If you experience back pain while doing crunches, stop and consult your physician. You may need to place a folded towel under the small of your back so that you start from a slightly arched position. This variation increases the range of motion and helps to build abdominal strength from the extended back position. Alternatively, if your back muscles are tight, you may need to perform several Two-Knee-to-Chest stretches (see under Flexibility Exercises) to relax your back prior to performing the crunch.

Still another way to reduce possible back strain is to use a technique developed by a famous neurologist—Vladimir Janda. His research led him to the conclusion that the psoas muscles tend to become activated even during the bent-knee crunch. He found that when you *pull down with your heels* while performing the crunch exercise, you contract your hamstrings and gluteus maximus muscles, which causes the psoas muscles to relax.

42. TWISTING CRUNCHES

This is performed just like the Straight Crunch, except that as you crunch, you twist and pull your right shoulder toward your left knee and vice versa (Fig. 5–42a,b). Alternate from side to side on each succeeding repetition.

Fig. 5–42a

Fig. 5–42b

43. SIDE CRUNCHES

Lie on the floor, partially on your side with your knees bent and your top leg slightly behind the bottom one. Try to orient yourself so that your hips are at approximately a 45° angle to the floor (Fig. 5–43). This will best recruit the oblique muscles. Place your hands across the back of your head and simultaneously crunch your head, shoulders and upper body up. Hold for a second and then return to the starting position. Perform the suggested number of repetitions. Make sure not to pull on your head, as this will strain your neck.

Fig. 5–43

44. ROPE CRUNCHES

Kneel several feet in front of a cable column. Attach a rope to the high pulley, pull it down, and hold the handle along each side of your head (Fig. 5–44a). Pretend that your hands, the rope, your head, and your shoulders are all one unit, and try to make them move together. Your knees should be at approximately a 100° angle, and your hips should be slightly flexed. Keep your knee and hip angle the same throughout the exercise. Starting from a straight or slightly arched back position, curl your spine and simultaneously bring your hands, head, and shoulders down in a circular motion toward you knees (Fig. 5–44b). Crunch down with your abdominals and breathe out. Hold for a second and then allow your hands, head, and shoulders to slowly return to the starting position. Feel your abdominals resist the uncurling.

Fig. 5–44a

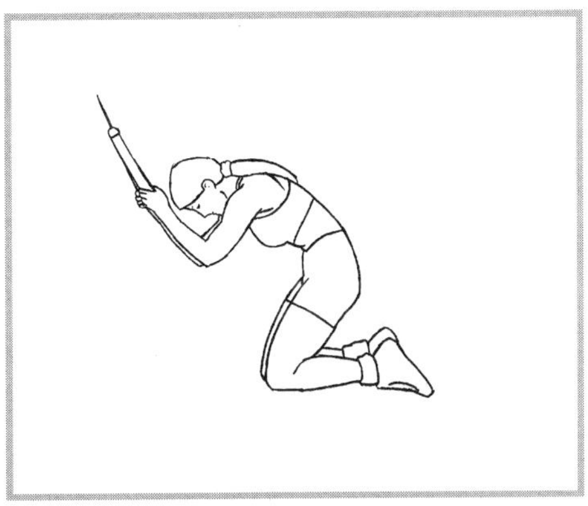

Fig. 5–44b

Avoid sitting back on your heels as you roll your arms and head down. This recruits the hip flexor muscles and may result in additional stress on your back. Keep your hips locked.

A variation is the twisting cable crunch, which involves a twist as you crunch down and direct one elbow toward the opposite knee. Another variation is to twist and lean to the same side as you crunch down. Both of these versions stress the obliques.

45. RUSSIAN TWISTS (ATHLETES ONLY)

This is an extremely advanced exercise and should be performed only by athletes who must regularly engage in rotational movements in their sports; for example, swinging a baseball bat or golf club. Perform it only if you have had no prior back injuries or have fully recovered from a back injury and are now in an advanced phase of rehabilitation.

This exercise can be performed either face up and extended off a back extension bench or on the floor in a bent-knee crunch position. Tighten your abdominals and try to keep your spine in a straight position, neither flexed nor arched. Hold your hands out, palms together, and your arms extended straight out in front of you (Fig. 5-45a). Slowly and under complete control, rotate your body in one direction and then the other (Fig. 5-45b). Start with a narrow range of motion—say 20° in each direction—and increase it as you feel comfortable, provided that you do not experience back pain. Don't let your abdominals relax, and make sure that your body does not dip into a hyperextended position during this exercise. You can hold a medicine ball or a weight plate in your hands to increase the difficulty of this exercise.

Fig. 5-45a

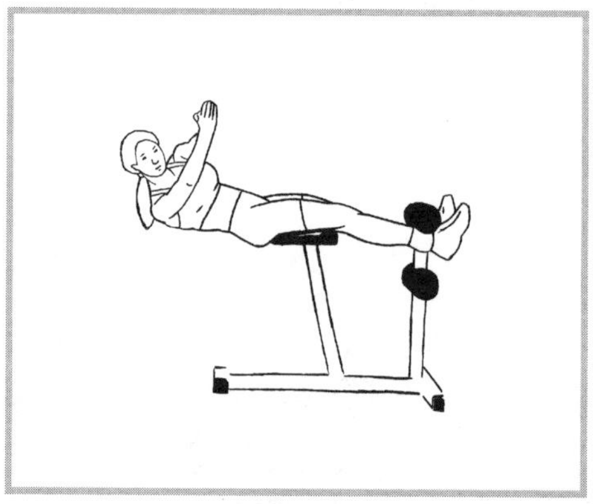

Fig. 5-45b

Medicine Ball Exercises for the Abs

Medicine ball exercises involve ballistic rotational movements and are potentially damaging to the spine. They are not worth the risk for the average person, but are often worthwhile for the athlete. You should perform these exercises only if you have had no prior back injuries or have fully recovered from a back injury and are in the advanced stages of rehabilitation. Athletes benefit from such exercises by preparing their bodies to handle the ballistic, back-strenuous positions and activities common in sport. Medicine ball exercises train the abdominals for speed and power, as well as for strength and endurance. There are many possible medicine ball exercises and drills. These are just a few to get you started. A good strength and conditioning specialist can develop additional exercises for you.

46. CATCH AND LOWER/SIT UP AND THROW

Lie on your back on the floor with your knees bent and hold a medicine ball in your hands (Fig. 5–46a). Perform an abdominal crunch and continue to come up in one smooth motion to a seated position. As you reach the top, throw the medicine ball to a partner (Fig. 5–46b). Hold yourself in this seated, crunched position and have your partner throw the medicine ball back to you. As you catch it, simultaneously lower yourself back to the floor. Control this motion using your abdominal muscles. Upon reaching the floor, immediately reverse direction and sit back up again.

This is a high-risk exercise, but it is an effective one. It trains the abdominal muscles to resist and generate the types of dynamic forces that occur regularly in sports.

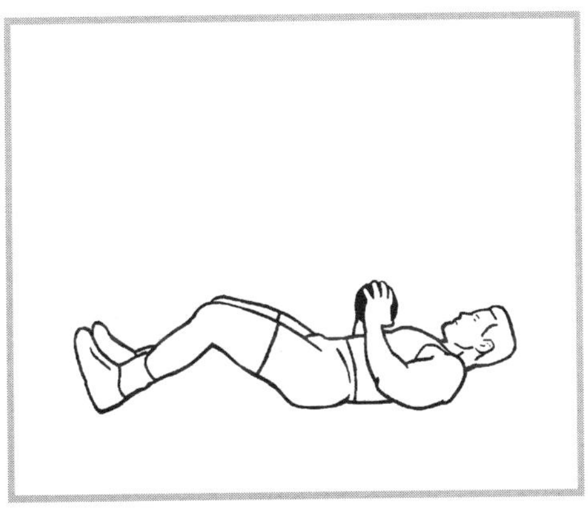

Fig. 5–46a

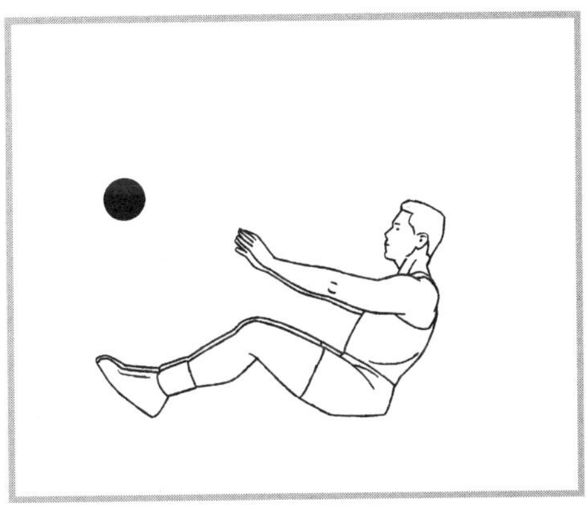

Fig. 5–46b

Fig. 5–47a

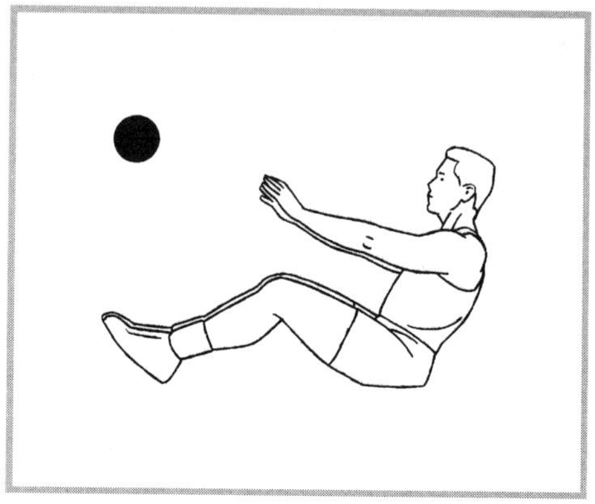

Fig. 5–47b

47. SIT CRUNCHED AND THROW AND CATCH

Sit in a crunched position either on the floor or on a decline crunch board (Fig. 5–47a). Have a partner throw the medicine ball to you from the front and slightly to the side. Have your partner vary the angle as this will recruit the abdominals slightly differently. Throw the ball back (Fig. 5–47b). You may vary your throws, using the chest toss, the side toss, and the overhead toss.

48. SEATED TWISTS

Sit on the floor with your knees bent and hold a medicine ball in your hands. Touch the ball to the floor to the left of your knees (Fig. 5–48a). Without pausing, lift the ball, rotate your trunk and touch the ball to the floor on the opposite side of your body (Fig. 5–48b). Rotate back and forth and perform multiple repetitions. Keep your abdominals tight. You will really feel your abdominal oblique muscles working on this exercise.

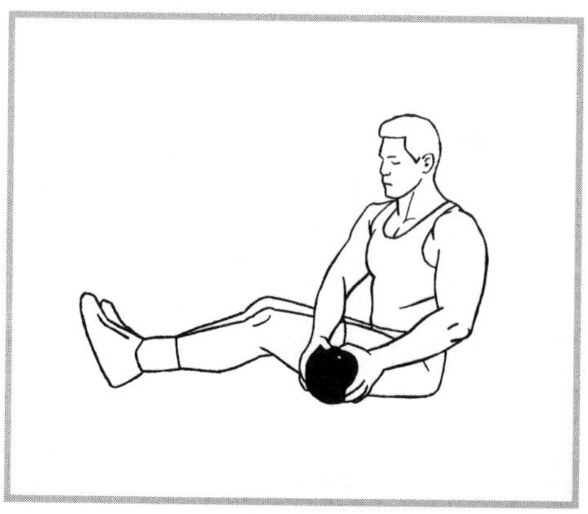

Fig. 5–48a

Fig. 5–48b

Fig. 5–49a

Fig. 5–49b

49. STANDING TWISTS W/PARTNER

Hold a medicine ball and stand back-to-back with a partner. Rotate and hand the ball to your partner (Fig. 5–49a). Turn to the other side to grab the ball. Your partner should similarly grab the ball, twist his body, and pass it back to you on the other side (Fig. 5–49b). Perform the designated repetitions. Repeat this sequence, rotating the opposite direction. If you do not have a partner, you can stand with your back to a wall and rotate back and forth. Start with a narrow range of motion, and work up to touching the wall on each side with the ball.

ISOLATION, QUADRATUS

Recent research indicates that the quadratus lumborum—the main muscle involved in side-bending exercises—plays a significant role in stabilizing your spine. Despite this, it is frequently ignored in rehabilitation programs.

Some caution should be used in exercising your quadratus lumborum, as overtightening of this muscle could exacerbate a low back problem, especially in cases of pelvic imbalance or scoliosis. Quadratus lumborum exercises can also, theoretically, lead to a thicker waistline, and this would not be aesthetically desirable, especially for a bodybuilder. This is unlikely, though, unless you combine side-bending movements with heavy loading. If this is a concern for you, however, you may elect to perform only the isometric side-support exercise. For most individuals, strengthening the quadratus lumborum is desirable and will create a more stable spine.

50. ISOMETRIC SIDE-SUPPORT EXERCISE

Lie on your side on the floor, supporting yourself with a straight lower arm. Bend your knees to 90° (Fig. 5–50a). Then raise your torso until it forms a straight line, on a diagonal to the floor (Fig. 5–50b). You should feel the bottom side of your waist region tighten up. Do not let your torso sag. Hold this position for 10 to 30 seconds. Repeat on the other side. Once you can do this easily, progress to doing the exercise with both legs straight (Fig. 5–50c). If you have shoulder problems or experience shoulder pain while performing this exercise, skip it. Substitute Side Bending on the Floor.

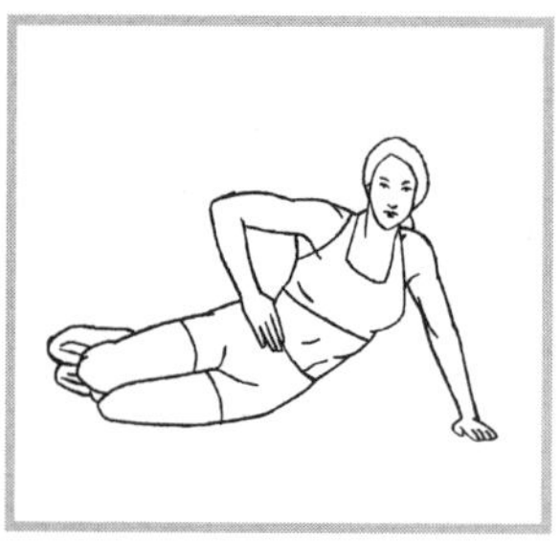

Fig. 5–50a

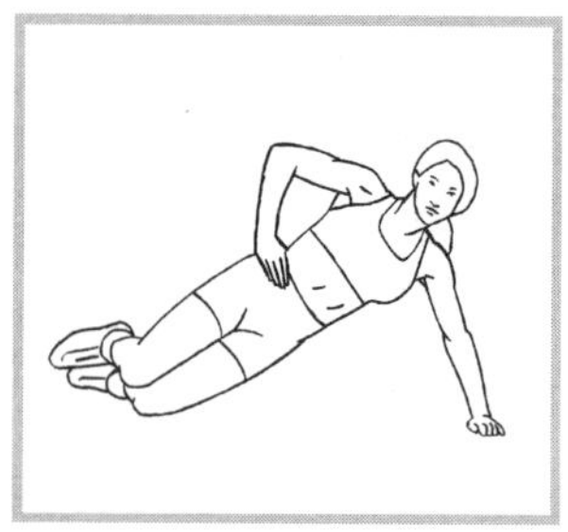

Fig. 5–50b

Fig. 5–50c

51. SIDE BENDING ON THE FLOOR

Lie on your side on the floor and place your hands behind your head. Your knees should be bent with one leg on top of the other. To better recruit the quadratus lumborum muscle, add internal rotation of the hip by rotating your top foot and leg up and away from your body (Fig. 5–51a). You should feel your side gently tightening. Then flex your upper body up, trying not to rotate your torso (Fig. 5–51b). Return slowly. Do 10 to 20 repetitions on each side. Perform 1 to 3 sets.

An easier version of this exercise can be done by eliminating the internal rotation of the hip. Simply keep your legs together on the floor. Hold for a second or two and then slowly return. Do 10 to 20 repetitions on each side. Perform 1 to 3 sets.

Fig. 5–51a

Fig. 5–51b

Fig. 5–52a

Fig. 5–52b

52. SIDE BENDING ON BENCH

Position yourself on your side on a 45° back extension bench so that your hip is anchored. Your spine should be in a straight line to start—not rotated or flexed. Hold your arms several inches in front of your body, parallel to it. Let your body slowly flex downward approximately 10° (Fig. 5–52a). Then slowly and smoothly flex your trunk in the opposite direction and come up until your body is flexed 10° upward (Fig. 5–52b). Repeat 5 to 15 times. Perform on the other side.

It is best to start with a narrow range of motion. Ten degrees is enough to recruit the quadratus lumborum and the abdominal oblique muscles that you are targeting. You can slowly increase the range to, say, 30° each direction, if this does not cause back pain.

STABILIZATION

While the exercises in the previous sections isolate and strengthen specific back and abdominal muscles, the following exercises engage the low back muscles to work along with the abdominal and other muscles of the body. The back and abdominal muscles contract to hold the spine in one position, while various forms of bending and lifting occur that involve other muscles. The back muscles thus develop increased ability to stabilize the spine in the neutral position and make it better able to resist strain from mechanical forces. It is more efficient to use the powerful muscles of the hips and thighs—the quadriceps, hamstrings, and gluteus maximus—to perform most of the work during bending and lifting activities. These muscles can handle significantly more loading than the back muscles. Stabilization exercises help you to learn safer and more efficient ways to move, bend, and lift. Watch out—these safe and efficient techniques can quickly become habit forming!

Some of the exercises in this section resemble normal, everyday activities. For example, you perform a squat every time you sit down and stand up. You perform a deadlift when you bend down to pick up a box from the floor. For this reason, these are often referred to as functional exercises.

You should maintain your spine in a slightly arched, neutral position during all of the following exercises. This stable, neutral position should be relatively pain-free. For individuals who have a lot of arch in their back, this may involve flattening the back slightly; for others, especially those with tight hamstrings, it may involve struggling to maintain arch in the back.

In some of these exercises, you will notice a tendency for your spine to become hyperextended, as when raising the hips during a hip extension. The abdominal muscles must contract forcefully to counter this tendency. On the other hand, while lowering your body during a hip extension, there is a tendency for your back to become flexed, and your back muscles must become more active to avoid this. To keep your spine in the neutral position, your back and your abdominal muscles must work together. Try to bear this in mind as you learn these exercises.

53. LYING 1-LEG HIP EXTENSIONS

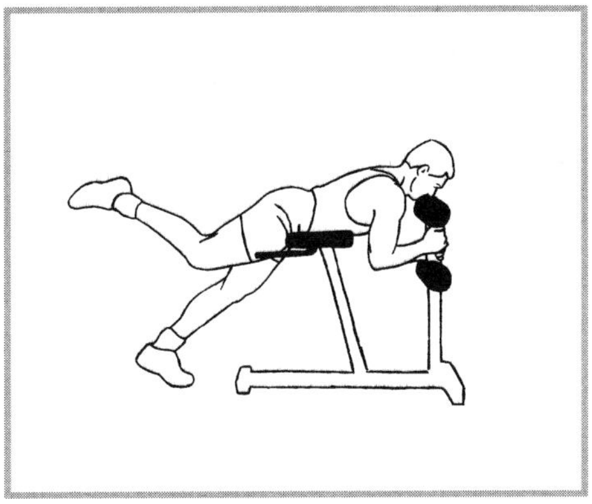

Fig. 5–53

Lie face down on a high bench or over the padded part of a horizontal back extension bench and hold on. Position your hip bones so that they are just on the pad. This will help to immobilize the pelvis. Make sure that there is sufficient padding to prevent bruising of your hips.

Start from a position where the legs hang down. Bend one knee—this will activate the gluteus maximus muscle—then extend that leg backward to the point where the spine starts to arch (Fig. 5–53). Hold this position for a second or so. Feel the buttocks muscles contract. Change legs and repeat.

Most of us have a very limited ability to extend the hip behind the plane of the body. If you have hip hyperextension of 10°, consider yourself very flexible. Make sure to keep your hips level during this exercise. Your low back muscles and your abdominals will be contracting isometrically to stabilize your pelvis. Spinal hyperextension should be avoided, and strong and active abdominals are required to prevent this. As you progress, you can wear ankle weights to increase the difficulty of this exercise.

54. LYING 2-LEG HIP EXTENSIONS

Lie face down on a high bench or over the padded part of a horizontal back extension bench and hold on. Position your hip bones so that they are just on the pad. This will help to immobilize the pelvis. Make sure that there is sufficient padding to prevent bruising of your hips. Pull your pelvis against the bench and tighten your abdominals to help prevent your low back from arching. Let your legs hang straight down with your knees bent to maximally activate the gluteus maximus muscles. Then extend both legs backward, making sure not to arch your low back (Fig. 5–54a). You may need to tense your abdominals to prevent your back from hyperextending as you raise your legs. As you lower your legs, keep your back muscles tight to avoid letting your back round. It is much more difficult to stabilize your back and prevent hyperextension in this exercise than in the one-leg version. Concentrate on the quality of the movement. When you can't maintain perfect form, it's time to stop.

You can also perform two-leg hip extensions while lying face down over a large gym ball (the average size is 65 cm). You will need to grab onto a bench or other stationary object with your hands (Fig. 5–54b). Lock your trunk into the neutral position by tensing your midsection. Then slowly extend your legs and hips while keeping your knees slightly bent. Hold for a second and return.

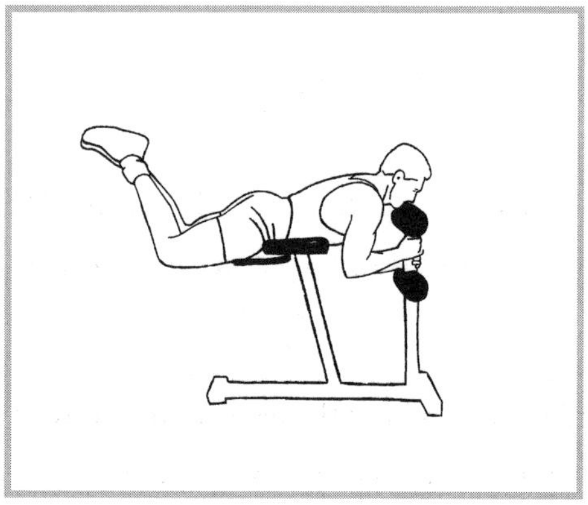

Fig. 5–54a

Fig. 5–54b

55. 45° HIP EXTENSIONS

Position yourself face down on the 45° back extension bench with your hips over the edge (Fig. 5–55a). Ideally, try to keep your knees bent, although this is almost impossible on many machines. Slowly lower yourself to a horizontal position with your back flat or slightly arched (Fig. 5–55b). As you go down, the tendency is to round your back, so consciously try to arch it. Then bring yourself back up using your hamstrings and buttocks. When you come back up, the tendency is to overarch your back, so consciously try to flatten it by slightly tensing your abdominals. Your back muscles will get some work as they contract isometrically, while your hip muscles perform most of the movement.

Fig. 5–55a

Fig. 5–55b

56. HORIZONTAL HIP EXTENSIONS

These are the same as 45° Hip Extensions except that they're performed on a horizontal back extension bench. Position yourself face down on the horizontal back extension bench with your hips over the edge (Fig. 5–56a). Again, although it is rather difficult—and on some benches, virtually impossible—try to keep your knees bent. Slowly lower yourself with your back flat or slightly arched (Fig. 5–56b). As you go down, the tendency is to round your back, so consciously try to arch it. Then bring yourself back up using your hamstrings and gluteal muscles. When you come back up, the tendency is to overarch your back, so consciously try to flatten it by tensing your abdominals. Your back muscles will get some work as they contract isometrically.

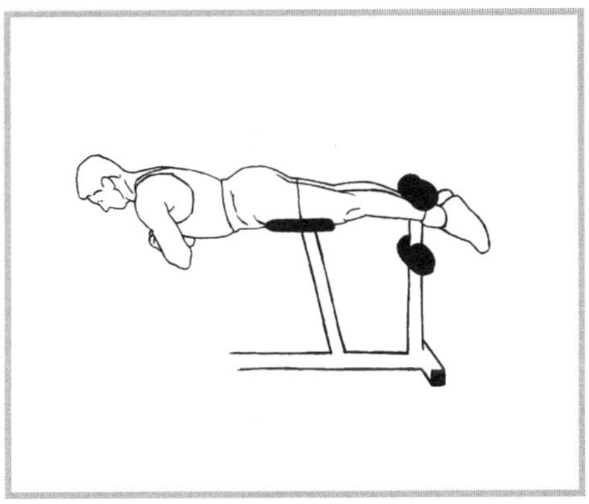

Fig. 5–56a

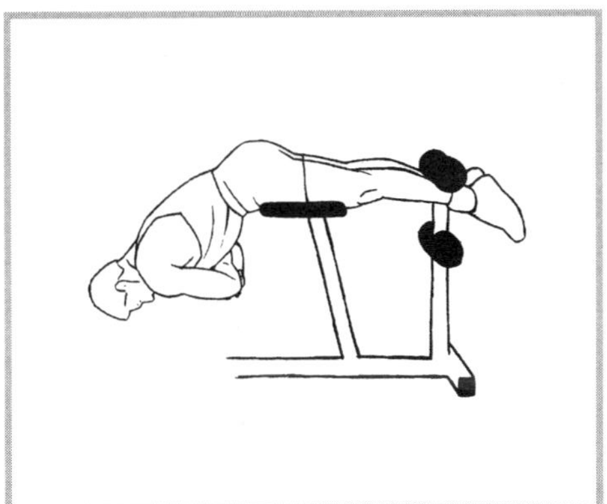

Fig. 5–56b

57. STANDING HIP EXTENSIONS

Assume a comfortable stance with your arms crossed over your chest (Fig. 5–57a). Bend your knees slightly and try to keep your spine in a stable position, maintaining the normal curvature. You do this by tensing your back muscles and holding them tight. Bend forward in a slow controlled manner as far as possible without losing the lumbar curvature (Fig. 5–57b). Then come back up slowly to the erect position.

The kneeling version involves kneeling on the floor or on something that slightly elevates the knees (several pillows, several mats, or a step-class step). Tense your gluteal muscles and slowly bend over with your back in a comfortable, slightly arched position (Fig. 5–57c). Then come back up to the starting position.

If you are trying this exercise for the first time or have had a back injury, start with a short range of motion, say 20° of forward bending. In general, the farther forward you bend, the more difficult the exercise. Slowly increase the degree of forward bending to make the exercise more difficult as you progress—provided that this does not cause back pain and that you can continue to maintain perfect form. "Back pain" here refers to pain related to your injury. It should be distinguished from the pain of the back muscles getting tired and burning. Fatigue and burning indicate that the muscles are getting a good workout.

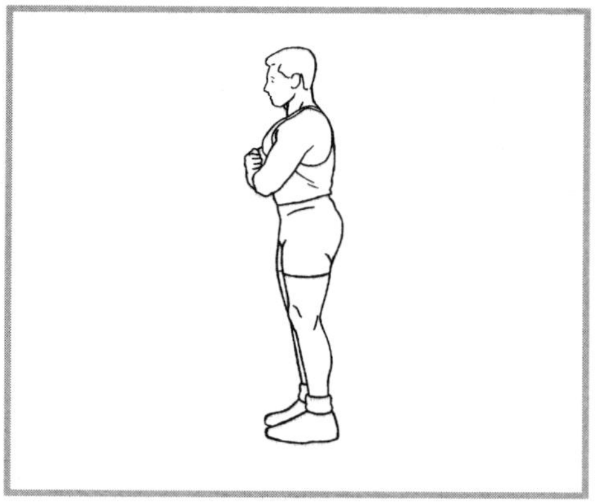

Fig. 5–57a

Fig. 5–57b

Fig. 5–57c

58. REVERSE CROSS-CABLE PULLS

Stand in the center of a cable crossover machine. Get your balance and tighten your abdominal and back muscles to hold your spine in a neutral position. Your goal will be to maintain this neutral position despite the changing loads supplied by the pulley weights as your arms move.

Bend your knees as though bending down to pick something up and let your arms move down and toward your right, toward the lower pulley origin. Grab the handle with both hands (Fig. 5–58a). Slowly and smoothly bring the handle across your body and toward your left shoulder as you stand up (Fig. 5–58b). Bring your arms up as though you were going to pass the handle above your left shoulder to someone behind you (Fig. 5–58c). Stop when the handle is even with the plane of your body or when the range of motion of your shoulder prevents further motion without sacrificing the neutral position of your spine.

You must keep your abdominals tight to prevent hyperextending your spine at the top of the movement. As much as possible, keep your hips facing straight ahead throughout this exercise; resist the tendency for them to rotate to the side of the cable origin when you lower the weight and to rotate to the opposite side when you raise the handle over your head. Perform the exercise on the opposite side.

Fig. 5–58a

Fig. 5–58b

Fig. 5–58c

Fig. 5–59a

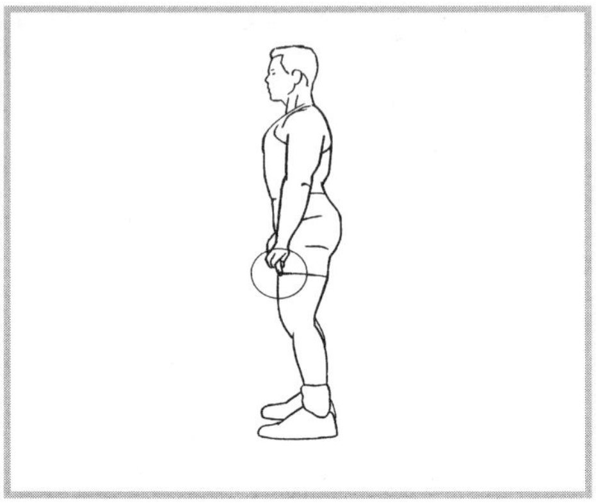
Fig. 5–59b

59. DEADLIFTS

Deadlifts involve bending down and then standing up while holding a barbell. They are good practice for lifting objects in everyday situations and involve the coordinated action of the low back muscles with the quadriceps and all the muscles of the body. Doing Deadlifts is a good way for you to integrate the strength derived from the isolation exercises.

Start with your feet shoulder-width apart or wider. Hold your arms alongside your legs. Squat down with your back arched and grab a barbell (Fig. 5–59a). You should bend forward only as far as you need to reach the bar. Keep your trunk as vertical as possible. Use an alternate grip—one palm facing your body and one palm facing away. Thrust your chest out and pull your shoulder blades together. This will help you to maintain an arched, stable back. Keep your midsection tense by bearing down, and look straight ahead.

Bring the bar straight up by simultaneously extending your knees, hips, and shoulders (Fig. 5–59b). The bar should travel upward in a path as close to your body as possible. Maintain your trunk in the same position as you lift. Once your knees are straight, continue to extend your hips until your body is vertical. Reverse this procedure when you slowly lower the weight, making sure all the while to maintain the back in an arched position and keep the trunk as vertical as possible.

The Deadlift is a difficult exercise to master, and you may need to seek individual training from a health care or fitness professional (such as a certified strength coach) to ensure correct form.

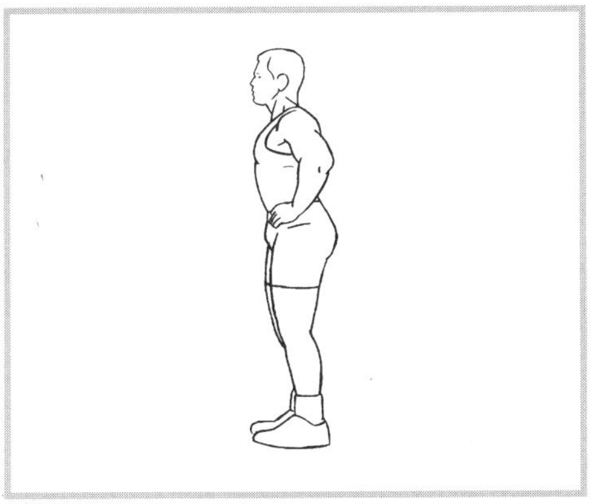

Fig. 5–60a

Fig. 5–60b

60. LUNGES

Stand up straight with your feet approximately shoulder-width apart, hands on hips. Both feet should face forward. Draw your abdomen in so that your navel is pulled toward your back (Fig. 5–60a). This will help to stabilize your spine by contracting your transverse abdominis and abdominal oblique muscles.

Step straight forward with one foot and slowly lower your body so that the rear knee comes to within an inch or so of touching the floor (Fig. 5–60b). Your rear foot should flex and the heel should lift off the floor. Use your hip and thigh muscles to push yourself up and back to the starting position. Avoid allowing the front knee to extend past your toes; it should not bend much beyond a 90° angle. There is a tendency to overarch (hyperextend) your back as you descend into a lunge. You may need to rock your hips under to prevent this, especially if you tend to have an exaggerated lordosis.

Initially, you can do Lunges without weights. As you get stronger, you can hold a medicine ball in front of you, hold dumbbells at your sides, or a grasp a barbell across the backs of your shoulders.

Fig. 5–61a

Fig. 5–61b

61. SQUATS

Stand up straight with your feet a bit more than shoulder-width apart and your toes pointed slightly outward. Draw your abdomen in so that your navel is pulled toward your back. This will help to stabilize your spine. Forcibly arch your low back by performing an anterior pelvic tilt (stick your butt out) and contracting your low back muscles. Maintain this arch in your back throughout the movement. Stick your chest out and squeeze your shoulder blades together to stabilize your upper back. You can practice with your hands empty or holding a medicine ball, as shown (Fig. 5–61a).

Slowly lower your hips so that they descend to a comfortable level, ideally to where your thighs are parallel to the floor. There is a tendency for your back to round and your body to lean forward as you lower yourself into the squat. Resist this by keeping your back muscles tight and sticking your chest up and out. If you can't maintain an arched spine, this may indicate short hamstrings or weak back muscles. Lower yourself only as far as you can maintain an arched back (Fig. 5–61b).

Remember to look straight ahead—not up at the ceiling or down at the floor. This will protect your neck. It will also ensure a synergistic contraction of the muscles along the upper back and the back of the neck. Hold your breath during the squat. Take a breath in at the top of the movement, and lower yourself while holding it. This will allow the intra-abdominal balloon support mechanism discussed in Chapter 2 to remain engaged throughout the movement, keeping the spine stiff. Do not breathe out until you are coming back up and are near the top of the movement.

Your knees should track over your feet and should not bend much beyond a 90° angle. Avoid the tendency for the knees to lean inward during the squat. Do not bounce when you reach the bottom position. Following these guidelines will protect you from a knee injury. If you do feel pain in your knees or any other joints during this exercise, stop and consult your physician.

As you get stronger, you can hold medicine balls of varying weights in front of you, hold dumbbells with your arms hanging at your sides, or a grasp a barbell across the backs of your shoulders. If the free-weight squat turns out to be too difficult or unstable for you, you may want to try performing this exercise with a Smith rack. This device has a bar, like a barbell, that slides up and down on two poles that guide it. The bar is locked in one plane of motion. The exercise using the Smith rack is performed in the same manner as the free-weight version.

62. SEATED CABLE ROWS

Place one foot on the forward foot plate of the cable row machine and grasp the handles with both hands. Slowly sit back into the bench in position to start the exercise. Maintain the normal curve in your back and keep your hips parallel to each other while getting into position.

Sit up straight and draw your abdomen in so that your navel is pulled toward your back (Fig. 5-62a). This will help to stabilize your spine. Make sure to maintain your neutral spine position by performing an anterior pelvic tilt and contracting your low back muscles. *It is important not to allow your back to round during this exercise.*

Lift your chest and thrust it out. Look straight ahead—not up at the ceiling or down at the floor. This will protect your neck. It will also ensure a synergistic contraction of the muscles along the back of the neck and the upper back.

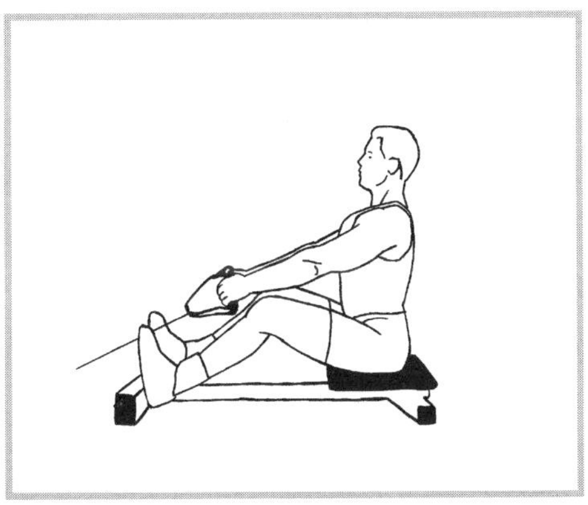

Fig. 5–62a

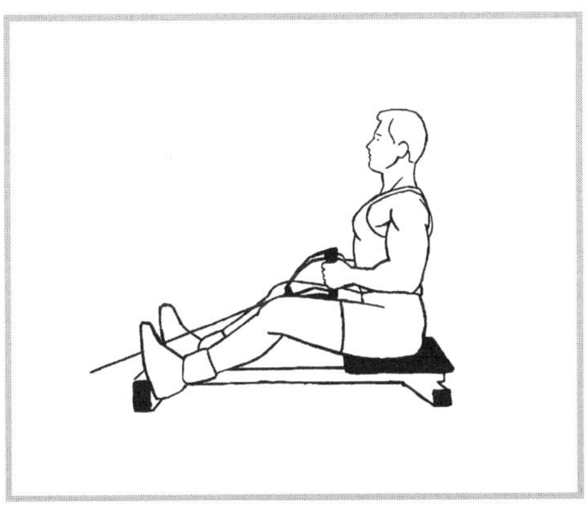

Fig. 5–62b

Keep your knees slightly bent, as this will keep your hamstrings from being stretched. As the hamstrings stretch, they tend to tilt the pelvis posteriorly, thus flattening the spine. This is undesirable. If you have tight hamstrings, this exercise will be more difficult to perform properly. If this is the case, bend your knees more to allow you to maintain your neutral posture.

Start the movement with your arms outstretched and your back upright. Your low back muscles are maintaining an isometric contraction in this position and developing both strength and endurance. Pull your hands into your torso at about the level of your lower rib cage (Fig. 5–62b). Your elbows should be approximately at a 90° angle. As you pull the weight toward you, your shoulder blades should come together. At the finish position, your shoulder blades should be pinched together. Then slowly allow your arms to extend out without changing your torso position and while keeping your back arched. Avoid the tendency to lean forward, and do not allow your back to round as you lower the weight.

COORDINATION

Most of the short muscles in your back are unable to exert enough torque to move the body in space. They are believed to play a large role, however, in providing proprioceptive feedback to the brain about the location of the body and its parts in space. The following exercises require balance and coordination of the various back muscles to prevent the spine and pelvis from twisting. These exercises can enhance your proprioceptive sense. The first two exercises below could also be considered stabilization exercises for the back. We have placed them in this category because they tend to target the smaller back muscles and because more balance is required than with some of the other stabilization exercises.

63. PRONE 1-ARM AND OPPOSITE-LEG RAISES

Lie face down with your arms extended alongside your head (Fig. 5–63a). Placing a pillow under your stomach may prevent excessive hyperextension and make this exercise more comfortable. The pillow also increases your lumbar range of motion. Keep your chin tucked in and your cervical spine in the neutral position. Avoid the tendency to lean your head back and hyperextend your neck.

Now, simultaneously lift one arm and the opposite leg, and hold this position for 1 to 10 seconds (Fig. 5–63b). Alternate with the opposite arm and leg. Perform the suggested number of repetitions. Be careful to avoid hyperextending the spine. Raise the leg only high enough to cause the back muscles to contract. There is no need to force the leg up to its highest level. Also, do not allow the back to twist; keep it in a neutral, balanced position.

For a simpler version of this exercise, lift only your arm. Hold this position for 1 to 10 seconds. Repeat with the other arm. Perform the suggested repetitions. This is the simplest version of the exercise. Then, lift only one leg and hold this position for 1 to 10 seconds. Repeat with the other leg and hip. Perform the suggested repetitions.

Fig. 5–63a

Fig. 5–63b

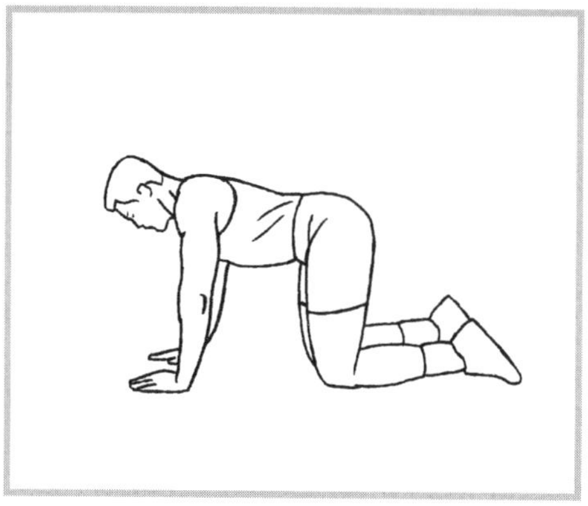

Fig. 5–64a

Fig. 5–64b

64. QUADRUPED EXERCISE - LEVEL 1

Fig. 5–64c

This exercise is actually a series of similar movements, each slightly harder than the last. When the exercise appears in a routine, you should treat it as a sort of *mini-routine*—start with the easiest version, then move up as each level becomes easy. In other words, the first few times you do a particular Chapter 6 routine, you may need to use the Level 1 version of the Quadruped Exercise. After that, use the Level 2 version for a few workouts, then the Level 3 version, and so on. Here's the Level 1 version:

Get down on your hands and knees on a mat. Your hands should be underneath your shoulders, and your knees should be underneath your hips. Then find the neutral position of your lumbar spine. Lock this position in by contracting your abdominals. Begin by holding this position (Fig. 5–64a). Then try picking up one hand just enough to slide a piece of paper under it. Hold this position for 5 to 10 seconds. Follow with the other hand and then with each knee (Fig. 5–64b). Keep your hips and shoulders level and avoid letting the position of your back change. At the same time keep your chin tucked in to counter the tendency to lean your head back and hyperextend your neck.

Next, while maintaining your neutral spine position, extend one arm forward over your head with your thumb pointing up (Fig. 5-64c). Hold this position for 10 seconds. Repeat with the other arm. Perform 5 to 15 repetitions. This is the simplest version of the exercise.

65. QUADRUPED EXERCISE - LEVEL 2

Slowly extend one leg directly behind you until the knee is straight (Fig. 5-65). Hold this position for 10 seconds. Avoid overarching the low back. Keep the hips level to avoid the tendency of the spine to rotate. Repeat with the other leg and hip. Perform 5 to 15 repetitions.

Fig. 5–65

66. QUADRUPED EXERCISE - LEVEL 3

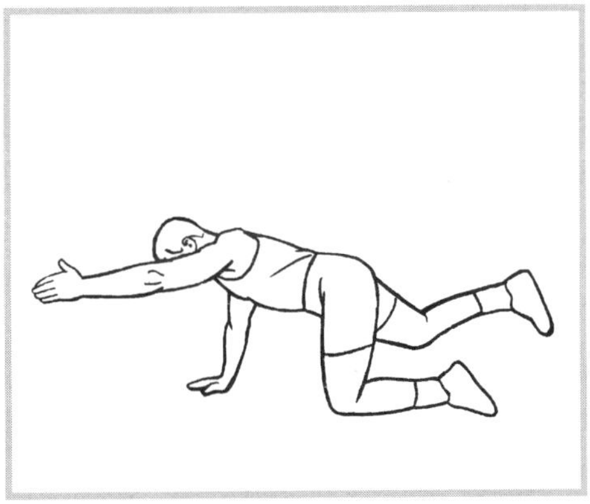

Fig. 5–66

Once you can perform the above exercises comfortably (it may take several sessions for this), try to simultaneously lift one arm and the opposite leg (Fig. 5-66). Hold this position for 5 seconds. Alternate with the opposite arm and leg. Perform 5 repetitions. Build up to 15 repetitions. Then drop back to 5 repetitions with a 10-second hold and work back up to 15 seconds. Remember to keep the spine in a neutral, balanced position. Once this becomes easy, ankle and/or wrist weights can be added. An interesting and more difficult variation is to use mismatched wrist and/or ankle weights.

67. QUADRUPED EXERCISE - LEVEL 4

While in the quadruped position, extend one arm and the opposite leg (Fig. 5-67). Write the letters of the alphabet in one-foot circles with your leg. Then reverse the arm and leg and repeat.

Fig. 5–67

Fig. 5–68

68. QUADRUPED EXERCISE - LEVEL 5

To further increase the proprioceptive/balance component of this exercise, you can place half-round foam rolls under each knee and hand with the round side down. This is an extremely challenging exercise (Fig; 5–68).

69. 1-LEGGED BALANCING

Stand up straight with your feet shoulder-width apart and your arms by your sides. If possible, stand in front of a full-length mirror. Grip the ground with your toes and feel the arches of your feet tighten. This will make it easier to balance. Raise one leg at least several inches off the ground by bending your knee and holding the foot in front of you (Fig. 5–69). Begin by trying to hold this position for a count of 10. Then attempt to balance on each leg for 30 seconds and repeat several times. Work up to doing this for at least a minute without wobbling. Alternate legs.

When 1-Legged Balancing becomes too easy, perform it with your eyes closed. Make sure that you stand next to a wall or something you can grab quickly if you start to lose your balance. You can also increase the difficulty of this exercise by standing on a gym mat or foam roll.

Fig. 5–69

If you suffer from dizziness or equilibrium problems, you should not perform these exercises without your doctor's permission.

70. WOBBLE-BOARD BALANCING

Fig. 5–70

Place a wobble board on a carpeted surface or place a towel under it to make it easier to start. The more padding under the board, the easier the exercise will be. Place the board near a wall or doorway so you can grab on if you lose your balance. Stand on the board with your feet several inches apart and parallel to each other (Fig. 5–70). Begin by finding your balance. This alone may take several sessions. Then slowly rock back and forth. Try to do this for 5 minutes to start with, building up to as much as 30 minutes. Experiment with various foot positions. For example, you can stand sideways on the board or try to balance on one leg.

71. GYM-BALL BALANCING

Sit on a large gym ball. The average size is 65 cm. You can determine the correct size by finding the ball that allows your knees to bend at a 90° angle when you sit on it.

Sit up straight on the ball and try to maintain the neutral position of your spine. Find your balance on the ball, and then gently bounce up and down on it, maintaining this neutral position of your spine (Fig. 5-71a). Bounce for several minutes. If you do this exercise in front of a full-length mirror, you will be able to check your form.

Next, perform a backward pelvic tilt by rolling your buttocks forward on the ball while letting your back round(Fig. 5-71b). Pretend you are slouching into a soft chair. Next, perform an anterior pelvic tilt by rolling the ball backward underneath you (Fig. 5-71c). Feel your low back arch. Perform the suggested number of repetitions.

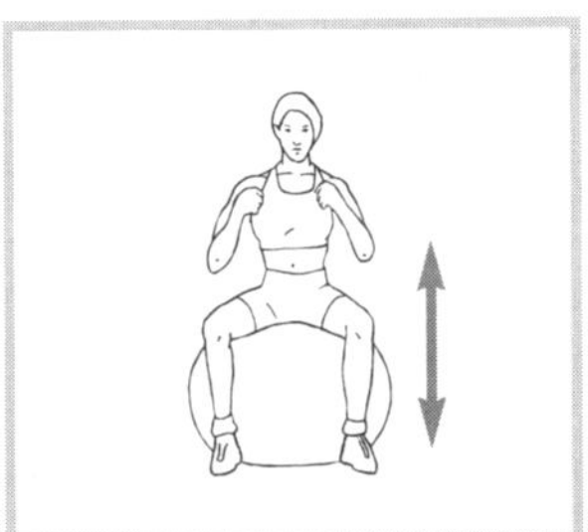

Fig. 5–71a

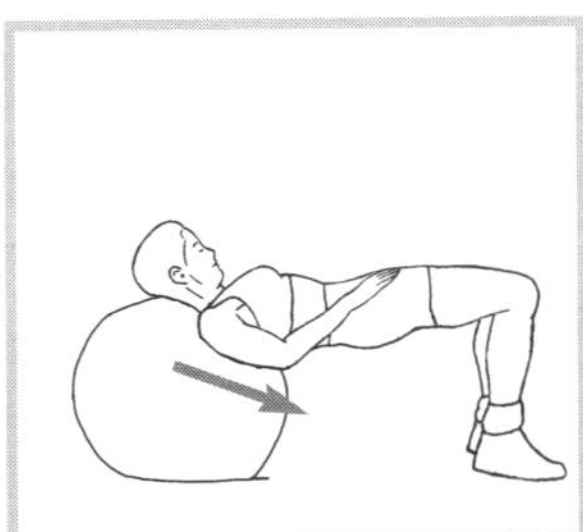

Fig. 5–71b

Fig. 5–71c

Other gym ball balancing drills: Lock in your neutral, slightly arched position and sit up straight. Pick up one foot an inch or so off the ground while remaining balanced on the ball. Try this on the other side. Perform 5 to 15 repetitions with each leg.

Then, extend one leg out straight in front of you while maintaining your balance. Hold this position for 5 to 10 seconds. Change legs and perform 5 to 15 repetitions with each leg. If you have difficulty maintaining your balance initially, you can hold onto the ball with your hands. Once you can perform 15 repetitions, drop back to 5 repetitions with a 10-second hold. Build back up to 15 repetitions.

FLEXIBILITY

The following stretching exercises are designed to improve the flexibility of muscles primarily in the hips and legs. Each of these muscles may affect the low back. For example, if your hamstrings are too tight, you will tend to bend more at the spine when you bend over to pick something up, thus increasing the stress placed on the spinal structures. Likewise, if the psoas (hip flexor) muscles are extremely tight, they will tend to take over when you perform abdominal exercises, and this increases compression of the spine. Stretching each of these muscle groups may therefore be of benefit in decreasing strain on the spine, as well as in facilitating your back strengthening program.

Take each stretch to the point where you feel mild discomfort but not pain. Increasing flexibility is a slow process. It will not happen overnight, so there is no benefit to stretching forcefully. Fast stretching may, in fact, engage the stretch reflex, which will cause the muscle to tighten up. Remember, stretching should not be painful; it should be relaxing. Breathe deeply while stretching. It is best to increase your stretch while exhaling. Exhalation enhances the relaxation of the muscle. Try to feel your muscles slowly elongate and lengthen, like rubber bands. You should hold each stretch for 10 to 30 seconds and repeat it 1 to 3 times. Stretching may be done several times per day.

Stretching is more effective when your body is warm. For this reason, it is good to stretch after your exercise routine. On the other hand, if your muscles are tight, they may affect your ability to properly perform your exercises. Performing some of your exercises slightly incorrectly due to muscle tightness may make whatever pain you're already experiencing worse. Therefore, we recommend stretching both before and after your training session.

To facilitate stretching before your workout, it is best to do a short warm-up to raise your body temperature several degrees. Warm muscles and tendons are more pliable and easily stretched. This warm-up could consist of 5 or 10 minutes of walking or stationary bicycling or even a hot shower or Jacuzzi. More warm-up is required if the weather is cold. Your stretching should immediately follow this warm-up.

None of the stretches described below should result in low back, knee, or hip pain, or in pain traveling down a leg. If you feel pain in any location other than the specific target muscle, stop and consult your physician or physical therapist. The following program is minimal; it incorporates only the exercises that we feel are necessary to stretch each of the important muscle groups related to the low back. We have included only those stretches that we believe to be safe and effective. There are many other possible stretches, some safe, some not so safe. Athletes, in particular, may have need of other stretches and may want to consult with a specialist to determine an appropriate individualized program.

72. CALF/HEEL CORD STRETCH

Target: Calf muscles, Achilles tendons.

To perform the calf stretch, stand with your feet side by side; face the wall and stand at least several feet away from it. Take a large step forward with one foot in the direction of the wall (Fig. 5–72a). Slowly lean your body toward the wall. Keep your head, shoulders, and back in one straight line. Keep the heel of your back foot on the ground. You should feel a stretch in the lower portion of your back leg. Increase the stretch by leaning farther into the wall. This stretches primarily the gastrocnemius (calf muscle) of the lower leg.

Then slightly bend the knee of the back leg (Fig. 5–72b). Hold and feel the stretch move down your leg closer to your foot. Increase the stretch by leaning farther into the wall. This stretches the soleus (lower calf muscle) and the Achilles tendon. Hold each version of the calf stretch for 10 seconds and repeat 1 to 3 times. Change legs.

Fig. 5–72a

Fig. 5–72b

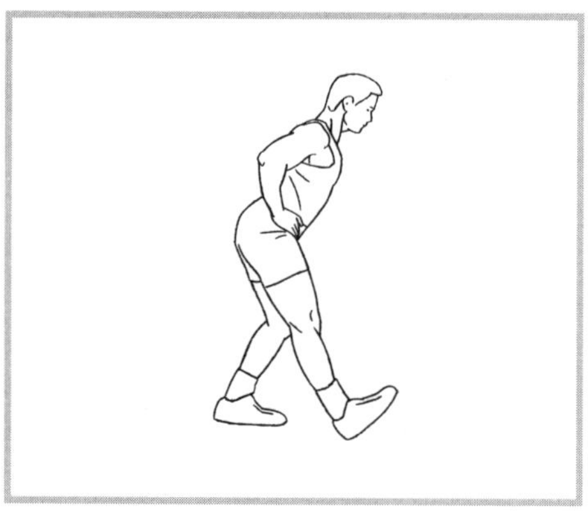

Fig. 5–73a

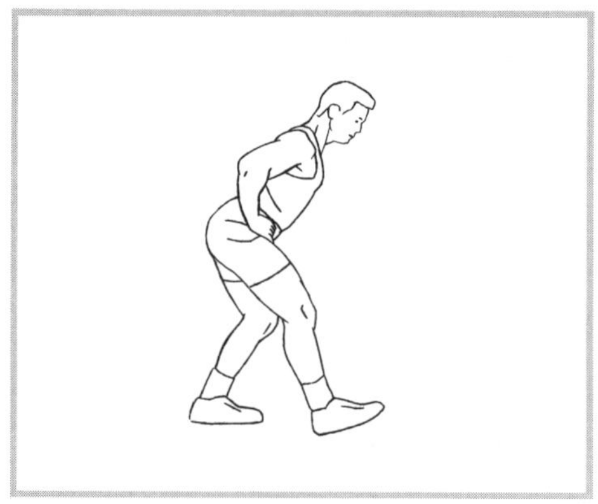

Fig. 5–73b

73. STANDING HAMSTRING STRETCH

Target: Hamstrings

Assume a comfortable stance with your hands on your hips. Extend one leg straight out in front of you and pull your foot up toward you (Fig. 5–73a). Slowly bend forward with your trunk, making sure to maintain the arch in your low back. It is crucial that you avoid rounding your back as you bend over. This is dangerous for your back, and it decreases the effectiveness of the stretch. You should feel a stretch in the back of the upper thigh (hamstring) of the raised leg. You should not feel pain in your back. Hold the stretch for 10 seconds and repeat 1 to 3 times. Change legs. You can allow the rear foot to point outward if that makes it easier to maintain your balance.

Maintaining the same body position, bend the knee of the front leg slightly and allow the foot to rest on the floor. Bend forward more from the hips, making sure to stick your butt out and keep your low back arched (Fig. 5–73b). You should feel this stretch in the upper part of the hamstring, closer to the hip.

74. STANDING QUADRICEPS STRETCH

Target: Quadriceps

Fig. 5–74

Stand with one hand braced against a wall or other support. Balance on one foot with your knee slightly bent. Flex the heel of the other foot toward your buttocks. Grab this raised foot with your free hand and pull it closer to your buttocks (Fig. 5–74). You can loop a towel around your foot and hold onto it if you have difficulty grasping your foot with your hand. Perform a slight posterior pelvic tilt and tighten your abdominals to avoid hyperextending your spine. You should feel this stretch along the front of your thigh. This stretch should not cause you any low back or knee pain. Hold the stretch for 10 seconds and repeat on the other side. Perform this stretch for each thigh 1 to 3 times.

75. KNEELING PSOAS STRETCH

Target: Psoas

Kneel in front of a wall. Bring one leg up, bend the knee, and place the foot some distance in front of the back knee. Your back knee and your back foot should both be resting on the floor, with the top of your back foot against the floor. Both hands should touch the wall in front of you. Slowly push your rear hip forward until you feel a stretch in the front of that hip (Fig. 5–75). Your trunk should remain in a vertical position. To avoid letting your back hyperextend, perform a slight posterior pelvic tilt. Since the

psoas produces anterior tilt, this will accentuate the stretch on the psoas. The stretch can be increased by reaching with the same-side hand up and toward the opposite side of the body; at the same time, slightly flex your body laterally to the opposite side. You should feel the stretch extend from the hip up along the side of your body.

Fig. 5–75

Avoid overflexing the front knee by moving the front foot closer to the wall. Try to keep this knee at close to a 90° angle. This will avoid strain on the knee. You can stretch a slightly different part of the front of the hip by very slightly and slowly rotating the rear hip outward. You will feel the area being stretched shift closer to the groin. Hold the stretch for 10 seconds and repeat on the other side. Perform this stretch for each side 1 to 3 times.

76. SEATED BENT-KNEE ADDUCTOR STRETCH

Target: Adductors

Sit on the ground, trying to maintain the normal lordotic curve in your back. Avoid the tendency to round your back and bend forward over your legs. Bend both knees and bring the bottoms of your feet together (Fig. 5–76). Place your forearms on the insides of your knees. Exhale and slowly push your knees down toward the floor. Feel the stretch on the insides of your legs and your groin. Hold for 10 seconds and repeat up to 3 times.

Fig. 5–76

If you are unable to perform this stretch without rounding your back, try sitting with your back flush up against the wall. If you have very tight hamstrings, even this version will be too difficult. Try lying on your back and placing your feet together against a wall. Place your hands on the insides of your legs and slowly move your knees outward until you feel a stretch on the insides of your hips and in the groin.

77. LYING HAMSTRING STRETCH

Target: Hamstrings

Fig. 5–77

Lie flat on your back with both knees bent. Straighten one knee until the leg is nearly straight. Bring the leg up toward your head till you can wrap your hands around it and clasp them behind the knee (Fig. 5–77). Try to fully straighten the knee by contracting the quadriceps muscles on the front of the thigh. You should feel a moderate stretch in the hamstring muscles on the back of the thigh. If not, pull the leg closer to your chest. Do not allow your buttocks to come off the floor. If you have trouble reaching your knee due to tight hamstrings, you can loop a towel around the bottom of your foot and grasp it to facilitate this stretch. You can also lean your foot against the wall. As you gain flexibility, you can inch closer to the wall. Eventually you can shift to a doorway, where your body can actually move past the wall while your leg is still against it. Hold for 10 seconds and repeat up to 3 times with each leg.

If you are suffering pain that radiates down one or both legs, stretching the hamstrings may not be advisable since this can also stretch the sciatic nerve and may make your pain worse. If the sciatic nerve is being pressed on by a bulging disc, stretching the hamstring will pull the nerve tighter against the disc, potentially making the problem worse. You should avoid any stretching that elicits nerve-type pain (burning pain that shoots down an arm or leg or a sensation of tingling or numbness).

78. 1-KNEE-TO-CHEST STRETCH

Target: Gluteus maximus and gluteus medius.

Lie flat on your back with both legs stretched out. Slowly slide one knee up to a bent position. Then slowly bring that knee up toward your chest. Place your hands around the knee and pull to increase the stretch (Fig. 5–78). You should feel a mild stretch across your hip and in your back. Hold for 10 seconds and repeat up to 3 times. Change legs.

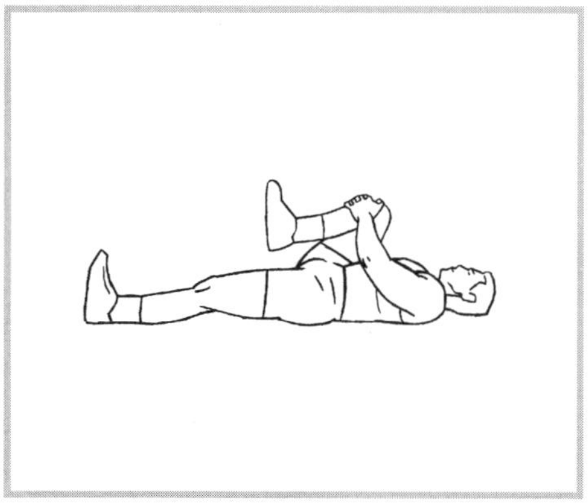

Fig. 5–78

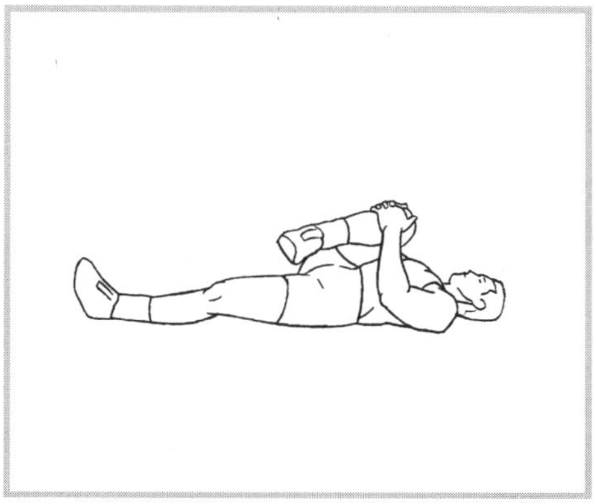

Fig. 5–79

79. 1-KNEE-TO-OPPOSITE-SHOULDER STRETCH

Target: Gluteus medius

While lying flat on your back, bend one knee, grasp your hands around it, and pull it up toward your chest and across to the opposite shoulder (Fig. 5–79). Avoid compressing the knee cap. You should feel the stretch across the outside of your buttocks and hip. Hold for 10 seconds and repeat up to 3 times. Change legs.

80. 2-KNEES-TO-CHEST STRETCH

Target: Gluteal and erector spinae muscles.

Lie flat on your back with your legs out straight. Bring one knee and then the other knee up. Grab your legs just behind your knees and pull them toward your chest (Fig. 5–80). By grabbing behind your knees, you will avoid overly compressing them. You should feel the stretch in both buttocks and across your low back. Hold the stretch for 10 seconds. When you relax, slowly extend your legs to the point where your knees are bent with your feet flat on the floor. Then repeat the stretch up to 3 times.

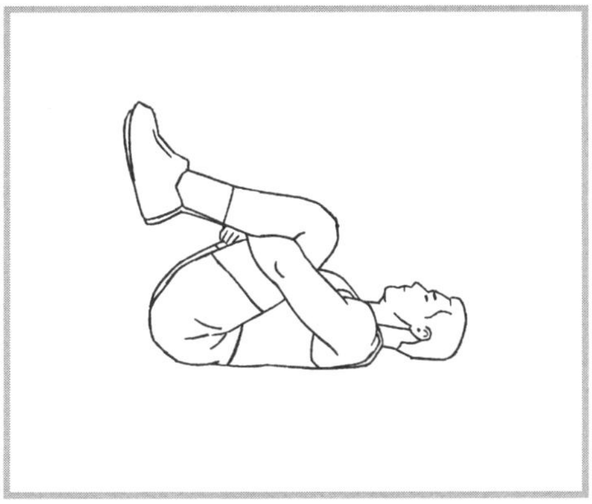

Fig. 5–80

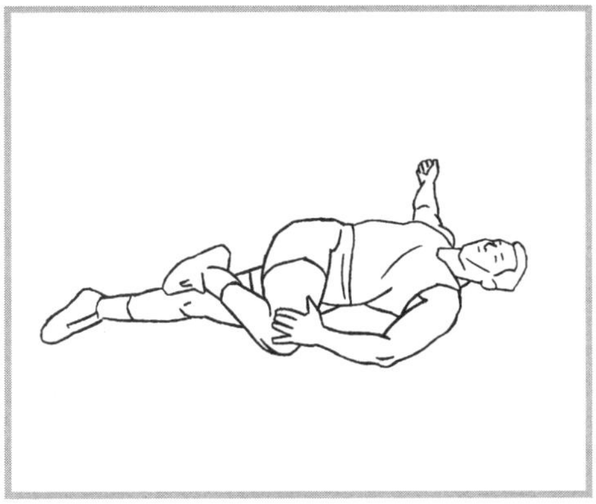

Fig. 5–81

81. CHIROPRACTIC STRETCH

Target: Erector spinae and tensor fascia lata.

Lie flat on your back on the floor with your legs stretched out. Bend your right knee toward your chest and then rotate that leg across your body to your left. Keep your right shoulder and arm on the floor, but let your torso twist. Grab your right knee with your left hand and pull it over closer to the floor (Fig. 5–81). You should feel a stretch across your low back. Hold for 10 seconds and repeat up to 3 times. Change legs.

82. LYING ADDUCTOR STRETCH

Target: Adductors

Lie on your back with your buttocks several inches from the wall and your legs up against it. Allow your legs to slowly spread apart. Inch your legs out along the wall as much as possible to heighten the stretch (Fig. 5–82). Feel the stretch on the insides of your thighs and in the groin. Hold for 10 seconds and repeat up to 3 times.

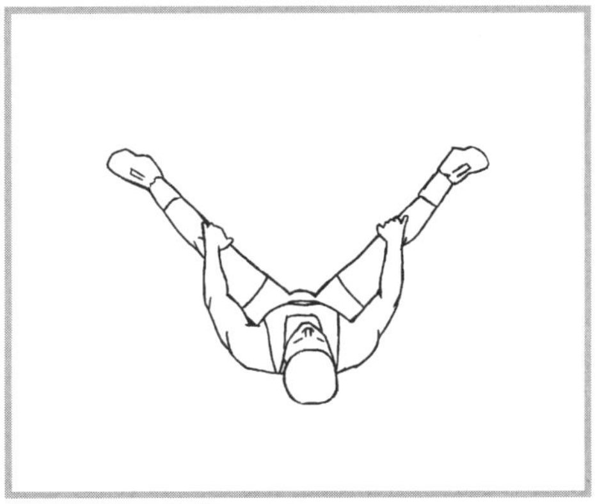

Fig. 5–82

Fig. 5–83a

Fig. 5–83b

83. CAT AND CAMEL STRETCH

Target: Spine, abdominals

Kneel on hands and knees with your knees directly under your hips and your hands under your shoulders. Let your stomach sag and arch your back like a cat, stretching by tipping your pelvis forward (Fig. 5–83a). Inhale and gently contract your back muscles to facilitate the stretch. Then slowly tilt your pelvis in the opposite direction. Exhale, contract your abdominals, and let your back round (Fig. 5–83b). You will look like a camel with a hump on its back. This stretch gently mobilizes the spine between the extended and the arched positions.

84. REPETITIVE COBRA EXERCISE

Target: Spine, abdominals

Lie face down with your hands directly under your shoulders. Use your arms to push your upper body up, letting the hips and low back sag. If possible, try to push yourself up until your elbows are straight while keeping your hips on the floor (Fig. 5–84a). The low back and buttocks muscles should remain relaxed. Remember, this is not a strengthening exercise, so there is no reason to tense your back muscles. Hold this position for a second or so and then lower yourself smoothly to the floor. Repeat 10 times. One variation is to turn your head in one direction as you push yourself up. Turn your head in the opposite direction on the next repetition.

You may be unable to perform this exercise initially due to back pain, but do not rush to eliminate it from your routine. You may need to prepare your back by lying flat on your stomach for a minute or so. Next, attempt to prop yourself up on your elbows (Fig. 5–84b). Lie in this position for another minute or so. Even if this causes back pain, give it a try and see if the pain begins to ease after several seconds. If so, then move on to the repetitive cobra. You may have pain on the first several repetitions. However, this pain should start to diminish with another 3 or 4 repetitions. If your level of pain continues or worsens, however, stop this exercise immediately. If you get pain that shoots down the leg and wasn't there before, stop this exercise immediately and consult your physician. Otherwise, continue.

The repetitive cobra is one of the most important exercises in this program, and you will see that it is specified many times in the routines described in Chapter 6. This exercise is derived from the McKenzie treatment program for low back pain. While it stretches the front wall of the body, its main benefit does not relate to the stretching of muscles. The repetitive cobra exercise helps to pump the fluid in your discs inward, thus relieving the posterior migration of the gel-like center of the disc that typically occurs as a result of a sedentary lifestyle. This exercise is an attempt to counter some of the potentially harmful effects of repetitively flexing the spine by repetitively extending it. It may help to relieve back and leg pain associated with posterior disc bulging and may also help to prevent future disc herniation.

This exercise can also be performed while standing. Simply stand with your hands on your hips. Then slowly lean backward, trying not to contract your back muscles (Fig. 5–84c). Try to support the weight of your upper body with your arms. Lean back as far as you can.

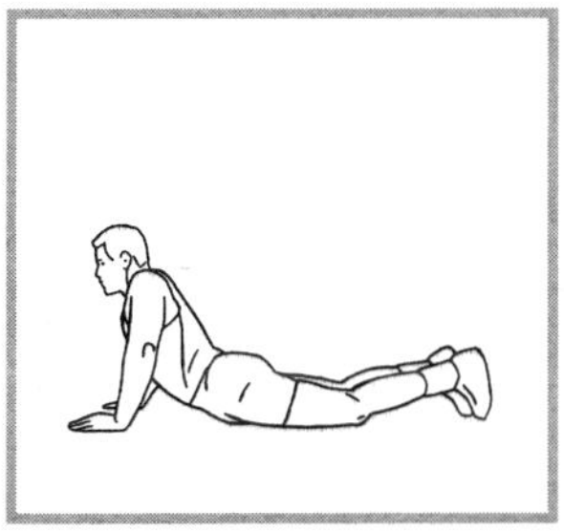

Fig. 5–84a

Fig. 5–84b

Fig. 5–84c

Although it may seem as though this exercise compresses the spine, research shows that it actually produces a mild traction effect on the discs. When prescribed for treatment of back pain, it is often recommended that 10 or more repetitions of this exercise be performed multiple times per day—even on an hourly basis in the case of acute back pain.

Despite its benefits for many, there will be individuals who will have trouble with the repetitive cobra. Those who suffer from spondylolisthesis or central stenosis will most likely want to avoid this exercise. They should consult a physician for further recommendations.

85. PRAYING TO MECCA STRETCH

Target: Spine

After completing the repetitive cobra exercise, get on your hands and knees. Make sure that your hands are directly under your shoulders and your knees directly under your hips (Fig. 5–85a). Leaving your hands where they are, sit back on your heels and allow your back to round forward (Fig. 5–85b). Feel the stretch across your back and your hips. Hold for 10 seconds and repeat up to 3 times.

Fig. 5–85a

Fig. 5–85b

AEROBIC EXERCISES

In general, aerobic training has been found to be beneficial for individuals with back pain. It promotes the release of endorphins, which are your body's natural pain relievers. Walking is often the most comfortable form of aerobic exercise. Individuals with back pain frequently remark that their pain is relieved by walking but returns when sitting or standing in one place.

We recommend that walking, cycling, swimming, or some other form of low impact aerobic exercise be performed for at least 20 minutes a day, 3 to 5 times per week, especially when you are recovering from a back injury. You should try to get your heart rate in the training zone, which is often defined as 60 to 80% of your estimated maximal heart rate (EMHR). EMHR is determined by subtracting your age from 220 and multiplying that number by .60 for the low end of the zone and then by .80 for the high end of the zone. If you are out of shape, start with a very slow pace and gradually work up to this zone. If you have to struggle to do more than 5 minutes, then start with 5 minutes. While in your training zone you should not be gasping for air; you should be able to carry on a conversation. For additional information on aerobic training, see *Max O2*, published by Health For Life.

While performing your aerobic exercise, make sure to maintain your spine in a neutral position. If you ride a bike or use the treadmill or stair machine, do not lean forward against the handles. Stand or sit up straight. You may find the recumbent cycle more effective than the conventional bicycle due to the back support it provides. You may also want to roll up a towel or place a back support pillow in the small of your back while riding the recumbent cycle. This will help to support your spine.

Of the commonly available stationary aerobic devices—bikes, treadmills, stair machines, ski machines, and rowing machines—stair machines seem to increase low back problems the most. This may be because they involve involve a psoas-dominated movement or because the user may adopt a lateral sway. However, if you enjoy using a stair machine and you experience no back discomfort while using it, then by all means, continue. It is important that you get some aerobic exercise, and your personal preferences and the availability of equipment should be taken into account. We have found walking, cycling, and swimming to be the activities best tolerated by those with back problems. Jogging, because of the forceful way that the foot strikes the ground, is actually more traumatic on the spine than running, and is not recommended.

While we have been focusing on the risk of low back pain, you should be aware there are other risks associated with exercise. In particular, there is a risk of cardiovascular problems arising from exercise, especially aerobic exercise. This risk is elevated if you have pre-existing cardiovascular problems. We strongly recommend, therefore, that you follow the guidelines provided by the American College of Sports Medicine: Even apparently healthy men over the age of 40 and women over the age of 50 should undergo a medical evaluation prior to engaging in vigorous exercise.

SPEED / POWER

Athletes must learn to stabilize their spines, not only during slow movements, but also during the types of rapid, ballistic movements that characterize their sports. They must also strengthen spinal muscles in isolation to increase their force-generating capabilities. Olympic lifts, such as power cleans and snatches, and medicine ball exercises are ideal for this.

Olympic Lifts

Olympic lifts are ideally suited to developing speed and power since they involve the coordinated use of most of the larger muscle groups in the body in pulling or pushing a bar rapidly. They can also help to stabilize the back, especially if the neutral spine position is maintained by keeping the abdominal and other trunk muscles tight. Although we provide brief descriptions of these exercises, keep in mind that they are extremely difficult and should only be performed by already well-conditioned athletes. Best bet: find a strength coach to work with you individually on performing these movements.

86. POWER CLEANS

This exercise begins from approximately the same position as the Deadlift with a barbell on the floor in front of you. Your feet should be shoulder-width apart or slightly wider. The hands should be outside of the thighs. Squat down and grasp the bar, palms down. The bar should be kept close to your legs. It is crucial that you maintain the normal arch in your back while in the bottom position, especially while pulling. You should also lift your chest up and out, and pull your shoulder blades toward each other. Look straight ahead.

Pull the bar up by simultaneously extending your knees and hips (Fig. 5-86a). Maintain your back in the neutral position. As you pull the bar above your knees, begin to thrust your hips forward (Fig. 5-86b). Then, as the bar reaches mid-thigh level, explosively extend your hips, knees, and ankles. Your body should leave the ground slightly. As the bar continues up past your thighs, your shoulder girdle should lift up. Then pull up your elbows, using your shoulder and arm muscles. The bar should be pulled as high as possible.

Once you reach that position, try to get under the bar and catch it (Fig. 5-86c). Slightly flex your knees and hips and rotate your elbows under and around the bar. The bar should be caught across the front of your shoulders. Slowly lower the bar back to the floor, maintaining the arch in the low back.

Fig. 5–86a

Fig. 5–86b

Fig. 5–86c

87. SNATCHES

This exercise begins from a starting position similar to that used in the Power Clean and Deadlift, except you use a wider hand placement. Your hands should be spaced approximately as far apart as your elbows are when you hold your arms straight out to the sides. Your feet should be shoulder-width apart or slightly wider. Squat down and grasp the bar. The bar should be kept close to your legs. It is crucial that you maintain the normal arch in your back in the bottom position, especially while pulling. You should also lift your chest up and out and pull your shoulders blades together. Look straight ahead.

Pull the bar up by simultaneously extending your knees and hips (Fig. 5–87a). Maintain your back in the neutral position. As you pull the bar above your knees, begin to thrust your hips forward (Fig. 5–87b). Then, as the bar reaches mid-thigh level, explosively extend your hips, knees, and ankles. Your body should leave the ground slightly. As the bar continues up past your thighs, your shoulder girdle should lift up. Then pull up your elbows, using your shoulder and arm muscles, and pull the bar as high as possible.

Fig. 5–87a

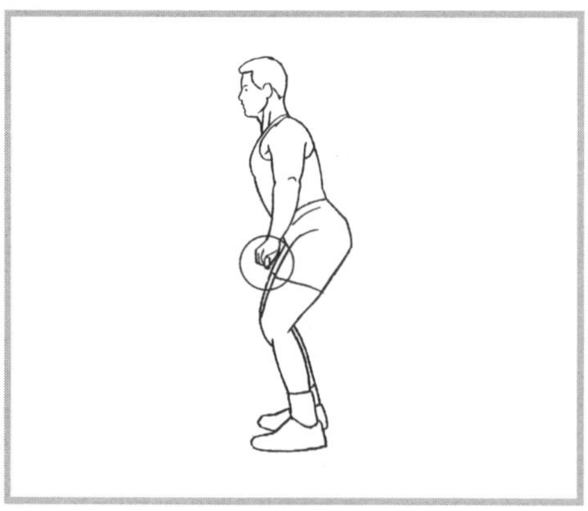

Fig. 5–87b

Fig. 5–87c

Once that position is reached, try to jump under the bar and catch it with your arms extended over your head (Fig. 5–87c). Flex your knees and hips and rotate your elbows under and around the bar. Catch the bar with your wrists hyperextended and your elbows straight.

Slowly lower yourself into a squat with the bar extended over your head. Make sure to control the weight in the low squat position. Slowly rise back to the standing position.

Slowly lower the bar back to the floor, maintaining the arch in your low back.

88. PUSH JERKS (PRESSES)

This exercise begins from the finishing position of the Power Clean with the bar resting across the fronts of your shoulders (Fig. 5–88a). You should be standing with your feet shoulder-width apart or slightly wider. Your hands should be spaced approximately at shoulder width, with your elbows pointing forward and slightly down.

Bend your knees and hips a little to generate some elastic energy. Then rapidly jump up using your legs and hips and simultaneously push the bar up over your head (Fig. 5–88b). As your knees and hips extend, your heels should also come off the floor. Your whole body is literally jerking the weight up over your head. Explode as you push it up. Then lower the weight back to your shoulders and repeat.

Your back will tend to hyperextend in this movement. You need to focus on drawing your waist in and tightening your abdominal muscles to keep your spine in a neutral position.

Fig. 5–88a

Fig. 5–88b

Medicine Ball Training

By using a medicine ball, you can perform ballistic, explosive exercises that will simultaneously develop strength and power. We recommend using one of the newer jelly balls, as they have an elastic quality that the older style balls do not have. This helps to blunt the trauma to your body as you catch the ball. Medicine ball training involves an elevated risk of injury and is recommended only for athletes who must prepare their bodies for the ballistic movements that occur in sports.

Medicine ball training is best done with a partner who can catch and return the ball to you. You will need a fairly large space—an aerobics room at a gym, a gymnasium, or a field—for some of these exercises; others require a back extension bench, which can be found in most gyms or weight rooms. If you don't have a partner or don't have the necessary space, use the non-release version of these exercises.

The medicine ball exercises listed here are aimed at strengthening the erector spinae and other back muscles. Additional medicine ball exercises are listed below, under "Resistance Exercises for the Abdominals."

89. OVER-THE-HEAD THROWS

Stand with your feet approximately shoulder-width apart and hold a medicine ball in both hands. Swoop the ball down between your legs in a circular motion while simultaneously bending your knees (Fig. 5–89a). Then rapidly reverse direction. Sweep the ball up and over your head while simultaneously straightening your legs (Fig. 5–89b).

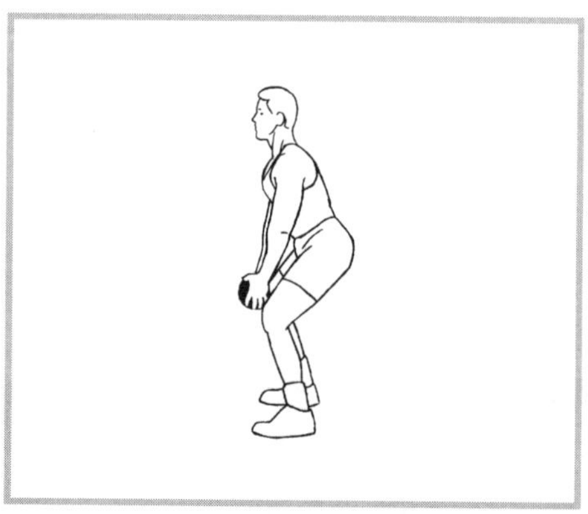

Fig. 5–89a

Fig. 5–89b

Fig. 5–89c

Fig. 5–89d

Let your back arch as you come up, but draw your midsection in slightly to avoid letting your back hyperextend. Your low back muscles help propel the ball, and your abdominal muscles must be activated to prevent your spine from hyperextending. There are two versions of this exercise—with and without ball release. If you release the ball for someone else to catch, this exercise is better for developing speed and power. If you hold on to the ball and bring it back down for another repetition, your muscles will need to work harder—especially your abdominal muscles—to break the speed of the ball.

The kneeling version of this exercise involves a similar movement. It isolates the back muscles more, but it resembles what actually happens in sports less. Kneel on the floor and hold the gel ball in front of you (Fig. 5–89c). Lower the ball toward the floor and then bring it in an arc across your body and over your head (Fig. 5–89d). Again, as with the standing version, there are two variations—with and without ball release. The ball-release version is better for developing power and speed, but it requires a partner to catch or retrieve the ball. The no-release version puts more strain on the abdominal muscles, which must contract to slow the ball down at the top.

90. OVER-THE-SHOULDER THROWS

This exercise is similar to the over-the-head throw except that it involves throwing the ball directly over one and then the other shoulder (Fig. 5–90a,b). Since it involves a slight twisting of the spine, it engages some of the rotational muscles in the back and the abdominal region. This exercise can also be done kneeling (Fig. 5–90c,d)

Fig. 5–90a

Fig. 5–90b

Fig. 5–90c

Fig. 5–90d

91. HANGING MEDICINE BALL TOSSES

Hold yourself in a straight position face down on the horizontal back extension bench with a medicine ball in your hands (Fig. 5–91a). With an underhand motion, sweep the medicine ball under your body and throw it in front of you (Fig. 5–91b). Try to keep your spine in a neutral position throughout the movement. Again, there are two versions—with and without ball release. The ball-release version is better for developing power and speed, but it requires a partner to catch the ball. The no-release version puts more strain on the abdominal muscles, which must contract to slow the ball down.

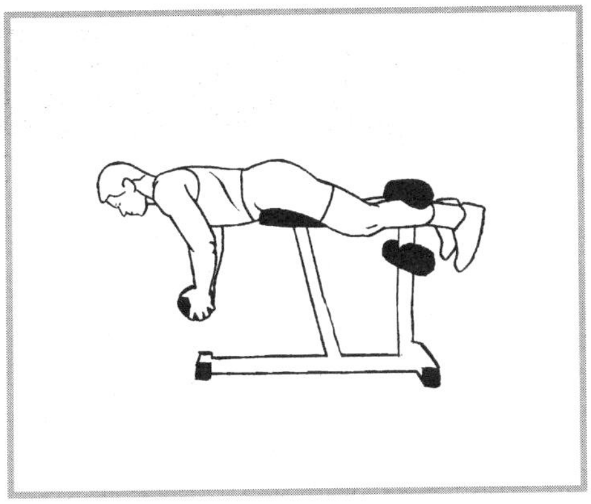

Fig. 5–91a

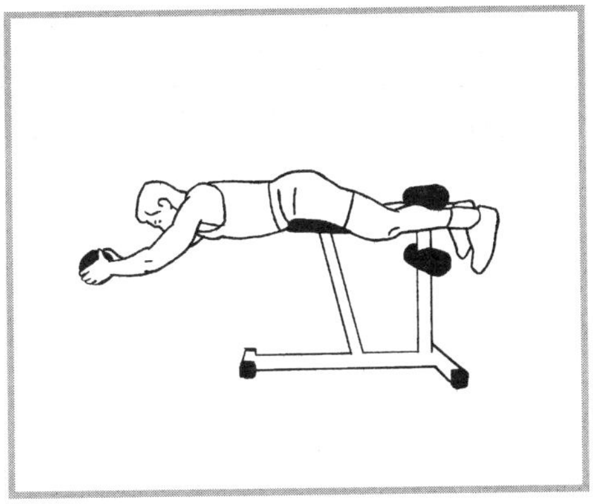

Fig. 5–91b

92. EXTEND AND THROW

This is the dynamic version of the hanging medicine ball toss. Get in position, with your torso hanging down from the hip over the back extension bench, and hold the medicine ball. Perform a rapid hip extension movement, keeping your spine in a neutral position throughout (Fig. 5–92 a,b). As you come back up to horizontal, rapidly sweep the ball over your body and your head. As with all of the above exercises, there are release and non-release versions. If you do not release the ball to a partner, rapidly lower your body and repeat the exercise.

Fig. 5–92a

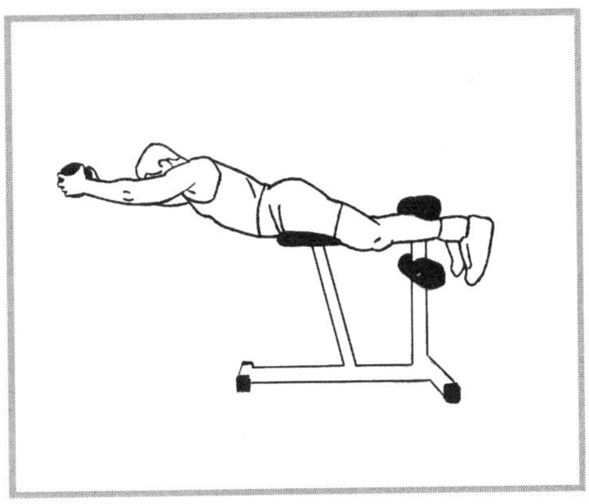

Fig. 5–92b

EXERCISES TO AVOID

There are many commonly performed strengthening and flexibility exercises that can aggravate low back problems and should be avoided or modified. These include abdominal exercises that overwork the hip flexors, exercises and stretches that might overstretch the ligaments of the spine, and exercises that involve uncontrolled, or ballistic, rotation.

Psoas/Ab Exercises

In many commonly performed abdominal exercises, the psoas (hip flexor) muscles actually do most of the work. The psoas muscle attaches to the front of the lumbar vertebrae and the discs, and when it contracts, it pulls down on them. This can increase compressive and shear forces on the spine, contributing to back injury and pain. This problem is compounded by the fact that many individuals have short and tight psoas muscles from sitting all day. Athletes tend to have highly developed and tight psoas muscles. For these reasons it may be even worse for them to overly strengthen these muscles, making them even tighter. Athletes generally need to strengthen their abdominals and the gluteals to balance the strength of their psoas muscles.

The following psoas/abdominal movements should, therefore, be avoided:

FULL SIT-UPS (AND SIT-UPS W/FEET ANCHORED)

If you are still doing full sit-ups or sit-ups with your feet fixed (Fig. 5–93), stop if you are at all concerned about the health of your low back. These exercises heavily recruit the psoas and may make a back problem worse.

IMPROPERLY PERFORMED STRAIGHT-LEG RAISES

This exercise involves lying on your back, locking your abdominal muscles, and lifting and lowering your legs using your hip flexors (Fig. 5–94). It is particularly harsh on the

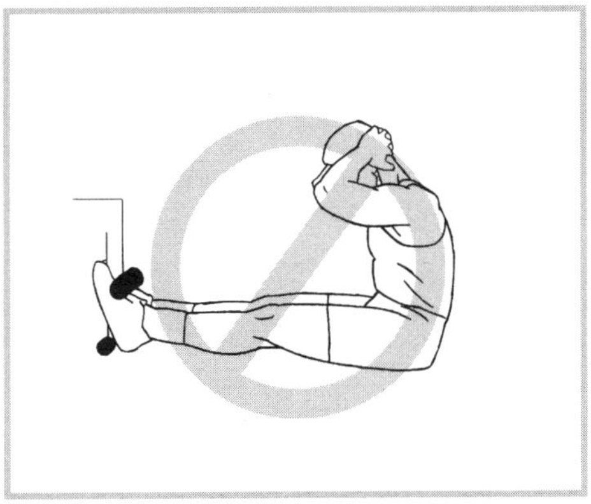

Fig. 5–93

Fig. 5–94

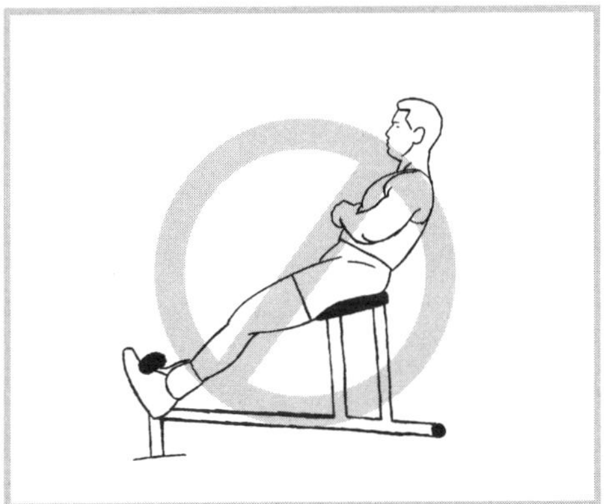

Fig. 5–95

Fig. 5–96

low back. Although you may feel a "burn" in the lower abdomen, this is probably coming from the psoas muscles. Some trainers feel that placing the hands under the hips makes this exercise safe, but this is not the case.

ROMAN CHAIR SIT-UPS

This exercise is performed while sitting on a small seat and rocking back and forth. The feet are hooked under a bar (Fig. 5–95). This is another psoas-dominated movement with only minimal isometric abdominal involvement. This exercise is not only unsafe, it is a waste of time.

HIGH-CHAIR LEG / KNEE RAISES

This exercise is still fairly common and is largely a hip exercise rather than an abdominal exercise (Fig. 5–96). You should leave this exercise out of your routine as well.

V-UPS

This exercise is sometimes also referred to as a jackknife (Fig. 5–97). It is performed sitting on the edge of a bench and simultaneously bringing your legs and upper body up to form a V-shape. It does work the abdominal muscles if performed properly; however, it probably involves the psoas too much for all but very advanced trainees.

Fig. 5–97

MOST ABDOMINAL MACHINES

No doubt, some abdominal machines are better than others. There is a tendency, however, when using these devices to hinge at the hips rather than rounding the back. When the feet are hooked, there is even more likelihood that the psoas will do most of the work. You will probably do best to avoid abdominal machines. Rope Crunches with weight make a more effective exercise.

Exercises Promoting Hyperflexion

The following exercises could overstretch your ligaments and the connective tissue in your back. They should be avoided.

STANDING TOE TOUCHES

In these exercises, you stand straight legged and bend over to touch your toes (Fig. 5–98). Because of the flexion-relaxation response, this exercise causes the full weight of your upper body to be placed on the ligaments and connective tissue of the spine. At worst this can result in a severe back injury. Over time it can gradually stretch the ligaments and produce an unstable lower spine.

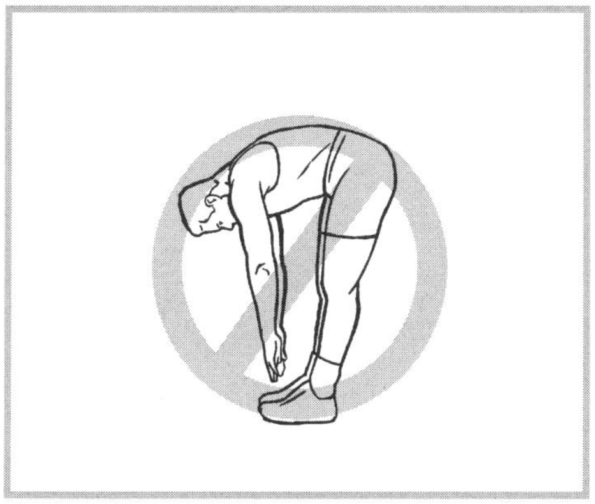

Fig. 5–98

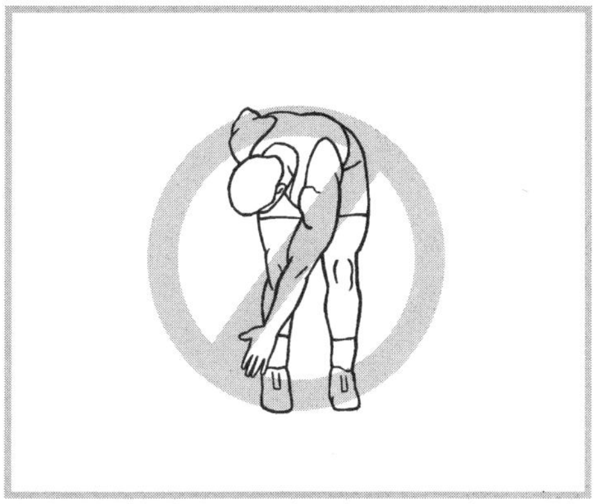

Fig. 5–99

WINDMILLS

The combination of full forward bending and twisting involved in this exercise is extremely dangerous and could result in a torn or herniated disc (Fig. 5–99). It is one of the most dangerous stretching exercises ever designed.

SEATED STRAIGHT-LEG TOE TOUCHES

This exercise duplicates the same fully flexed position that occurs with Standing Toe Touches. The only difference is that gravity is not pushing you down, so you have more control (Fig. 5–100). Of course, if you have an overzealous trainer pushing on your upper back from behind, the strain on the low back could be greater than what you get from the Standing Toe Touches.

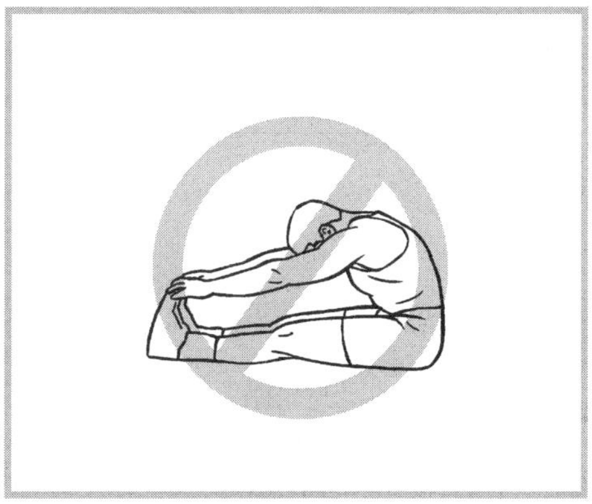

Fig. 5–100

Fig. 5–101a

Fig. 5–101b

IMPROPERLY PERFORMED ROWS

Performing Bent-Over Rows (Fig. 5–101a) or Seated Cable Rows (Fig. 5–101b) and letting your back round as you extend the weight at the end of the repetition could result in injury to the ligaments, muscles, or discs. Bending over and rounding your back is dangerous due to the flexion-relaxation response that transfers all of the weight of the upper body to the ligaments, which are ill equipped to handle it. Bending over and rounding your back while holding a heavy weight is even more dangerous.

We recommend that you perform rowing exercises with your low back in a straight or slightly arched position and that you pull back and forth with your arms. This will greatly reduce your risk of back injury. If you are a competitive rower and this exercise duplicates the rowing that you do in competition, then assume the risk and keep on rowing by stretching out and pulling back with the hip and back muscles. If you are a bodybuilder and you are convinced that you must stretch forward while performing seated cable rows, then at least restrict the forward motion to hip flexion/extension and keep your back arched or flat. At all costs, try to avoid rounding your back while holding a heavy weight.

Fig. 5–102

Fig. 5–103

DEADLIFTS – BACK ALLOWED TO ROUND

Deadlifts consist of bending down and then standing back up while holding a barbell or dumbbells. If deadlifts are performed, every attempt should be made to maintain the normal curvature in the lumbar spine. This will help you to avoid disc and ligamentous injuries that may occur if it is allowed to round (Fig. 5–102). It is especially important to focus on maintaining the lumbar curvature because extremely heavy weights are often used in the deadlift. This is because it is a fairly basic exercise that involves many of the largest muscle groups of the body.

SEATED LEG PRESS MACHINE – KNEES TOO CLOSE TO CHEST

As your knees come back to the chest, your back is pressed into the seat and your pelvis tilts backward. If the knees come back too far, the back becomes flexed forward in a position similar to bending over and holding a weight. This can result in a hyperflexion injury to the spine (Fig. 5–103).

Ideally, you should maintain the normal curvature in your low back when doing this exercise; however, this is impossible without the aid of a very firm lumbar pad. Some machines actually have a built-in lumbar support. If the pad hits you at the right height, this is ideal. If you are too tall or too short, however, this pad may do you more harm than good.

Ballistic or Uncontrolled Rotation

The following exercises involve ballistic, or uncontrolled, rotational stresses and could potentially lead to facet or disc injury:

BROOMSTICK OR BARBELL TWISTS

Twisting exercises such as broomstick twists (Fig. 5–104) place rotational stresses on the spine and can lead to tearing of the discs or injury to the facet joints. Bending forward, as is commonly done during twists performed while seated on a decline V bench, increases the risk of disc injury. Adding extension, as with the Nautilus rotation machine, increases the risk of a facet injury. Rotation must occur in a very controlled fashion so that the strain is placed on the oblique muscles and not on the spinal structures. Furthermore, if doing twists with a broomstick is dangerous, performing them with a barbell is even worse. Compression added to rotation is a surefire recipe for a back injury. Avoid this exercise!

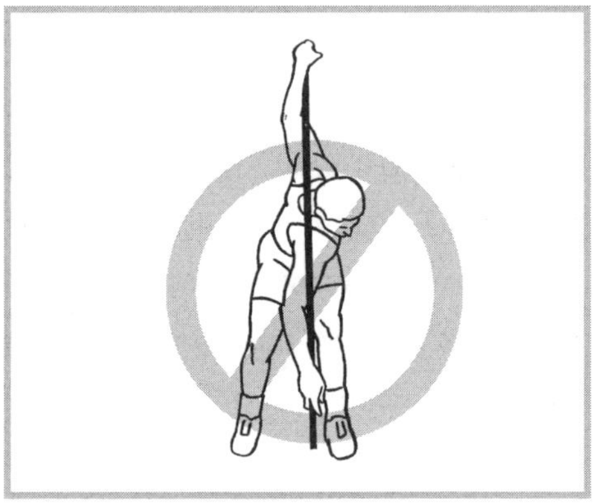

Fig. 5–104

ROTARY TORSO MACHINES

Unless you're an athlete in a sport that involves considerable rotation, rotary torso machines should be avoided (Fig. 5–105). Rotational movements against resistance can lead to overdeveloped oblique muscles. In addition, rotational forces may be injurious to the spine unless they are kept within a very controlled range. It is very easy to misuse this type of machine and to exceed the optimum range of motion of the lumbar spine.

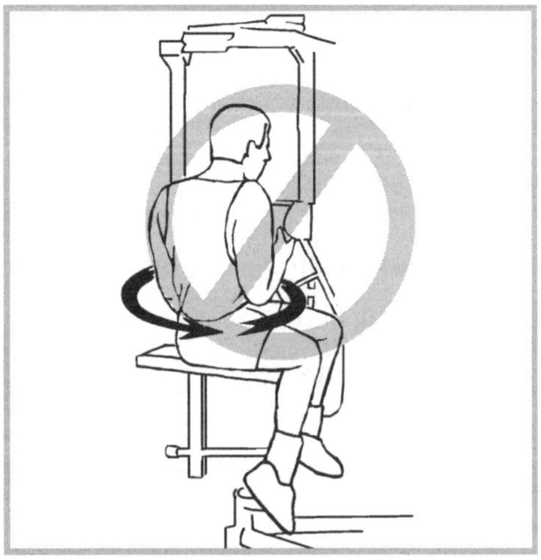

Fig. 5–105

BALLISTIC HYPEREXTENSION

When you see someone flying up and down on the back extension bench and crashing up into a hyperextended position on each repetition, you are most likely witnessing low back pain in the making. Do yourself a favor and avoid this exercise (Fig. 5-106).

Fig. 5–106

The Routines

The exercise routines detailed below are organized into three major categories according to your fitness profile: non-athlete, bodybuilder, or athlete. Further distinctions allow for different levels of conditioning within the non-athlete category and for the special requirements of different sports within the athlete category. There are routines designed to rehabilitate an injured or painful back and others aimed at the prevention of back injury for both the non-athlete and athlete. There's even a routine specifically for bodybuilders, aimed at the prevention of back injury and maintenance of appearance.

6 THE ROUTINES

First, some general guidelines: If you are lucky and your back is currently pain-free, choose a **prevention** routine appropriate to your level of fitness to ensure it stays that way. If you've recently injured your back or suffer from chronic pain, your first step should be to consult with your physician. Your physician knows your case history and is in the best position to recommend the appropriate **rehabilitation** routine and to suggest modifications, if any are necessary.

Rehabilitation

The rehab routines aim to strengthen and condition while decreasing risk of further injury. Here's the basic scheme: Initially, you avoid exercises that place much of a load on your spine. You then slowly increase exercise demands, taking care not to exceed the tolerance of your still-healing spinal tissues.

This can be a delicate balance! Pain is your guide. If an exercise causes increased pain, skip it and continue with the rest of the routine. But keep in mind that an exercise that causes pain one day may not do so on another.

While you should avoid anything that causes significant increases in your pain, most likely you'll experience some low-grade pain as a result of exercising and mobilizing muscles and tissues you may not have used that way before. This typically low-grade pain should be localized to your back.

Another perspective: If you require a rehab routine, you're obviously in some pain now. The right kind of exercise routine is the best way to help you out of it. You should start exercising as soon as you are out of the acute pain phase. At this point, the initial inflammation of your back injury has subsided and your pain level has become more moderate. Your physician can best determine for you when you have reached this stage.

If you wait until all your pain is gone before starting activities, you can fall into the "chronic pain/deconditioning syndrome," where pain promotes inactivity, and failure to exercise delays recovery. If your physician approves, you may be better off starting your rehab program while you are still experiencing some pain.

Although you should try to find those exercises and ranges of motion where the least pain exists, your goal should be to get into better shape so you can feel in control of your life again. Most likely you'll find that as your muscles get stronger and you become more flexible and fit, your pain will diminish and, ultimately, disappear. *You should not make decreasing pain your goal.* If you focus on pain, it may actually become worse. If, however, you suffer any of the following symptoms while performing these exercises, you should stop immediately and consult your physician:

- Increased pain
- Sharper pain
- Pain down the leg that you were not feeling before
- Tingling or numbness in one or both legs or feet

Provided all goes well and you do not experience any of these symptoms, you should move to the intermediate phase of your rehabilitation routine as soon as you no longer feel challenged by the initial phase. This should typically be no longer than six weeks after beginning. By this point, you should either be pain free or have entered a chronic pain phase and experienced a decrease in the severity of your pain. As you become stronger, more flexible, more aerobically fit, and better able to keep your spine stabilized while performing various activities, your pain will continue to abate.

In a rehab routine you do back and abdominal exercises first. Your emphasis is on strengthening these weak links, and you need to exercise these areas first when you have the most energy. Then, follow up with a light full-body training program.

Prevention

In a prevention routine, you do the overall weight-training routine first, followed by the abdominal and back exercises. The abdominal and lower back muscles are stabilizing muscles and should ideally not be exhausted before they are required for lifting relatively heavy weights. You want them fresh so they can stabilize your spine while you perform your lunges, curls, and all of your other exercises.

5-MINUTE CORE ROUTINE

Time is at a premium for just about everybody. Perhaps you can't perform 10 or 20 exercises no matter how much your back hurts. What can you do? The core of our back conditioning program can be completed in five minutes or less. If all you do is this core routine, you will notice considerable benefit. Your spine will become more stable, your stomach and back muscles will become stronger, your hip muscles will become more flexible, your balance will improve, and even your vertebrae will become stronger. Your back pain will also probably decrease, and when it does, it will be less likely to return—provided, of course, that you continue doing your exercises.

Perform the following exercises on a daily basis.

STRETCHES

1 rep	**2-Knees-to-Chest Stretch** *(p. 126)*	10 sec hold
1 rep	**Lying Hamstring Stretch** *(p. 125)*	10 sec hold

EXERCISES

1 set	**Pelvic Tilting Exercises** *(p. 79)*	2 min or until fatigued
1 set	**Repetitive Cobra Exercise** *(p. 128)*	10 reps
1 set	**Quadruped Exercises** *(p. 116)*	2 min or until fatigued

NON-ATHLETE/REHAB

Level 1

Begin this routine with your physician's approval as soon as your acute pain phase is over, and continue it until your pain is almost gone. You can usually start this phase one to ten days after your injury. Your physician, chiropractor, or therapist may want you to use pain-controlling modalities—such as oral medications, cortisone injections, manipulation, massage, electrical stimulation, ultrasound, or ice—during this initial phase to help facilitate your transition into active rehabilitative exercise. Ice applied immediately following exercise is recommended to lessen the impact to your main injury.

Perform these exercises once or twice daily.

WARMUP

1 set	**Walking or Cycling**	5–10 min

STRETCHES

2–3 reps	**1-Knee-to-Chest Stretch** *(p. 126)*	10–30 secs
2–3 reps	**2-Knees-to-Chest Stretch** *(p. 126)*	10–30 secs
2–3 reps	**Lying Hamstring Stretch*** *(p. 125)*	10–30 secs
2–3 reps	**Chiropractic Stretch** *(p. 127)*	10–30 secs
2–3 reps	**Cat and Camel Stretch** *(p. 128)*	10–30 secs
2–3 reps	**Repetitive Cobra Exercise** *(p. 128)*	10–30 secs
2–3 reps	**Praying to Mecca Stretch** *(p. 130)*	10–30 secs

**Skip Lying Hamstring Stretches if they elicit pain down the leg or tingling or numbness in the leg or foot.*

EXERCISES

5 sets	**1-Legged Balancing** *(p. 118)*	alt. legs, 30 secs each
1 set	**Pelvic Tilting Exercises** *(p. 79)*	5–15 reps
1 set	**Bridging With Pelvic Tilt Exercises** *(p. 86)*	5–15 reps
1 set	**Repetitive Cobra Exercise** *(p. 128)*	10 reps
1 set	**Quadruped Exercises** *(p. 116)*	5–15 reps

AEROBICS

1 set	**Walking, Cycling or Swimming**	10–30 min

REPEAT STRETCHES LISTED ABOVE.

Level 2

As soon as you no longer find the initial phase challenging, proceed to this phase. Typically, this phase should start after the first month or so. By this point, you may be going to the gym to complete your workout. If your gym does not have exercise balls available, you can perform your ball exercises at home before you go to the gym. If you don't want to go to the gym, you can perform all of these exercises at home with minimal equipment.

Perform exercises marked with a "d" daily, if possible. Perform the other exercises 3 times a week.

WARMUP (D)

1 set	**Walking or Cycling**	5–10 min

STRETCHES (D)

1–3 reps	**Calf/Heel Cord Stretch** *(p. 121)*	10 secs (each leg)
1–3 reps	**Standing Hamstring Stretch** *(p. 122)*	10 secs (each leg)
1–3 reps	**Standing Quadriceps Stretch** *(p. 123)*	10 secs (each leg)
1–3 reps	**Kneeling Psoas Stretch** *(p. 123)*	10 secs (each side)
1–3 reps	**Seated Bent-Knee Abductor Stretch** *(p. 124)*	10 secs
1–3 reps	**Lying Hamstring Stretch*** *(p. 125)*	10 secs (each leg)
1–3 reps	**1-Knee-to-Chest Stretch** *(p. 126)*	10 secs (each leg)
1–3 reps	**1-Knee-to-Opposite-Shoulder Stretch** *(p. 126)*	10 secs (each leg)
1–3 reps	**2-Knees-to-Chest Stretch** *(p. 126)*	10 secs
1–3 reps	**Chiropractic Stretch** *(p. 127)*	10 secs (each side)
1–3 reps	**Lying Adductor Stretch** *(p. 127)*	10 secs
10 reps	**Cat and Camel Stretch** *(p. 128)*	
10 reps	**Repetitive Cobra Exercise** *(p. 128)*	
1–3 reps	**Praying to Mecca Stretch** *(p. 130)*	10 secs

**Skip Lying Hamstring Stretches if they elicit pain down the leg or tingling or numbness in the leg or foot.*

EXERCISES

5 sets	**1-Legged Balancing** *(p. 118)*	alt. legs, 30 secs each
1 set	**Pelvic Tilting Exercises** *(p. 79)*	5–15 reps (d)
1 set	**Gym Ball Balancing** *(p. 119)*	10 pelvic tilts (all dirs) (d)
1 set	**Bridging With Pelvic Tilts** *(p. 86)*	5–15 reps (d)
2 supersets	**Reverse Crunches** *(p. 90)*	10–30 reps
	Lying Hip Thrusts *(p. 92)*	10–30 reps
2 sets	**Isometric Side-Support Exercises*** *(p. 102)*	10–30 secs (each side)

**If you experience any pain in your shoulders, elbows, or wrists while performing this exercise, substitute Side Bending on the Floor for 2 sets of 10–20 reps on each side.*

1 set	**Twisting Crunches** *(p. 96)*	10–30 reps
1 set	**Quadruped Exercises** *(p. 116)*	5–15 reps (d)
2 sets	**Ball Extensions*** *(p. 74)*	10–15 reps

**If you don't have a ball, then do Prone Shoulder and Leg Lifts for 2 sets of 10–15 reps.*

2 sets	**Lunges** *(p. 111)*	10–15 reps

AEROBICS

1 set	**Walking, Cycling or Swimming**	20–60 mins (d)

REPEAT STRETCHES LISTED ABOVE.

Level 3

Perform exercises marked with a "D" daily, if possible. Perform the other exercises 3 times a week.

WARMUP (D)

1 set	**Walking or Cycling**	5–10 min

STRETCHES (D)

1–3 reps	**Calf/Heel Cord Stretch** *(p. 121)*	10 secs (each leg)
1–3 reps	**Standing Hamstring Stretch** *(p. 122)*	10 secs (each leg)
1–3 reps	**Standing Quadriceps Stretch** *(p. 123)*	10 secs (each leg)
1–3 reps	**Kneeling Psoas Stretch** *(p. 123)*	10 secs (each side)
1–3 reps	**Seated Bent-Knee Abductor Stretch** *(p. 124)*	10 secs
1–3 reps	**Lying Hamstring Stretch*** *(p. 125)*	10 secs (each leg)
1–3 reps	**1-Knee-to-Chest Stretch** *(p. 126)*	10 secs (each leg)
1–3 reps	**1-Knee-to-Opposite-Shoulder Stretch** *(p. 126)*	10 secs (each leg)
1–3 reps	**2-Knees-to-Chest Stretch** *(p. 126)*	10 secs
1–3 reps	**Chiropractic Stretch** *(p. 127)*	10 secs (each side)
1–3 reps	**Lying Adductor Stretch** *(p. 127)*	10 secs
10 reps	**Cat and Camel Stretch** *(p. 128)*	
10 reps	**Repetitive Cobra Exercise** *(p. 128)*	
1–3 reps	**Praying to Mecca Stretch** *(p. 130)*	10 secs

**Skip Lying Hamstring Stretches if they elicit pain down the leg or tingling or numbness in the leg or foot.*

EXERCISES

2 supersets	**Reverse Crunches** *(p. 90)*	15–30 reps
1 set	**Lying Hip Thrusts** *(p. 92)*	15–30 reps
1 set	**Pelvic Tilting Exercises** *(p. 79)*	5–15 reps (d)
2 sets	**Side Bending on the Floor** *(p. 102)*	15–30 reps (each side)
1 set	**Side Crunches** *(p. 97)*	15–30 reps (each side)
1 set	**Twisting Crunches** *(p. 96)*	15–30 reps (each side)
2 sets	**Rope Crunches** *(p. 97)*	15–30 reps
2 sets	**Cross-Cable Pulls** *(p. 94)*	10–15 reps (each side)
1 set	**Quadruped Exercises** *(p. 116)*	5–15 reps (d)
3 sets	**Lying 1-Leg Hip Extensions** *(p. 105)*	10–20 reps
3 sets	**45-Degree Lumbar Ext.** *(p. 74)*	10–20 reps

We recommend you also do a full-body weight-training program such as the one described in *Secrets of Advanced Bodybuilders*, published by Health For Life. If you don't have time or are unwilling to perform such a program, then do lunges and squats (2 sets of each for 10–20 reps).

AEROBICS (D)

1 set	**Walking, Cycling or Swimming**	20–60 min (d)

REPEAT STRETCHES LISTED ABOVE. (D)

NON-ATHLETE/PREVENTION

Level 1

This is an exercise routine designed to help prevent back injuries, especially for the average sedentary individual who does not exercise regularly, such as an office worker. If you exercise regularly, you should start with the intermediate routine. Sitting most of the day and working at a computer or over a desk definitely has negative consequences for the body: the hamstring and hip flexor muscles tend to become shortened; the abdominal, back, and buttocks muscles tend to weaken; the back and shoulders tend to round forward into a slumping posture.

To help counter some of these effects, this routine includes exercises to help lengthen the hamstring and hip flexor muscles; to strengthen the abdominal, back, and buttocks muscles; and to help correct slumping posture.

We also recommend a full-body weight-training routine such as the one described in *Secrets of Advanced Bodybuilders*, published by Health For Life. If you don't have time for this, however, don't worry. You will still get good results.

Perform all exercises 2 times a week.

WARMUP

1 set	**Walking or Cycling**	5–10 min

STRETCHES

1–3 reps	**Calf/Heel Cord Stretch** *(p. 121)*	10 secs (each leg)
1–3 reps	**Standing Hamstring Stretch** *(p. 122)*	10 secs (each leg)
1–3 reps	**Standing Quadriceps Stretch** *(p. 123)*	10 secs (each leg)
1–3 reps	**Kneeling Psoas Stretch** *(p. 123)*	10 secs (each side)
1–3 reps	**Seated Bent-Knee Abductor Stretch** *(p. 124)*	10 secs
1–3 reps	**Lying Hamstring Stretch*** *(p. 125)*	10 secs (each leg)
1–3 reps	**1-Knee-to-Chest Stretch** *(p. 126)*	10 secs (each leg)
1–3 reps	**1-Knee-to-Opposite-Shoulder Stretch** *(p. 126)*	10 secs (each leg)
1–3 reps	**2-Knees-to-Chest Stretch** *(p. 126)*	10 secs
1–3 reps	**Chiropractic Stretch** *(p.127)*	10 secs (each side)
1–3 reps	**Lying Adductor Stretch** *(p. 127)*	10 secs
10 reps	**Cat and Camel Stretch** *(p. 128)*	
10 reps	**Repetitive Cobra Exercise** *(p. 128)*	
1–3 reps	**Praying to Mecca Stretch** *(p. 130)*	10 secs

**Skip Lying Hamstring Stretches if they elicit pain down the leg or tingling or numbness in the leg or foot.*

EXERCISES

(OPTIONAL FULL-BODY WEIGHT-TRAINING PROGRAM)

1 set	**Gym Ball Balancing** *(p. 119)*	10 pelvic tilts (all directions)
2 sets	**Reverse Crunches** *(p. 90)*	10–30 reps
1 set	**Pelvic Tilting Exercises** *(p. 79)*	5–15 reps (each leg)
2 sets	**Twisting Crunches** *(p. 96)*	10–30 reps (each side)
1 set	**Isometric Side-Support Exercise*** *(p. 102)*	10–30 secs (each side)

**If you experience any pain in your shoulders, elbows, or wrists while performing this exercise, substitute Side Bending on the Floor for 1 set of 10–20 reps (each side).*

1 set	**Quadruped Exercises** *(p. 116)*	5–15 reps
1 set	**Prone Shoulder and Leg Lifts** *(p. 72)*	5–15 reps
1 set	**Horizontal Isometric Holds** *(p. 69)*	10 secs–2 min

AEROBICS

1 set	**Walking, Cycling or Swimming**	10–30 min

REPEAT STRETCHES LISTED ABOVE. Emphasize the Lying Hamstring Stretch and the Kneeling Psoas Stretch.

Level 2

This routine is for the individual who engages in some activity other than sitting during the day—including some light lifting. If you regularly do light housework or yard work, it's right for you. This is also a good starting routine if you regularly do light exercise but have never focused on attempting to stabilize the back. In addition, if you have been doing the beginner routine and it no longer challenges you, you can move up to this level.

Level 2 places particular emphasis on developing the isometric strength of the back and other trunk muscles. Many individuals tend to have weak lower abdominals—especially women who have had C-sections or other abdominal surgery. Level 2 works to reverse the trend. It also targets the gluteals and begins to focus on balanced training.

Perform all exercises 2 to 3 times a week.

WARMUP

1 set	**Bike or Treadmill**	5–10 min

STRETCHES

1–3 reps	**Calf/Heel Cord Stretch** *(p. 121)*	10 secs (each leg)
1–3 reps	**Standing Hamstring Stretch** *(p. 122)*	10 secs (each leg)
1–3 reps	**Standing Quadriceps Stretch** *(p. 123)*	10 secs (each leg)
1–3 reps	**Kneeling Psoas Stretch** *(p. 123)*	10 secs (each side)
1–3 reps	**Seated Bent-Knee Abductor Stretch** *(p. 124)*	10 secs
1–3 reps	**Lying Hamstring Stretch*** *(p. 125)*	10 secs (each leg)
1–3 reps	**1-Knee-to-Chest Stretch** *(p. 126)*	10 secs (each leg)
1–3 reps	**1-Knee-to-Opposite-Shoulder Stretch** *(p. 126)*	10 secs (each leg)
1–3 reps	**2-Knees-to-Chest Stretch** *(p. 126)*	10 secs

1–3 reps	**Chiropractic Stretch** *(p. 127)*	10 secs (each side)
1–3 reps	**Lying Adductor Stretch** *(p. 127)*	10 secs
10 reps	**Cat and Camel Stretch** *(p. 128)*	
10 reps	**Repetitive Cobra Exercise** *(p. 130)*	
1–3 reps	**Praying to Mecca Stretch** *(p. 130)*	10 secs

**Skip Lying Hamstring Stretches if they elicit pain down the leg or tingling or numbness in the leg or foot.*

EXERCISES

(FULL-BODY WEIGHT-TRAINING PROGRAM)

2 supersets	**Reverse Crunches** *(p. 90)*	15–30 reps
	Lying Hip Thrusts *(p. 92)*	15–30 reps
1 set	**Pelvic Tilting Exercises** *(p. 79)*	5–15 reps (each leg)
1 set	**Bridging With Pelvic Tilt Exercises** *(p. 86)*	5–15 reps
2 sets	**Isometric Side-Support Exercises*** *(p. 102)*	30 secs (each side)

**If you experience any pain in your shoulders, elbows, or wrists while performing this exercise, substitute Side Bending on the Floor for 2 sets of 10–20 reps (each side).*

2 sets	**Isometric Cross-Cable Holds** *(p. 89)*	10–30 secs (each side)
2 sets	**Twisting Crunches** *(p. 196)*	15–30 reps (each side)
2 sets	**Side Crunches** *(p. 97)*	15–30 reps (each side)
1 set	**Repetitive Cobra Exercise** *(p. 128)*	10 reps
1 set	**Quadruped Exercises** *(p. 116)*	5–15 reps
1 set	**Prone 1-Arm & Opp.-Leg Raises** *(p. 115)*	10–15 reps (each side)
1 set	**Horiz. Iso. Holds or Kneeling** *(pp.68-69)*	10 secs–2 min

AEROBICS

1 set	**Walking, Cycling or Swimming**	15–45 min

REPEAT STRETCHES LISTED ABOVE.

Level 3

This routine would be appropriate for the individual who regularly does a lot of lifting and bending and who sits less than half of the workday, but who does not follow a regular exercise program. A parcel delivery person or a construction worker would fit into this category. If you're performing the intermediate routine, you should progress to this routine as soon as you no longer feel challenged.

This advanced injury prevention routine emphasizes strengthening the abdominal and the erector spinae muscles and then integrating them into proper lifting procedures through the use of the deadlift.

If you need to lift fairly heavy objects a relatively few times per day, then your need for overall strength is increased, while your need for muscular endurance is decreased. On the other hand, if you lift lighter objects a number of times per day, then your need for muscular endurance is greater than your need for muscular strength. Perform Deadlifts accordingly.

Perform all exercises 3 times a week.

WARMUP

1 set	**Bike or Treadmill**	5–10 min

STRETCHES

1–3 reps	**Calf/Heel Cord Stretch** *(p. 121)*	10 secs (each leg)
1–3 reps	**Standing Hamstring Stretch** *(p. 122)*	10 secs (each leg)
1–3 reps	**Standing Quadriceps Stretch** *(p. 123)*	10 secs (each leg)
1–3 reps	**Kneeling Psoas Stretch** *(p. 123)*	10 secs (each side)
1–3 reps	**Seated Bent-Knee Abductor Stretch** *(p. 124)*	10 secs
1–3 reps	**Lying Hamstring Stretch*** *(p. 125)*	10 secs (each leg)
1–3 reps	**1-Knee-to-Chest Stretch** *(p. 126)*	10 secs (each leg)
1–3 reps	**1-Knee-to-Opposite-Shoulder Stretch** *(p. 126)*	10 secs (each leg)
1–3 reps	**2-Knees-to-Chest Stretch** *(p. 126)*	10 secs
1–3 reps	**Chiropractic Stretch** *(p. 127)*	10 secs (each side)
1–3 reps	**Lying Adductor Stretch** *(p. 127)*	10 secs
10 reps	**Cat and Camel Stretch** *(p. 128)*	
10 reps	**Repetitive Cobra Exercise** *(p. 128)*	
1–3 reps	**Praying to Mecca Stretch** *(p. 130)*	10 secs

**Skip Lying Hamstring Stretches if they elicit pain down the leg or tingling or numbness in the leg or foot.*

THE ROUTINES

EXERCISES

(FULL-BODY WEIGHT-TRAINING PROGRAM)

2 sets	**Reverse Crunches** *(p. 90)*	15–30 reps
2 sets	**Twisting Crunches** *(p. 96)*	15–30 reps (each side)
1 set	**Pelvic Tilting Exercises** *(p. 79)*	5–15 reps (each leg)
1 set	**Bridging Back on Ball** *(p. 87)*	2 min or until fatigued
2 sets	**Side Bending on the Floor** *(p. 102)*	10–20 reps (each side)
2 sets	**Cross-Cable Pulls** *(p. 94)*	10–15 reps
2 sets	**Rope Crunches** *(p. 97)*	10–30 reps
1 set	**Repetitive Cobra Exercise** *(p. 128)*	10 reps
1 set	**Dynamic Quadruped Exercise** *(p. 72)*	10–20 reps (each side)
1 set	**Quadruped With Rotation** *(p. 73)*	5–15 reps (each side)
3 sets	**Lying 2-Leg Hip Extensions** *(p. 105)*	10–15 reps
3 sets	**45-Degree Lumbar Extensions*** *(p. 74)*	10–20 reps

**Perform before Deadlifts if your goal is endurance, or after Deadlifts if your goal is strength.*

3 sets	**Conventional-Style Deadlifts**	15–20 for endurance or
	(Avoid heavy weights.)	3 sets of 6–12 for strength.

AEROBICS

1 set	**Walking, Cycling or Swimming**	20–60 min

REPEAT STRETCHES LISTED ABOVE.

BODYBUILDER

This routine emphasizes hypertrophy of the erector spinae muscles. It also focuses on the isometric strength that bodybuilders need on stage, where they are often required to hold isometric contractions of their back, abdominal, and other muscles for up to ten seconds at a time on a repeated basis. Bodybuilders need functional strength only so that they can perform other bodybuilding movements, such as squats and rows, without injury.

Perform all exercises 3 times a week.

WARMUP

1 Set	**Bike or Treadmill**	5–10 min

STRETCHES

1–3 reps	**Calf/Heel Cord Stretch** *(p. 121)*	10 secs (each leg)
1–3 reps	**Standing Hamstring Stretch** *(p. 122)*	10 secs (each leg)
1–3 reps	**Standing Quadriceps Stretch** *(p. 123)*	10 secs (each leg)
1–3 reps	**Kneeling Psoas Stretch** *(p. 123)*	10 secs (each side)
1–3 reps	**Seated Bent-Knee Abductor Stretch** *(p. 124)*	10 secs
1–3 reps	**Lying Hamstring Stretch*** *(p. 125)*	10 secs (each leg)
1–3 reps	**1-Knee-to-Chest Stretch** *(p. 126)*	10 secs (each leg)
1–3 reps	**1-Knee-to-Opp.-Shoulder Stretch** *(p. 126)*	10 secs (each leg)
1–3 reps	**2-Knees-to-Chest Stretch** *(p. 126)*	10 secs
1–3 reps	**Chiropractic Stretch** *(p. 127)*	10 secs (each side)
1–3 reps	**Lying Adductor Stretch** *(p. 127)*	10 secs
10 reps	**Cat and Camel Stretch** *(p. 128)*	
10 reps	**Repetitive Cobra Exercise** *(p. 128)*	
1–3 reps	**Praying to Mecca Stretch** *(p. 130)*	10 secs

**Skip Lying Hamstring Stretches if they elicit pain down the leg or tingling or numbness in the leg or foot.*

EXERCISES

3 supersets	**Reverse Crunches** *(p. 90)*	15–30 reps
3 sets	**Lying Hip Thrusts** *(p. 92)*	15–30 reps
1 set	**Pelvic Tilting Exercises** *(p. 79)*	5–15 reps (each leg)
3 sets	**Twisting Crunches** *(p. 96)*	15–30 reps (each side)
3 sets	**Rope Crunches** *(p. 97)*	15–30 reps
1 set	**Repetitive Cobra Exercise** *(p. 128)*	10 reps
3 sets	**Conventional-Style Deadlifts** *(p. 110)*	6–8 reps

Include the Deadlifts if you are in the mass phase of training, but phase them out if you are in the pre-contest phase, or if you have a history of lumbar disc injury or spondylolisthesis.

Although this exercise is a good mass builder, it carries a high risk of injury due to the heavy weights involved and the severe compressive forces imposed on the spine while lifting them. If you have a history of low back injury, you should probably skip this exercise.

3 sets	**Lying 2-Leg Hip Extensions** *(p. 105)*	15–20 reps
3 sets	**Horizontal Lumbar Extensions** *(p. 75)*	1 min hold

Horizontal Lumbar Extensions or 45-Degree Lumbar Extensions: Perform 3 sets with a 1-minute hold at the end of each set while performing a muscular pose with the biceps flexed. Attempt to feel all your back muscles contract simultaneously. Move your arms up and down slowly while flexing your back, as though performing a shoulder press. Pull your shoulder blades down and back to contract the lower trapezius muscles, which will add definition to the mid-back. Visualize yourself on stage, posing your back.

As with any rehabilitation program, you should begin your routine only after the acute stage of your back injury has passed and only with the approval of your sports physician. The low back rehabilitation exercises come with two guidelines: the pain guideline and the centralization of pain guideline.

The Pain Guideline

The *pain guideline* says that if an exercise causes you increased or more intense pain within a certain range of motion, avoid that range or the exercise completely. Later, when your recovery has progressed, you can improve the functional range, including what is currently painful.

The Centralization of Pain Guideline

The *centralization of pain guideline* applies if you experience pain radiating from the back down a leg. Avoid anything that increases your leg pain or makes the leg pain extend farther down the leg.

For example, if an exercise or position causes no back pain but causes leg pain to extend down to the foot—whereas formerly it had only extended to the knee—you should avoid this exercise or position. If an exercise or position causes slightly increased back pain but a decrease or elimination of leg pain, it is considered acceptable, since it is helping to "centralize" the pain.

Keep in mind that one exercise may decrease pain on one day (for any number of reasons) and may increase it on another.

It is important that a slow sense of progression occur in rehabilitation programs. You should not work until burn or failure, as is often done in standard exercise programs. The "no pain, no gain" formula that often governs conventional training programs is too risky for rehab programs. (For that matter, there is some debate as to whether training to failure is the best way to exercise for the non-injured athlete!)

Mechanisms of Injury

We have categorized the rehabilitation routines for athletes by mechanism of injury. This, however, can sometimes be difficult to determine. You may not experience pain until the practice or game is over. Many times a combination of forces or movements contributes to an injury. If you are uncertain about which category you fit into, use the "Flexion-Type Injury" routine. Each of these routines starts with you training in the neutral protected position, so you will not go wrong by following any of them. Your physician, physical therapist, or trainer can help you to modify one of these programs to fit your specific needs.

ATHLETES REHAB 1

Following a Diagnosed Disc Injury or after a Flexion-Type Injury

Initially after a flexion or disc injury, the athlete should avoid flexion and rotation, instead primarily doing exercises that are performed in the neutral position and extension. Flexion movements can be reintroduced as recovery progresses and they no longer elicit significant pain.

Level 1

Begin this routine with physician approval as soon as your acute pain phase is over. You can usually start it one to ten days after your injury and continue it for several weeks until your pain is gone. Progress to the intermediate phase as quickly as possible with the approval of your physician or therapist. But keep in mind that it often takes several months or even several years for a disc injury to heal completely.

Perform all exercises daily.

WARMUP

1 set	**Bike or Treadmill**	5–10 min

STRETCHES

2–3 reps	**Kneeling Psoas Stretch** *(p. 123)*	10–30 secs
2–3 reps	**Lying Hamstring Stretch*** *(p. 125)*	10–30 secs
2–3 reps	**1-Knee-to-Chest Stretch** *(p. 126)*	10–30 secs
2–3 reps	**2-Knees-to-Chest Stretch** *(p. 126)*	10–30 secs
2–3 reps	**Chiropractic Stretch** *(p. 127)*	10–30 secs
2–3 reps	**Seated Bent-Knee Abductor Stretch** *(p. 124)*	10–30 secs
2–3 reps	**Cat and Camel Stretch** *(p. 128)*	10–30 secs

**Skip Lying Hamstring Stretches if they elicit pain down the leg or tingling or numbness in the leg or foot.*

EXERCISES

5 sets	**1-Legged Balancing** *(p. 118)*	alt. legs, 30 secs each
1 set	**Pelvic Tilting Exercises** *(p. 79)*	5–15 reps (each leg)
1 set	**Bridging with Pelvic Tilt Exercises** *(p. 86)*	5–15 reps
1 set	**Repetitive Cobra Exercise** *(p. 128)*	10 reps
1 set	**Prone 1-Arm and Opp.-Leg Raises** *(p. 115)*	10-sec hold, 15 reps (each side)
1 set	**Gym Ball Balancing** *(p. 119)*	2 min
1 set	**Quadruped Exercises** *(p. 116)*	5–15 reps

AEROBICS

1 set	**Walking, Cycling or Swimming**	20–60 min

REPEAT STRETCHES LISTED ABOVE.

Level 2

Perform exercises marked with a "D" daily, if possible. Perform the other exercises 3 times a week.

WARMUP (D)

1 set	**Bike or Treadmill**	5–10 min

STRETCHES (D)

1–3 reps	**Quadruped Exercises** *(p. 116)*	10 secs (each leg)
1–3 reps	**Standing Hamstring Stretch** *(p. 122)*	10 secs (each leg)
1–3 reps	**Standing Quadriceps Stretch** *(p. 123)*	10 secs (each leg)
1–3 reps	**Kneeling Psoas Stretch** *(p. 123)*	10 secs (each side)
1–3 reps	**Seated Bent-Knee Abductor Stretch** *(p. 124)*	10 secs
1–3 reps	**Lying Hamstring Stretch*** *(p. 125)*	10 secs (each leg)
1–3 reps	**1-Knee-to-Chest Stretch** *(p. 126)*	10 secs (each leg)
1–3 reps	**1-Knee-to-Opposite-Shoulder Stretch** *(p. 126)*	10 secs (each leg)
1–3 reps	**2-Knees-to-Chest Stretch** *(p. 126)*	10 secs
1–3 reps	**Chiropractic Stretch** *(p. 127)*	10 secs (each side)
1–3 reps	**Lying Adductor Stretch** *(p. 127)*	10 secs
10 reps	**Cat and Camel Stretch** *(p. 128)*	
10 reps	**Repetitive Cobra Exercise** *(p. 128)*	
1–3 reps	**Praying to Mecca Stretch** *(p. 130)*	10 secs

**Skip Lying Hamstring Stretches if they elicit pain down the leg or tingling or numbness in the leg or foot.*

EXERCISES

1 set	**Pelvic Tilting Exercises**	3–4 min (d)
1 set	**Bridging with Pelvic Tilt Exercises**	5–15 reps (d)

2 supersets	**Reverse Crunches** *(p. 90)*	15–30 reps
	Lying Hip Thrusts *(p. 92)*	15–30 reps
2 sets	**Isometric Side-Support Exercise** *(p. 102)*	10–30 secs (each side)
2 sets	**Cross-Cable Pulls** *(p. 94)*	10–20 reps
2 sets	**Side Crunches** *(p. 97)*	15–30 reps (each side)
2 sets	**Straight Crunches** *(p. 95)*	10–30 reps (each side)
1 set	**Repetitive Cobra Exercise** *(p. 128)*	10 reps (d)
1 set	**Quadruped Exercises** *(p. 116)*	5–15 reps (d)
2 sets	**Ball Extensions** *(p. 74)*	10–20 reps
3 sets	**45-Degree Hip Extensions** *(p. 106)*	10–20 reps

AEROBICS (D)

1 set	**Walking, Cycling or Swimming**	20–60 min

REPEAT STRETCHES LISTED ABOVE. (D)

Level 3

Perform exercises marked with a "D" daily, if possible. Perform the other exercises 3 times a week.

WARMUP (D)

1 set	**Bike or Treadmill**	5–10 min

STRETCHES (D)

1–3 reps	**Calf/Heel Cord Stretch** *(p. 121)*	10 secs (each leg)
1–3 reps	**Standing Hamstring Stretch** *(p. 122)*	10 secs (each leg)
1–3 reps	**Standing Quadriceps Stretch** *(p. 123)*	10 secs (each leg)
1–3 reps	**Kneeling Psoas Stretch** *(p. 123)*	10 secs (each side)
1–3 reps	**Seated Bent-Knee Abductor Stretch** *(p. 124)*	10 secs
1–3 reps	**Lying Hamstring Stretch*** *(p. 125)*	10 secs (each leg)
1–3 reps	**1-Knee-to-Chest Stretch** *(p. 126)*	10 secs (each leg)
1–3 reps	**1-Knee-to-Opposite-Shoulder Stretch** *(p. 126)*	10 secs (each leg)
1–3 reps	**2-Knees-to-Chest Stretch** *(p. 126)*	10 secs
1–3 reps	**Chiropractic Stretch** *(p. 127)*	10 secs (each side)
1–3 reps	**Lying Adductor Stretch** *(p. 127)*	10 secs
10 reps	**Cat and Camel Stretch** *(p. 128)*	
10 reps	**Repetitive Cobra Exercise** *(p. 128)*	
1–3 reps	**Praying to Mecca Stretch** *(p. 130)*	10 secs

**Skip Lying Hamstring Stretches if they elicit pain down the leg or tingling or numbness in the leg or foot.*

EXERCISES

1 set	**Pelvic Tilting Exercises** *(p. 79)*	5–15 reps (d)
2 supersets	**Reverse Crunches** *(p. 90)*	15–30 reps
	Lying Hip Thrusts *(p. 92)*	15–30 reps

2 sets	**Lying Hip Rotations** *(p. 93)*	15–30 reps
2 sets	**Cross-Cable Pulls** *(p. 94)*	10–15 reps
2 sets	**Side Bending on the Floor** *(p. 102)*	10–20 reps
2 sets	**Rope Crunches** *(p. 97)*	20–40 reps
1 set	**Repetitive Cobra Exercise** *(p. 128)*	10 reps (d)
1 set	**Medicine Ball Training** *(p. 99)*	15 min (stop when fatigued)
3 sets	**Power Cleans** *(p. 133)*	10 reps
3 sets	**Push Jerks** *(p. 135)*	10 reps
3 sets	**45° Lumbar Extensions*** *(p. 74)*	10–20 reps

AEROBICS (D)

1 set	**Walking, Cycling or Swimming**	20–60 min

REPEAT STRETCHES LISTED ABOVE.

ATHLETES REHAB 2

Following a Torsional-Type Injury

Following a torsional-type injury, you should avoid rotational movements until you are essentially pain-free. You can then gradually introduce them into your routine. In the interim, you need to emphasize strengthening your oblique muscles. They act to decelerate the trunk and prevent excessive rotation. Being able to control rotational forces with your obliques will help you to decrease the strain on your spine.

Level 1

Begin this routine with physician approval as soon as your acute pain phase is over. You can usually start it 1 to 10 days after your injury and continue for 2 to 6 weeks until your pain is gone.

Perform exercises daily if possible.

WARMUP

1 set	**Bike or Treadmill**	5–10 min

STRETCHES

2–3 reps	**Calf/Heel Cord Stretch** *(p. 121)*	10 secs (each leg)
2–3 reps	**Standing Hamstring Stretch** *(p. 122)*	10 secs (each leg)
2–3 reps	**Standing Quadriceps Stretch** *(p. 123)*	10 secs (each leg)
2–3 reps	**Kneeling Psoas Stretch** *(p. 123)*	10 secs (each side)
2–3 reps	**Seated Bent-Knee Abductor Stretch** *(p. 124)*	10 secs
2–3 reps	**Lying Hamstring Stretch*** *(p. 125)*	10 secs (each leg)
2–3 reps	**1-Knee-to-Chest Stretch** *(p. 126)*	10 secs (each leg)
2–3 reps	**1-Knee-to-Opp.-Shoulder Stretch** *(p. 126)*	10 secs (each leg)
2–3 reps	**2-Knees-to-Chest Stretch** *(p. 126)*	10 secs
2–3 reps	**Lying Adductor Stretch** *(p. 127)*	10 secs
10 reps	**Cat and Camel Stretch** *(p. 128)*	
10 reps	**Repetitive Cobra Exercise** *(p. 128)*	

2–3 reps	**Praying to Mecca Stretch** *(p. 130)*	10 secs

**Skip Lying Hamstring Stretches if they elicit pain down the leg or tingling or numbness in the leg or foot.*

EXERCISES

5 sets	**1-Legged Balancing** *(p. 118)*	alt. legs, 30 secs each
1 set	**Pelvic Tilting Exercises** *(p. 79)*	5–15 reps
1 set	**Bridging with Pelvic Tilt Exercise** *(p. 86)*	5–15 reps
1 set	**Repetitive Cobra Exercise** *(p. 128)*	10 reps
1 set	**Prone 1-Arm and Opp.-Leg Raises** *(p. 115)*	10-second hold, 15 reps (each side)
1 set	**Gym Ball Balancing** *(p. 119)*	2 min
1 set	**Quadruped Exercises** *(p. 116)*	5–15 reps

AEROBICS

1 set	**Walking, Cycling or Swimming**	20–60 min

REPEAT STRETCHES LISTED ABOVE.

Level 2

Perform exercises marked with a "D" daily, if possible. Perform the other exercises 3 times a week.

WARMUP (D)

1 set	**Bike or Treadmill**	5–10 min

STRETCHES (D)

1–3 reps	**Calf/Heel Cord Stretch** *(p. 121)*	10 secs (each leg)
1–3 reps	**Standing Hamstring Stretch** *(p. 122)*	10 secs (each leg)
1–3 reps	**Standing Quadriceps Stretch** *(p. 123)*	10 secs (each leg)
1–3 reps	**Kneeling Psoas Stretch** *(p. 123)*	10 secs (each side)
1–3 reps	**Seated Bent-Knee Abductor Stretch** *(p. 124)*	10 secs
1–3 reps	**Lying Hamstring Stretch*** *(p. 125)*	10 secs (each leg)
1–3 reps	**1-Knee-to-Chest Stretch** *(p. 126)*	10 secs (each leg)
1–3 reps	**1-Knee-to-Opp.-Shoulder Stretch** *(p. 126)*	10 secs (each leg)
1–3 reps	**2-Knees-to-Chest Stretch** *(p. 126)*	10 secs
1–3 reps	**Chiropractic Stretch** *(p. 127)*	10 secs (each side)
1–3 reps	**Lying Adductor Stretch** *(p. 127)*	10 secs
10 reps	**Cat and Camel Stretch** *(p. 128)*	
1–3 reps	**Praying to Mecca Stretch** *(p. 130)*	10 secs

**Skip Lying Hamstring Stretches if they elicit pain down the leg or tingling or numbness in the leg or foot.*

EXERCISES

1 set	**Pelvic Tilting Exercises** *(p. 79)*	5–15 reps (d)
2 sets	**Reverse Crunches** *(p. 90)*	15–30 reps
2 sets	**Lying Hip Thrusts** *(p. 92)*	15–30 reps
2 sets	**Isometric Cross-Cable Holds** *(p. 89)*	30 secs (add weight as needed)

2 sets	**Side Crunches** *(p. 97)*	15–30 reps (each side)
2 sets	**Twisting Crunches** *(p. 96)*	15–30 reps (each side)
2 sets	**Straight Crunches** *(p. 95)*	10–30 reps
1 set	**Repetitive Cobra Exercise** *(p. 128)*	10 reps
2 sets	**Isometric Side-Support Exercise** *(p. 102)*	10–30 secs (each side)
1 set	**Quadruped Exercises** *(p. 116)*	5–15 reps (d)
2 sets	**Ball Extensions** *(p. 74)*	15 reps
3 sets	**45-Degree Hip Extensions** *(p. 106)*	10–20 reps (add weight as needed)

AEROBICS (D)

1 set	**Walking, Cycling or Swimming**	20–60 min

REPEAT STRETCHES LISTED ABOVE. (D)

Level 3

Perform exercises marked with a "D" daily, if possible. Perform the other exercises 3 times a week.

WARMUP (D)

1 set	**Bike or Treadmill**	5–10 min

THE ROUTINES

STRETCHES (D)

1–3 reps	**Calf/Heel Cord Stretch** *(p. 121)*	10 secs (each leg)
1–3 reps	**Standing Hamstring Stretch** *(p. 122)*	10 secs (each leg)
1–3 reps	**Standing Quadriceps Stretch** *(p. 123)*	10 secs (each leg)
1–3 reps	**Kneeling Psoas Stretch** *(p. 123)*	10 secs (each side)
1–3 reps	**Seated Bent-Knee Abductor Stretch** *(p. 124)*	10 secs
1–3 reps	**Lying Hamstring Stretch*** *(p. 125)*	10 secs (each leg)
1–3 reps	**1-Knee-to-Chest Stretch** *(p. 126)*	10 secs (each leg)
1–3 reps	**1-Knee-to-Opposite-Shoulder Stretch** *(p. 126)*	10 secs (each leg)
1–3 reps	**2-Knees-to-Chest Stretch** *(p. 126)*	10 secs
1–3 reps	**Chiropractic Stretch** *(p. 127)*	10 secs (each side)
1–3 reps	**Lying Adductor Stretch** *(p. 127)*	10 secs
10 reps	**Cat and Camel Stretch** *(p. 128)*	
10 reps	**Repetitive Cobra Exercise** *(p. 128)*	
1–3 reps	**Praying to Mecca Stretch** *(p. 130)*	10 secs

**Skip Lying Hamstring Stretches if they elicit pain down the leg or tingling or numbness in the leg or foot.*

EXERCISES

1 set	**Pelvic Tilting Exercises** *(p. 79)*	5–15 reps (d)
1 set	**Bridging with Pelvic Tilt Exercise** *(p. 86)*	5–15 reps (d)
2 sets	**Reverse Crunches** *(p. 90)*	15–30 reps

2 sets	**Lying Hip Thrusts** *(p. 92)*	15–30 reps
2 sets	**Lying Hip Rotations** *(p. 93)*	15–30 reps
2 sets	**Cross-Cable Pulls** *(p. 94)*	10–15 reps
2 sets	**Isometric Cross-Cable Holds** *(p. 89)*	30 secs (add weight as tolerated)
2 sets	**Side Crunches** *(p. 97)*	15–30 reps (each side)
2 sets	**Twisting Crunches** *(p. 96)*	15–30 reps (each side)
2 sets	**Rope Crunches** *(p. 97)*	15–30 reps
2 sets	**Side Bending on Bench** *(p. 103)*	10–15 reps
1 set	**Medicine Ball Exercises Abs** *(p. 99)*	25 min
3 sets	**Power Cleans** *(p. 133)*	10 reps
3 sets	**Snatches** *(p. 134)*	10 reps
3 sets	**Conventional-Style Deadlifts** *(p. 110)*	10–15 reps (if you are a power or strength athlete)
3 sets	**45° Lumbar Extensions*** *(p. 74)*	8–20 reps (add weight as tolerated)

AEROBICS (D)

1 set	**Walking, Cycling or Swimming**	20–60 min

REPEAT STRETCHES LISTED ABOVE. (D)

ATHLETES REHAB 3

Athlete with a Known Spondylolisthesis or Following a Hyperextension Injury

Athletes in these categories need to avoid hyperextension to allow healing to occur. The emphasis in this rehabilitation routine is on stabilization exercises and on strengthening the abdominal muscles so they help to prevent hyperextension and keep the spine in a neutral position. If the athlete is involved in a sport where hyperextension of the spine is likely to occur again, then developing abdominal strength from an extended position is crucial to prevent reinjury.

Level 1

Begin this routine with physician approval as soon as your acute pain phase is over. You can usually start 1 to 10 days after your injury and continue for 2 to 6 weeks until your pain is gone.

Perform the exercises daily, if possible.

WARMUP

1 set	**Bike or Treadmill**	5–10 min

STRETCHES

2–3 reps	**Lying Hamstring Stretch*** *(p. 125)*	10–30 sec
2–3 reps	**1-Knee-to-Chest Stretch** *(p. 126)*	10–30 sec
2–3 reps	**1-Knee-to-Opposite-Shoulder Stretch** *(p. 126)*	10–30 sec
2–3 reps	**2-Knees-to-Chest Stretch** *(p. 126)*	10–30 sec

2–3 reps	**Cat and Camel Stretch** *(p. 128)*	10–30 sec
2–3 reps	**Praying to Mecca Stretch** *(p. 130)*	10–30 sec

EXERCISES

1 set	**Pelvic Tilting Exercises** *(p. 79)*	5–15 reps
1 set	**Bridging with Pelvic Tilt Exercise** *(p. 86)*	5–15 reps
2 sets	**Straight Crunches** *(p. 95)*	15–30 reps
2 sets	**Twisting Crunches** *(p. 96)*	15–30 reps (each side)
1 set	**Gym Ball Balancing** *(p. 119)*	2 min or until fatigued
1 set	**Quadruped Exercises** *(p. 116)*	5–15 reps

AEROBICS

1 set	**Walking, Cycling or Swimming**	20–60 min

REPEAT STRETCHES LISTED ABOVE.

Level 2

Perform exercises marked with a "D" daily, if possible. Perform the other exercises 3 times a week.

WARMUP (D)

1 set	**Bike or Treadmill**	5–10 min

STRETCHES (D)

1–3 reps	**Calf/Heel Cord Stretch** *(p. 121)*	10 secs (each leg)
1–3 reps	**Standing Hamstring Stretch** *(p. 122)*	10 secs (each leg)
1–3 reps	**Standing Quadriceps Stretch** *(p. 123)*	10 secs (each leg)
1–3 reps	**Kneeling Psoas Stretch** *(p. 123)*	10 secs (each side)
1–3 reps	**Seated Bent-Knee Abductor Stretch** *(p. 124)*	10 secs
1–3 reps	**Lying Hamstring Stretch*** *(p. 125)*	10 secs (each leg)
1–3 reps	**1-Knee-to-Chest Stretch** *(p. 126)*	10 secs (each leg)
1–3 reps	**1-Knee-to-Opposite-Shoulder Stretch** *(p. 126)*	10 secs (each leg)
1–3 reps	**2-Knees-to-Chest Stretch** *(p. 126)*	10 secs
1–3 reps	**Chiropractic Stretch** *(p. 127)*	10 secs (each side)
1–3 reps	**Lying Adductor Stretch** *(p. 127)*	10 secs
10 reps	**Cat and Camel Stretch** *(p. 128)*	
1–3 reps	**Praying to Mecca Stretch** *(p. 130)*	10 secs

**Skip Lying Hamstring Stretches if they elicit pain down the leg or tingling or numbness in the leg or foot.*

EXERCISES

1 set	**Pelvic Tilting Exercises** *(p. 79)*	5–15 reps (d)
1 set	**Bridging with Pelvic Tilt Exercise** *(p. 86)*	5–15 reps (d)
2 sets	**Reverse Crunches** *(p. 90)*	15–30 reps
2 sets	**Lying Hip Thrusts** *(p. 92)*	15–30 reps
2 sets	**Cross-Cable Pulls** *(p. 94)*	10–15 reps
2 sets	**Side Crunches** *(p. 97)*	15–30 reps (each side)
2 sets	**Straight Crunches** *(p. 95)*	15–30 reps
2 sets	**Ball Extensions** *(p. 74)*	10–20 reps
3 sets	**45° Hip Extensions** *(p. 106)*	10–20 reps

AEROBICS (D)

1 set	**Walking, Cycling or Swimming**	20–60 min

REPEAT ALL STRETCHES ABOVE. (D)

Level 3

Perform exercises marked with a "D" daily, if possible. Perform the other exercises 3 times a week.

WARMUP (D)

1 set	**Bike or Treadmill**	5–10 min

STRETCHES (D)

1–3 reps	**Calf/Heel Cord Stretch** *(p. 121)*	10 secs (each leg)
1–3 reps	**Standing Hamstring Stretch** *(p. 122)*	10 secs (each leg)
1–3 reps	**Standing Quadriceps Stretch** *(p. 123)*	10 secs (each leg)
1–3 reps	**Kneeling Psoas Stretch** *(p. 123)*	10 secs (each side)
1–3 reps	**Seated Bent-Knee Abductor Stretch** *(p. 124)*	10 secs
1–3 reps	**Lying Hamstring Stretch*** *(p. 125)*	10 secs (each leg)
1–3 reps	**1-Knee-to-Chest Stretch** *(p. 126)*	10 secs (each leg)
1–3 reps	**1-Knee-to-Opp.-Shoulder Stretch** *(p. 126)*	10 secs (each leg)
1–3 reps	**2-Knees-to-Chest Stretch** *(p. 126)*	10 secs
1–3 reps	**Chiropractic Stretch** *(p. 127)*	10 secs (each side)
1–3 reps	**Lying Adductor Stretch** *(p. 127)*	10 secs
10 reps	**Cat and Camel Stretch** *(p. 128)*	
1–3 reps	**Praying to Mecca Stretch** *(p. 130)*	10 secs

**Skip Lying Hamstring Stretches if they elicit pain down the leg or tingling or numbness in the leg or foot.*

EXERCISES

1 set	**Pelvic Tilting Exercises** *(p. 79)*	5–15 reps (d)
1 set	**Bridging with Pelvic Tilt Exercise** *(p. 86)*	5–15 reps (d)
1 set	**Sit Crunched/ Throw and Catch** *(p. 100)*	15 min
2 supersets	**Reverse Crunches** *(p. 90)*	15–30 reps
	Lying Hip Thrusts *(p. 92)*	15–30 reps

2 sets	**Reverse Crunches (Off Bench)** *(p. 90)*	15–30 reps
2 sets	**Cross-Cable Pulls** *(p. 94)*	10–15 reps (each side)
2 sets	**Side Crunches** *(p. 97)*	15–30 reps (each side)
2 sets	**Straight Crunches** *(p. 95)*	15–30 reps
3 sets	**Power Cleans** *(p. 133)*	10 reps
1 set	**Prone 1-Arm and Opp.-Leg Raises** *(p. 115)*	10-sec hold, 15 reps
2 sets	**Side Bending on Bench** *(p. 103)*	10–15 reps
3 sets	**45° or Horizontal Hip Extensions** *(pp. 106-7)*	8–20 reps

AEROBICS (D)

1 set	**Walking, Cycling or Swimming**	20–60 min

REPEAT ALL STRETCHES ABOVE. (D)

ATHLETES/PREVENTION 1

Emphasis on Rotational Strength—Prevention Routine for the Athlete

Athletes such as soccer, hockey, and baseball players; football quarterbacks; bowlers; golfers; and javelin throwers need to develop rotational strength to avoid injury in the course of their sports. The general guidelines that follow can be modified by a competent strength coach or sports physician to meet the needs of the individual athlete.

Perform all exercises 3 times a week.

WARMUP

1 set	**Bike or Treadmill**	5–10 min

STRETCHES

1–3 reps	**Calf/Heel Cord Stretch** *(p. 121)*	10 secs (each leg)
1–3 reps	**Standing Hamstring Stretch** *(p. 122)*	10 secs (each leg)
1–3 reps	**Standing Quadriceps Stretch** *(p. 123)*	10 secs (each leg)
1–3 reps	**Kneeling Psoas Stretch** *(p. 123)*	10 secs (each side)
1–3 reps	**Seated Bent-Knee Abductor Stretch** *(p. 124)*	10 secs
1–3 reps	**Lying Hamstring Stretch*** *(p. 125)*	10 secs (each leg)
1–3 reps	**1-Knee-to-Chest Stretch** *(p. 126)*	10 secs (each leg)
1–3 reps	**1-Knee-to-Opp.-Shoulder Stretch** *(p. 126)*	10 secs (each leg)
1–3 reps	**2-Knees-to-Chest Stretch** *(p. 126)*	10 secs
1–3 reps	**Chiropractic Stretch** *(p. 127)*	10 secs (each side)
1–3 reps	**Lying Adductor Stretch** *(p. 127)*	10 secs
10 reps	**Cat and Camel Stretch** *(p. 128)*	
10 reps	**Repetitive Cobra Exercise** *(p. 128)*	
1–3 reps	**Praying to Mecca Stretch** *(p. 130)*	10 secs

**Skip Lying Hamstring Stretches if they elicit pain down the leg or tingling or numbness in the leg or foot.*

EXERCISES

2 supersets	**Lying Hip Thrusts** *(p. 92)*	15–30 reps
	Reverse Crunches *(p. 90)*	15–30 reps
2 sets	**Lying Hip Rotations** *(p. 93)*	15–30 reps
1 set	**Pelvic Tilting Exercises** *(p. 79)*	5–15 reps
1 set	**Bridging with Pelvic Tilt Exercise** *(p. 86)*	5–15 reps
1 set	**Medicine Ball Exercises** *(p. 99)*	5 min or until fatigued
2 sets	**Russian Twists** *(p. 98)*	10–15 reps
2 sets	**Side Bending on the Floor** *(p. 102)*	10–20 reps
2 sets	**Rope Crunches (Twisting)** *(p. 97)*	15–30 reps
2 sets	**Cross-Cable Pulls** *(p. 94)*	10–15 reps
1 set	**Repetitive Cobra Exercise** *(p. 128)*	10 reps
1 set	**Prone 1-Arm and Opp.-Leg Raises** *(p. 115)*	15 reps (each side)
2 sets	**45˚ or Horizontal Lumbar Ext.** *(pp. 74-75)*	10–20 reps
1 set	**Reverse Russian Twists** *(p. 78)*	10–20 reps
3 sets	**Seated 1-Arm Cable Rows** *(p. 113)*	8–15 reps

AEROBICS

1 set	**Walking, Cycling or Swimming**	20–60 min

REPEAT STRETCHES LISTED ABOVE.

ATHLETES/PREVENTION 2

Emphasis on Abdominal Strength

The emphasis in this routine is on abdominal strength. This is needed to get out of an extended position and to avoid a hyperextended position. This routine is especially suited to athletes—such as football linemen, ballet dancers, gymnasts, divers, and pole vaulters—who are involved in sports in which hyperextension is a common mechanism of back injury.

Perform all exercises 3 times a week.

WARMUP

1 set	**Bike or Treadmill**	5–10 min

STRETCHES

1–3 reps	**Calf/Heel Cord Stretch** *(p. 121)*	10 secs (each leg)
1–3 reps	**Standing Hamstring Stretch** *(p. 122)*	10 secs (each leg)
1–3 reps	**Standing Quadriceps Stretch** *(p. 123)*	10 secs (each leg)
1–3 reps	**Kneeling Psoas Stretch** *(p. 123)*	10 secs (each side)
1–3 reps	**Seated Bent-Knee Abductor Stretch** *(p. 124)*	10 secs
1–3 reps	**Lying Hamstring Stretch*** *(p. 125)*	10 secs (each leg)
1–3 reps	**1-Knee-to-Chest Stretch** *(p. 126)*	10 secs (each leg)
1–3 reps	**1-Knee-to-Opposite-Shoulder Stretch** *(p. 126)*	10 secs (each leg)
1–3 reps	**2-Knees-to-Chest Stretch** *(p. 126)*	10 secs
1–3 reps	**Chiropractic Stretch** *(p. 127)*	10 secs (each side)

1–3 reps	**Lying Adductor Stretch** *(p. 127)*	10 secs
10 reps	**Cat and Camel Stretch** *(p. 128)*	
10 reps	**Repetitive Cobra Exercise** *(p. 128)*	
1–3 reps	**Praying to Mecca Stretch** *(p. 130)*	10 secs

**Skip Lying Hamstring Stretches if they elicit pain down the leg or tingling or numbness in the leg or foot.*

EXERCISES

1 set	**Pelvic Tilting Exercises** *(p. 79)*	5–15 reps
2 supersets	**Reverse Crunches (Off bench)** *(p. 90)*	15–30 reps
	Lying Hip Thrusts *(p. 92)*	15–30 reps
2 sets	**Side Bending on Bench** *(p. 103)*	10–15 reps
2 sets	**Straight Crunches** *(p. 95)*	15–30 reps
2 sets	**Rope Crunches** *(p. 97)*	15–30 reps
2 sets	**Cross-Cable Pulls** *(p. 94)*	8–15 reps
1 set	**Prone 1-Arm and Opp.-Leg Raises** *(p. 115)*	10-sec hold, 15 reps (each side)
3 sets	**45˚ Hip Extensions** *(p. 106)*	8–15 reps
3 sets	**Lunges** *(p. 111)*	8–15 reps
3 sets	**Push Jerks (Presses)** *(p. 135)*	10 reps

AEROBICS

1 set	**Walking, Cycling or Swimming**	20–60 min

REPEAT STRETCHES LISTED ABOVE.

ATHLETES/PREVENTION 3

Emphasis on Back Muscle Strength to Prevent Hyperflexion

This routine is especially for athletes who are likely to suffer flexion injuries of the spine, such as football running backs and linebackers, baseball infielders, skiers, and speed skaters. While it focuses on abdominal support, it places slightly greater emphasis on the development of hip and lumbar extensor strength.

Perform all exercises 3 times a week.

WARMUP

1 set	**Bike or Treadmill**	5–10 min

STRETCHES

1–3 reps	**Calf/Heel Cord Stretch** *(p. 121)*	10 secs (each leg)
1–3 reps	**Standing Hamstring Stretch** *(p. 122)*	10 secs (each leg)
1–3 reps	**Standing Quadriceps Stretch** *(p. 123)*	10 secs (each leg)
1–3 reps	**Kneeling Psoas Stretch** *(p. 123)*	10 secs (each side)
1–3 reps	**Seated Bent-Knee Abductor Stretch** *(p. 124)*	10 secs
1–3 reps	**Lying Hamstring Stretch*** *(p. 125)*	10 secs (each leg)
1–3 reps	**1-Knee-to-Chest Stretch** *(p. 126)*	10 secs (each leg)
1–3 reps	**1-Knee-to-Opposite-Shoulder Stretch** *(p. 126)*	10 secs (each leg)
1–3 reps	**2-Knees-to-Chest Stretch** *(p. 126)*	10 secs
1–3 reps	**Chiropractic Stretch** *(p. 127)*	10 secs (each side)
1–3 reps	**Lying Adductor Stretch** *(p. 127)*	10 secs

10 reps	**Cat and Camel Stretch** *(p. 128)*	
10 reps	**Repetitive Cobra Exercise** *(p. 128)*	
1–3 reps	**Praying to Mecca Stretch** *(p. 130)*	10 secs

**Skip Lying Hamstring Stretches if they elicit pain down the leg or tingling or numbness in the leg or foot.*

EXERCISES

1 set	**Pelvic Tilting Exercises** *(p. 79)*	5–15 reps
1 set	**Medicine Ball Exercises for Abs** *(p. 99)*	15 min
2 supersets	**Reverse Crunches** *(p. 90)*	15–30 reps
	Lying Hip Thrusts *(p. 92)*	15–30 reps
1 set	**Repetitive Cobra Exercise** *(p. 128)*	10 reps
1 set	**Prone 1-Arm and Opp.-Leg Raises** *(p. 115)*	15 reps (each side)
2 sets	**Reverse Cross-Cable Pulls** *(p. 109)*	8–15 reps
2 sets	**Side Crunches** *(p. 97)*	15–30 reps
2 sets	**Rope Crunches** *(p. 97)*	15–30 reps
3 sets	**Power Cleans** *(p. 133)*	10 reps
2 sets	**Side Bending on Bench** *(p. 103)*	10–15 reps
3 sets	**45° Hip Extensions** *(p. 106)*	10–20 reps
3 sets	**Medicine Ball Exercises for Back** *(p. 136)*	5–10 mins

AEROBICS

1 set	**Walking, Cycling or Swimming**	20–60 min

REPEAT STRETCHES LISTED ABOVE.

Glossary

Biomechanics

The scientific study of the mechanics of human movement. Also called kinesiology.

Compressive Loading

A force that pushes together the vertebrae and discs of the spinal column. This occurs when standing or when lifting a heavy weight.

Extension, Low Back

Bending backward at the waist.

Flexion, Low Back

Bending forward at the waist.

Hyperextension, Low Back

Bending backward at the waist beyond the normal range.

Isometric Exercises

Exercises that require tight contraction of a muscle followed by its release, but involve no movement at the joint.

Isotonic Exercises

Exercises that involve a range of motion and help to build strength.

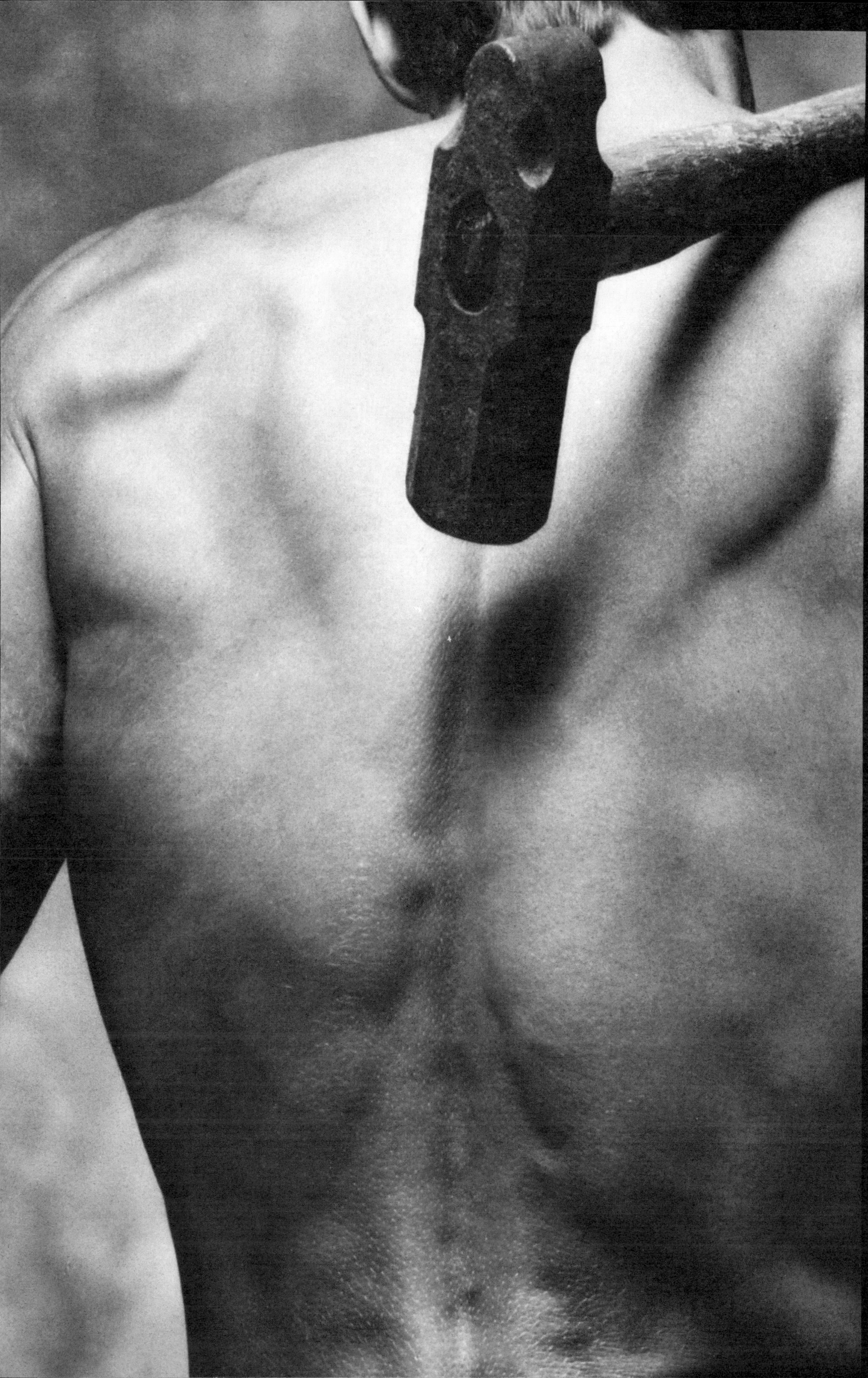

GLOSSARY

GLOSSARY

Lateral flexion, Low Back

Bending to the side at the waist.

Ligament

A strong fibrous band that connects bone to bone and functions to limit excessive motion.

Load

The opposition to motion provided by weight.

Lordosis

The normal curvature of the low back when standing.

Muscle

Soft tissue that contracts when stimulated by the nervous system.

Neutral Position

For most people, this is the normal, pain-free, moderately arched position of the low back when standing.

Resistance Exercises

Exercises that aim to strengthen by isolating and working specific muscles.

Rotation, Low Back

Turning in one direction around the axis of the spine

Shear Loading

A stress that causes one of the vertebrae to slide forward or backward on the one below it. This typically happens when bending over or lifting a heavy weight.

Stabilization Exercises

Exercises that integrate back, abdominal, and hip muscles, working them in combination to increase the stability of the back.

Synergism

Combining elements to create a whole greater than just the sum of those elements.

Bibliography

Introduction

Frymoyer, J.W., Introduction to *Rehabilitation of the Spine.* Ed. S.H. Hochschuler, H.B. Cotler & R.D. Guyer. St. Louis: Mosby, 1993.

Grazier, K.L., Holbrook, T., Kelsy, J., et al (eds.), *The Frequency of Occurrence, Impact, and Cost of Selected Musculoskeletal Conditions in the United States.* Chicago: American Academy of Orthopedic Surgeons, 1984.

Porterfield, J.A. & DeRosa, C., *Mechanical Low Back Pain.* Philadelphia: W. B. Saunders Co., 1991.

Chapter 1

Adams, M.A. & Dolan, P., "Recent Advances in Lumbar Spine Mechanics and Their Clinical Significance," *Clinical Biomech* 10 (1995): 3–19.

Adams, M.A. & Hutton, W.C., "The Effect of Posture on the Role of the Apophyseal Joints in Resisting Intervertebral Compressive Forces," *J Bone Joint Surg* 62–B (1980): 358–62.

Adams, M.A., Hutton, W.C. & Stott, M.A., "The Resistance to Flexion of the Lumbar Intervertebral Joint," *Spine* 5 (1980): 245.

Alexander, M.J.L., "Biomechanical Aspects of Lumbar Spine Injuries in Athletes: A Review," *Can J Appl Spt Sci* 10 (1985): 9.

Bogduk, N. & Twomey, L.T., *Clinical Anatomy of the Lumbar Spine* 2nd. ed. New York: Churchill Livingstone, 1991.

BIBLIOGRAPHY

Bogduk, N., Pearcy, M. & Hadfield, G., "Anatomy and Biomechanics of Psoas Major," *Clinical Biomech* 7 (1992): 109–19.

Cholewicki, J. & McGill, S.M., "Mechanical Stability of the In Vivo Lumbar Spine: Implications for Injury and Chronic Low Back Pain," *Clinical Biomech* 11 (1996): 1–15.

Granhed, H., Jonson, R. & Hansson, T., "The Loads on the Lumbar Spine During Extreme Weight Lifting," *Spine* 12 (1987): 146–49.

Heylings, D.J.A., "Supraspinous and Interspinous Ligaments of the Human Lumbar Spine," *J Anat* 125 (1978): 127–31.

Holm, S. & Nachemson, A., "Variations in the Nutrition of the Canine Intervertebral Disc Induced by Motion," *Spine* 8 (1983): 866–74.

McGill, S.M., Juker, D. & Kropf, P., "Quantitative Intramuscular Myoelectric Activity of Quadratus Lumborum During a Wide Variety of Tasks," *Clinical Biomech.* 11 (1996): 170–72.

Nordin, M. & Frankel, V.H., *Basic Biomechanics of the Musculoskeletal System.* 2nd ed. Philadelphia: Lea and Febiger, 1989.

Rissanen, P.M., "The Surgical Anatomy and Pathology of the Supraspinous and Interspinous Ligaments of the Lumbar Spine with Special Reference to Ligament Ruptures," *Acta Orthop Scand*, suppl. 46 (1960): 1–100.

Sharma, M., Langrana, N.A. & Rodriguez, J., "Role of Ligaments and Facets in Lumbar Spinal Stability," *Spine* 20 (1995): 887–900.

Valencia, F.P. & Munro, R.R., "An Electromyographic Study of the Lumbar Multifidus in Man," *Electromyogr Clin Neurophysiol* 25 (1985): 205–21.

Vleeming, A., et al., "The Posterior Layer of the Thoracolumbar Fascia," *Spine* 20 (1995): 753–58.

Chapter 2

Adams, M.A., Dolan, P. & Hutton.,W.C., "Diurnal Variations in the Stresses on the Lumbar Spine," *Spine* 12 (1987): 130–37.

Bartelink, D.L., "The Role of Abdominal Pressure in Relieving Pressure on the Lumbar Intervertebral Discs," *J Bone Joint Surg* 39B (1957): 718–25.

Bogduk, N. & Macintosh, J.E., "The Applied Anatomy of the Thoracolumbar Fascia," *Spine* 9 (1984): 168.

Farfan, H.F., *Mechanical Disorders of the Low Back.* Philadelphia: Lea and Febiger, 1973.

Floyd, W.F. & Silver, P.H.S., "The Function of the Erectores Spinae Muscles in Certain Movements and Postures in Man," *J Physiology* 129 (1955): 184–203.

Gracovetsky, S., Farfan, H. & Helleur, C., "The Abdominal Mechanism," *Spine* 10 (1985): 317–24.

Gracovetsky, S., Farfan, H. & Lamy, C., "The Mechanism of the Lumbar Spine," *Spine* 6 (1981): 249–62.

Hukins, D.W.L., Aspden, R.M. & Hickey, D.S., "Thoracolumbar Fascia Can Increase the Efficiency of the Erector Spinae Muscles," *Clinical Biomech* 5 (1990): 30–34.

Hyman, J. & Liebenson, C., "Spinal Stabilization Exercise Program," In *Rehabilitation of the Spine* Ed. C. Liebenson. Baltimore: Williams and Wilkins, 1996.

Krag, M.H., Byrne, K.B., Gilbertson, L.G. & Haugh, L.D., "Failure of Intra-abdominal Pressurization to Reduce Erector Spinae Loads During Lifting Tasks," In *Proceedings of the North American Congress on Biomechanics* Ed. P. Allard and M. Gagnon. 1986: 87-88.

Kumar, S., Narayan, Y & Zodka, M., "An Electromyographic Study of Unresisted Trunk Rotation with Normal Velocity Among Healthy Subjects," *Spine* 21 (1996): 1500–12.

Macintosh, J.E., Bogduk, N. & Gracovetsky, S., "The Biomechanics of the Thoracolumbar Fascia," *Clinical Biomech* 2 (1987): 78–83.

McGill, S.M. & Norman, R.W., "Potential of Lumbodorsal Fascia Forces to Generate Back Extension Movements During Squat Lifts," *J Biomed Eng* 10 (1988): 312–18.

Morgan, D., "Concepts in Functional Training and Postural Stabilization for the Low-Back-Injured," *Top Acute Care Trauma Rehabil* 2, no. 4 (1988): 8–17.

Tesch, K.M., Dunn, J.S. & Evans, J.H., "The Abdominal Muscles and Vertebral Stability," *Spine* 12 (1987): 501.

Chapter 3

"Disc Herniation in the Athlete," *Sports Med Digest* 17 (1995): 5.

Adams, M.A. & Dolan, P., "Posture and Spinal Mechanisms During Lifting," In *The Integrated Function of the Lumbar Spine and Sacroiliac Joint* Ed. A. Vleeming, V. Mooney, T. Dorman, and C. Snijders. San Diego: Second Interdisciplinary World Congress on Low Back Pain,1995.

Adams, M.A. & Hutton, W.C., "The Relevance of Torsion to the Mechanical Derangement of the Lumbar Spine," *Spine* 6 (1981): 241–48.

Anderson, C.K. & Chaffin, D.B., "A Biomechanical Evaluation of Five Lifting Techniques," *Applied Ergonomics* 17 (1986): 2–8.

Armstrong, C.P. & Blower, A.L., "Non-steroidal Anti-inflammatory Drugs and Life-Threatening Complications of Peptic Ulceration," *Gut* 28 (1987): 527– 32.

Aro, S. & Leino, P., "Overweight and Musculoskeletal Morbidity: A Ten-Year Follow-up," *Int J Obes* 9 (1985): 267–75.

Aspden, R.M., "Intra-abdominal Pressure andIits Role in Spinal Mechanics," *Clinical Biomech* 2 (1987): 168–74.

Bednar, D.A., Orr, F.W. & Simon, G.T., "Observations on the Pathomorphology of the Thoracolumbar Fascia in Chronic Mechanical Back Pain," *Spine* 20 (1995): 1161–64.

Bigos, S., et al., "Acute Low Back Problems in Adults," *Clinical Practice Guideline 14, AHCPR Publication* 95–0642. Rockville, Maryland: AHCPR, 1994.

Boden, S.D., Davis, D.O., Dina, T.S., et al., "Abnormal Magnetic-Resonance Scans of the Lumbar Spine in Asymptomatic Patients," *J Bone Joint Surg* 72 (1990): 40.

Boden, S., et al., "Orientation of the Lumbar Facet Joints: Association with Degenerative Disc Disease," *J Bone Joint Surg* 78-A (1996): 403–11.

Bogduk, N., "The Anatomical Basis for Spinal Pain Syndromes," *JMPT* 18 (1995): 603–5.

Bogduk, N.,"The Lumbar Disc and Low Back Pain," *Neurosurg Clin N Am* 2 (1991): 791–806.

Bogduk, N. & Jull, G., "The Theoretical Pathology of Acute Locked Back: A Basis for Manipulative Therapy," *J Manual Medicine* 1 (1985): 78–82.

Bogduk, N. & Modic, M.T., "Controversy: Lumbar Discography," *Spine* 21 (1996): 402–4.

Bongers, P.M., Hulshof, C.T.J., Dijkstra, L. & Boshuizen, H.C., "Back Pain and Exposure to Whole Body Vibration in Helicopter Pilots," *Ergonomics* 33 (1990): 1007–26.

Bongers, P.M., Boshuizen, H.C., Hulshof, C.T.J. & Koemeester, A.C., "Back Disorders in Crane Operators," *Int Arch Occup Environ Health* 60 (1988):129–37.

Bovenzi, M. & Zadini, A., "Self-Reported Low Back Symptoms in Urban Bus Drivers Exposed to Whole Body Vibration," *Spine* 17 (1992): 10478–59.

Brinckmann P., Biggemann, M. & Hilweg, D., "Fatigue Fracture of Human Lumbar Vertebrae," *Clinical Biomech* 3 , suppl. 1 (1988).

Cady, L.D., et al., "Strength and Fitness and Subsequent Back Injuries in Firefighters," *J Occup Med* 21 (1979): 269–72.

Cailliet, R., *Low Back Pain Syndrome* Philadelphia: F. A. Davis Co., 1988.

Carlson, C.R., et al., "Ambulatory Electromyogram Activity in the Upper Trapezius Region," *Spine* 21 (1996): 595–99.

Cassidy, J.D., "The Pathoanatomy and Clinical Significance of the Sacroiliac Joints," *JMPT* 15 (1992): 41–42.

Cinotti, G., et al., *Sports Med Digest* 18 (August 1996): 89.

Dabbs, V.M. & Dabbs, L.G., "Correlation Between Disk Height Narrowing and Low-Back Pain," *Spine* 15 (1990): 1366.

Deyo, R.A., "Conservative Therapy for Low Back Pain," *JAMA* 250 (1983): 1057–62.

Deyo, R.A., Diehl, A.K. & Rosenthal, M., "How Many Days of Bed Rest for Acute Low Back Pain? A Randomized Clinical Trial," *N Eng J Med 315 (1986): 1064–70.*

Deyo, R.A. & Bass, J.E., "Lifestyle and Low-Back Pain: The Influence of Smoking and Obesity," *Spine* 14 (1989): 501–6.

Don Tigny, R.L., "Function of the Lumbosacral Complex as a Self- Compensating Force Coupled with a Variable, Force-Dependent Transverse Axis: A Theoretic Analysis," *J Man and Manipulative Therapy* 2 (1994): 87–93.

Don Tigny, R.L., "Anterior Dysfunction of the Sacroiliac Joint as a Major Factor in the Etiology of Idiopathic Low Back Pain Syndrome," *Physical Therapy* 70 (1990): 250–62.

Dupuis, H. & Zerlett, G., "Whole Body Vibration and Disorders of the Spine," *Int Arch Occup Environ Health* 59 (1987):323–36.

Farfan, H., et al., "The Effects of Torsion on the Lumbar Intervertebral Joints: The Role of Torsion in the Production of Disc Degeneration," *The Journal of Bone and Joint Surgery* 52A (1970): 496.

Friberg, O., "Clinical Symptoms and Biomechanics of Lumbar Spine and Hip Joint in Leg Length Inequality," *Spine* 8 (1983): 643–50.

Fries, J.F., "Assessing and Understanding Patient Risk" *Scand J Rheumatol* 92, suppl. (1992): 21–24.

Frymoyer, J.W., Newberg, A., Pope, M.H., et al., "Spine Radiographs in Patients with Low-Back Pain: An Epidemiological Study in Men," *J Bone Joint Surg* 66 (1984): 1048.

Frymoyer, J.W., et al., "Epidemiological Study of Acute Herniated Lumbar Intervertebral Discs," *Rheumatol Rehabil* 14 (1975): 144–59.

Gabriel, S.E., Jaakkimainen, L. & Bombardier, C., "Risk for Serious Gastrointestinal Complications Related to Use of Nonsteroidal Anti-inflammatory Drugs: A Meta-analysis," *Ann Int Med* 115 (1991): 787–96.

Garzillo, M.J.D. & Garzillo, T.A.F., "Does Obesity Cause Low Back Pain?" *JMPT* (1994): 17.

Giles, L.G.F., Taylor, J.R. & Cockson, A., "Human Zygapophyseal Joint Synovial Folds," *Acta Anat* 126 (1986): 110–14.

Giles, L.G.F., "Pathoanatomic Studies and Clinical Significance of Lumbosacral Zygapophyseal (Facet) Joints," *JMPT* 15 (1992): 36–40.

Giles, L.G.F. & Harvey, A.R., "Immunohistochemical Demonstration of Nociceptors in the Capsule and Synovial Folds of Human Zygapophyseal Joints," *British J of Rheumatology* 26 (1987): 362–64.

Giles, L.G.F. & Taylor, J.R., "Low Back Pain Associated with Leg Length Inequality," *Spine* 6 (1981): 510–21.

Giles, L.G.F. & Taylor, J.R., "Lumbar Spine Structural Changes Associated with Leg Length Inequality," *Spine* 7 (1982): 159–62.

Giles, L.G.F. & Taylor, J.R., "The Effect of Postural Scoliosis on Lumbar Apophyseal Joints," *Scand J Rheumatol* 13 (1984): 209–20.

Gordon, S.J., Yang, K.H., Mayer, P.J., et al., "Mechanism of Disc Rupture," *Spine* 16 (1991): 450–56.

Gracovetsky, S., Farfan, H. & Helleur, C., "The Abdominal Mechanism," *Spine* 10 (1985): 317–24.

Guyer, R.D., Collier, R., Stith, W.J., et al., "Discitis After Discography," *Spine* 13 (1988): 1532–34.

Hanai, F., Matsui, N. & Hongo, N., "Changes in Responses of Wide Dynamic Range Neurons in the Spinal Horn after Dorsal Root or Dorsal Root Ganglion Compression," *Spine* 21 (1996): 1408–15. Also see the accompanying editorial by Marshall Devor in the same issue, pp. 1414–15. Hanley, E. N. *Clinical Efficacy and Outcome in the Diagnosis and Treatment of Low Back Pain* Ed. J. F. Weinstein. New York: Raven Press, 1992.

Hardcastle, P., Annear, P. & Foster, D., "Spinal Abnormalities in Young Fast Bowlers," *J Bone Joint Surgery* 74-B (1992): 421–25.

Hedberg, G.E., "The Period Prevalence of Musculoskeletal Complaints Among Swedish Professional Drivers," *Scan J Soc Med* 16 (1988): 5–13.

Hirsch, C., Ingelmark, B. & Miller, M., "The Anatomical Basis for Low Back Pain," *Acta Orthop Scand* 33 (1963): 1–17.

Holm, S. & Nachemson, A., "Nutrition Changes in the Canine Intervertebral Disc After Spinal Fusion," *Clin Orthop* 169 (1982): 243–58.

Holmes, J.A., Damaser, M.S. & Lehman, S.L., "Erector Spinae Activation and Movement Dynamics about the Lumbar Spine in Lordotic and Kyphotic Squat-Lifting," *Spine* 17 (1992): 327–34.

Hukins, D.W.L., Kirby, M.C., Sikoryn, T.A., Aspden, R.M. & Cox, A.J., "Comparison of Structure, Mechanical Properties, and Functions of Lumbar Spinal Ligaments," *Spine* 15 (1990): 787–95.

Jackson, R.P., "The Facet Syndrome—Myth or Reality?" *Clin Orthop* 279 (1992): 110.

Jensel, M.C., Brant-Zawadzki, M.N., Obuchowki, N., et al., "Magnetic Resonance Imaging of the Lumbar Spine in People without Back Pain," *N Engl J Med* 2 (1994): 69.

Johnson, K.E., Rosen, I. & Uden, A., "The Natural Course of Lumbar Stenosis," *Clin Orthop* 279 (1992): 82.

Kelsey, J.L. & White, A.A., "Epidemiology and Impact of Low-Back Pain," *Spine* 5 (1980): 133–142.

Kelsey, J.L. & Hardy, R.L., "Driving of Motor Vehicles as a Risk Factor for Acute Herniated Lumbar Intervertebral Disc." *Am J Epidemiol* 102 (1975): 63–73.

Kelsey, J.L., et al., "An Epidemiologic Study of Lifting and Twisting on the Job and Risk for Acute Prolapsed Lumbar Intervertebral Disc," *Journal of Orthopaedic Research* 2 (1984): 61–66.

Koes, B.W., Bouter, L.M., Van Mameren, H., et al., "Randomized Clinical Trial of Manipulative Therapy and Physiotherapy for Persistent Back and Neck Complaints: Results of a One Year Follow-up," *Br Med J* 304 (1992): 601–5.

Krag, M.H., Seroussi, R.E., Wilder, D.G. & Pope, M.H., "Internal Displacement Distribution from In Vitro Loading of Human Thoracic and Lumbar Spinal Motion Segments: Experimental Results and Theoretical Predictions," *Spine* 12 (1987): 1001–7.

Kramer, J., *Intervertebral Disc Disease.* New York: Thieme Medical Publishers, Inc., 1990.

Kristiansson, P., Svardsudd, K. & Von Schoultz, B., "Back Pain During Pregnancy," *Spine* 21 (1996): 702–9.

Kuslich, S.D., Ulstrom, C.L. & Michael, C.J., "The Tissue Origin of Low Back Pain and Sciatica," *Orthop Clin N Am* 22 (1991): 183.

Lantz, C.A., "A Review of the Evolution of Chiropractic Concepts of Subluxation," *Topics in Clinical Chiropractic* 2 (1995): 3.

Larsson, U., Choler, U., Lidstrom, A., et al., "Auto-Traction for Treatment of Lumbago-Sciatica: A Multicentre Controlled Investigation," *Acta Orthop Scan* 51 (1980): 791–98.

Leboeuf-Yde, C., Yashin, A. & Torsten, L., "Does Smoking Cause Low Back Pain? Results from a Population-Based Study," *JMPT* 19 (1996): 99–108.

Magora, A. & Schwartz, A., "Relation Between the Low Back Pain Syndrome and X-Ray Findings: 1. Degenerative Osteoarthritis," *Scand J Rehab Med* 8 (1976): 115–25.

Mayer, T.G., Barnes, D., Kishino, N.D., et al., "Progressive Isoinertial Lifting Evaluation: 1. A Standardized Protocol and Normative Database," *Spine* 13 (1988): 993–97.

McGill, S.M., "Estimation of Force and Extensor Moment Contributions of the Disc and Ligaments at L4/5," *Spine* 13 (1988): 1395.

McGill, S.M. & Brown, S., "Creep Response of the Lumbar Spine to Prolonged Full Flexion," *Clinical Biomech* 7 (1992): 43–46.

McGill, S.M., Seguin, J. & Bennett, G., "Passive Stiffness of the Lumbar Torso About the Flexion-Extension, Lateral Bend and Axial Twist Axes: the Effect of Belt Wearing and Breath Holding," *Spine* 19 (1994): 696–704.

McGill, S.M., Patt, N. & Norman, R.W., "Measurement of the Trunk Musculature Of Active Males Using CT Scan Radiography: Implications for Force and Moment Generating Capacity about the L4/5 Joint," *J Biomech* 21 (1988): 329–41.

McGoey, B., Deitel, M., Saplys, R. & Kliman, M., "Effect of Weight Loss on Musculoskeletal Pain in the Morbidly Obese," *J Bone Joint Surg* 72-B (1990): 322–23.

McKenzie, R.A., *The Lumbar Spine: Mechanical Diagnosis and Therapy.* Waikanae, New Zealand: Spinal Publications, 1981.

Meade, T.W., Dyer, S., Browne, W., et al., "Low Back Pain of Mechanical Origin: Randomized Comparison of Chiropractic and Hospital Outpatient Treatment," *Br Med J* 300 (1990): 1431.

Mooney, V. & Robertson, J., "The Facet Syndrome," *Clin Orthop* 115 (1976): 149–56.

Mundt, D.J., Githens, P.J., White, A.A., et al., "An Epidemiological Study of Non-Occupational Lifting as a Risk Factor for Herniated Lumbar Intervertebral Disc," *Spine* 18 (1993): 595–602.

Nachemson, A., "The Lumbar Spine: An Orthopedic Challenge," *Spine* 1 (1976): 59–71.

Nachemson, A. L., "Newest Knowledge of Low Back Pain," *Clin Orthop* 8 (1992): 279.

Nichols, P.J.R., "Short-Leg Syndrome," *Br Med J* (1960): 1863–65.

Palmer, D.D., *The Science, Art, and Philosophy of Chiropractic.* Portland: Portland Printing House, 1910.

Panjabi, M.M., "The Stabilizing System of the Spine: Part I," *J Spinal Disord* 5 (1992): 383–89.

Parker, L.M., Murrell, S.E., Boden, S.D. & Horton, W.C., "The Outcome of Posterolateral Fusion in Highly Selected Patients with Discogenic Low Back Pain," *Spine* 21 (1996): 1909–17.

Parkola, R., Rytokoski, U. & Kormano, M., "Magnetic Resonance Imaging of the Discs and Trunk Muscles in Patients With Chronic Low Back Pain and Healthy Controlled Subjects," *Spine* 18 (1993): 833.

Postacchini, R., Lami, R. & Pugliese, O., "Familial Predisposition to Discogenic Low-Back Pain: An Epidemiologic and Immunogenetic Study," *Spine* 13 (1988): 1403–6.

Potvin, J.R., Norman, R.W. & McGill, S.M., "Reduction in Anterior Shear Forces on the L4/5 Disc by the Lumbar Musculature." *Clin Biomech* 6 (1991): 88–96.

Rossi, F., "Spondylolysis, Spondylolisthesis, and Sports," *J Sports Med Phys Fitness* 18 (1978): 317.

Saal, J.A., Saal, J.S. & Herzog, R.J., "The Natural History of Lumbar Intervertebral Disc Extrusions Treated Nonoperatively," *Spine* 15 (1990): 683.

Sarno, J., *Healing Back Pain: The Mind-Body Connection.* New York: Warner Books, Inc., 1991.

Schonstrom, N., "Lumbar Spinal Stenosis," In *Physical Therapy of the Low Back* Ed. L. T. Twomey and J. R. Taylor. 2nd ed. New York: Churchill Livingstone, 1994.

Schwarzer, A.C., Aprill, C.N. & Bogduk, N., "The Sacroiliac Joint in Chronic Low Back Pain," *Spine* 20 (1995): 31–37.

Schwarzer, A.C., Aprill, C.N., Derby, N.R., Fortin, J., Kine, G. & Bogduk, N., "The Prevalence and Clinical Features of Internal Disk Disruption in Patients with Chronic Low Back Pain," *Spine* 20 (1995): 1878–83.

Shekelle, P.S., Adams, A.H., Chassin, M.R., Hurwitz, E.L. & Brook, R.H., "Spinal Manipulation for Low Back Pain," *Ann Intern Med* 117 (1992): 590–98.

Sturesson, B., Slevik, G. & Uden, A., "Movements of the Sacroiliac Joints: A Roentgen Stereophotogrammetric Analysis," *Spine* 14 (1989): 162–65.

Svensson, H.O., Vedin, A., Wilhelmsson, C. & Andersson, G.B.J., "Lower Back Pain in Relation to Other Diseases and Cardiovascular Risk Factors," *Spine* 8 (1983): 277–85.

Troup, J.D.G., "Clinical Effects of Shock and Vibration on the Spine," *Clin Biomech* 3 (1988): 227–31.

Twomey, L. & Taylor, J., "Spine Update: Exercise and Spinal Manipulation in the Treatment of Low Back Pain," *Spine* 20 (1995): 617.

Vernon-Roberts, B. & Pirie, C.J., "Healing Trabecular Microfractures in the Bodies of Lumbar Vertebrae," *Ann Rheum Dis* 32 (1973): 406–12.

Videman T., Nurminen, M. & Troup, J.D.G., "Lumbar Spinal Patholgy in Cadaveric Material in Relation to History of Back Pain, Occupations, and Physical Loading." *Spine* 15 (1990): 728–40.

Videman, T., "Connective Tissue and Immobilization: Key Factors in Musculoskeletal Degeneration?" *Clin Orthop* 221 (1987): 26–32.

Waddell, G., "A New Clinical Model for the Treatment of Low-Back Pain," *Spine* 12 (1987): 632–44.

Waddell, G., Main, C.J., Morris, E.W., et al., "Chronic Low Back Pain, Psychological Distress, and Illness Behavior," *Spine* 9 (1984): 209.

Watkins, R., "Lumbar Spine Problems in the Athlete," presented at the American Medical Society for Sports Medicine, Orlando, 1996. Quoted in *Sports Med Digest* 18 (August 1996): 85.

Weber, H., "Lumbar Disc Herniation: A Controlled Prospective Study with Ten Years of Observation," *Spine* 8 (1983): 131–40.

Weinstein, J., Claverie, W. & Gibson, S.S., "The Pain of Discography," *Spine* 13 (1988): 1344.

White, A.A. & Panjabi, M.M., *Clinical Biomechanics of the Spine.* Philadelphia, J. B. Lippincott Co., 1978.

Wiesel, S.E., Tsourmans, N., Feffer, H.L., et al., "A Study of Computer-Assisted Tomography I: The Incidence of Positive CAT Scans in an Asymptomatic Group of Patients," *Spine* 9 (1984): 549.

Wilder, D.G., Pope, M.H. & Frymoyer, J.W., "The Biomechanics of Lumbar Disc Herniation and the Effect of Overload and Instability," *J Spinal Disorders* 1 (1988): 29.

Yahia, L.H., Rhalmi, S., Newman, N., et al., "Sensory Innervation of Human Thoracolumbar Fascia," *Acta Orthop Scand* 63 (1992): 195–97.

Young, D.M., "The Diagnosis of Sacroiliac Sprain: A Review," *Journal of the Am Chiro Assoc* (December 1995): 55.

Zdeblick, T.A., "The Treatment of Degenerative Lumbar Disorders: A Critical Review of the Literature," *Spine* 20 (1995): 127S.

Chapter 4

Biering-Sorensen, F., "Physical Measurements as Risk Indicators for Low Back Trouble Over a One Year Period," *Spine* 9 (1984): 106–19.

Byl, N.N. & Sinnott, P.L., "Variations in Balance and Body Sway in Middle-Aged Adults: Subjects with Healthy Backs Compared with Subjects with Low-Back Dysfunction," *Spine* 16 (1991): 325–30.

Cady, L.D., et al., "Strength and Fitness and Subsequent Back Injuries in Firefighters," *J Occup Med* 21 (1979): 269–72.

Chafin, D.B., Herrin, G.D. & Keyserling, W.M., "Preemployment Strength Testing," *J Occup Med* 67 (1978): 403–408.

Dolan P. & Adams, M.A., "Influence of Lumbar and Hip Mobility on the Bending Stresses Acting on Lumbar Spine," *Clinical Biomech* 8 (1993): 185–92.

Biering-Sorensen, F., "Physical Measurements as Risk Indicators for Low Back Trouble Over a One-Year Period," *Spine* 9 (1984): 106–19.

Freeman, M., Dean, M. & Hanham, I., "The Etiology and Prevention of Functional Instability of the Foot," *J Bone Joint Surg* 47B (1965): 669–77.

Gundewell, B., Liljeqvist, M. & Hansson, T., "Primary Prevention of Back Symptoms and Absence from Work," *Spine* 18 (1993): 587–94.

Hupli, M., Hurri, H., Luoto, S., et al., "Low Synthesis Rate of Type I Procollagen is Normalized During Active Back Rehabillitation," *Spine* 22 (1997): 850–54.

Hilton, R.C., Ball, J. & Ben, R.T., "In Vitro Mobility of the Lumbar Spine," *Ann Rheum Dis* 38 (1979): 378–83.

Hultman, G., Nordin, M., Saraste, H. & Ohlsen, H., "Body Composition, Endurance, Strength, Cross-Sectional Area and Density of Erector Spinae Muscles in Men with and without Low Back Pain," *J Spinal Disorders* 6 (1993): 114–23.

Hides, J.A., Stokes, M.J., Saide, M., Hull, G.A. & Cooper, D.H., "Evidence of Lumbar Multifidus Wasting Ipsilateral to Symptoms in Patients with Chronic Low Back Pain," *Spine* 19 (1994): 165–72.

Janda, V. & Va 'Vrova,' M., "Sensory Motor Stimulation," In *Rehabilitation of the Spine* Ed. C. Liebenson. Baltimore: Williams and Wilkins, 1996.

Janda, V., "Muscles, Central Nervous system Motor Regulation and Back Problems," In *Neurobiologic Mechanisms in Manipulative Therapy* Ed. M. Korr. New York: Plenium Press, 1978.

Jull, G.A. & Janda, V., "Muscles and Motor Control in Low Back Pain: Assessment and Management," In *Physical Therapy of the Low Back* Ed. L. T. Twomey and J. R. Taylor. New York: Churchill Livingstone, 1987.

Kellet, K.M., Kellett, D.A. & L.A. Nordholm., "Effects of an Exercise Program on Sick Leave Due to Back Pain," *Physical Therapy* 71 (1991): 283–91.

Luoto, S., Heliovaara, M., Hurri, H. & Alaranta, H., "Static Back Endurance and the Risk of Low-Back Pain," *Clinical Biomech* 10 (1995): 323–24.

Manniche, C., Lundberg, E., Christensen, I., et al., "Intensive Dynamic Back Exercises for Chronic Low Back Pain: A Clinical Trial," *Pain* 47 (1991): 53–64.

McGill, S., "Low Back Exercises: Prescription for the Healthy Back and When Recovering from Injury," In *American College of Sports Medicine Resource Manual for Guidlelines for Exercise Testing and Prescription* 3rd ed. Philadelphia: Lea and Febiger, forthcoming.

McQuade, K.J., Turner, J.A. & Buchner, D.M., "Physical Fitness and Chronic Low Back Pain," *Clin Orthop Relat Res* 233 (1988): 198–204.

Melin, G., "Correlations of Hip Mobility with Degree of Back Pain and Lumbar Spinal Mobility in Chronic Low-Back Pain Patients," *Spine* 13 (1988): 688–70.

Nordgren, B., Scheile, R. & Linroth, K., "Evaluation and Prediction During Military Field Service," *Scand J Rehab Med* 12 (1980): 1–7.

Nutter, P., "Aerobic Exercise in the Treatment and Prevention of Low Back Pain," *State of the Art Rev Occ Med* 3 (1988): 137–45.

Saal, J.A. & Saal, J.S., "Nonoperative Treatment of Herniated Lumbar Intervertebral Disc with Radiculopathy," *Spine* 14 (1989): 431–37.

Salter, R.B., "The Biologic Concept of Continuous Passive Motion of Synovial Joints," *Clin Orthop* 242 (1989): 12–25.

Takemasa, R., Yamamoto, H. & Tani, T., "Trunk Muscle Strength in and Effect of Trunk Muscle Exercises for Patients with Chronic Low Back Pain," *Spine* 20 (1995): 2522–30.

Twomey, T., Salter, R.B., Keane, G.P. & Saal, J.A., "The Sports Medicine Approach to Occupational Low Back Pain," *W J Medicine* 154 (1991): 526.

Uppal, G.S. & Dillin, W.H., "Aerobic Conditioning," In *The Spine in Sports* Ed. R. G. Watkins. St. Louis: Mosby, 1996.

Videman, T., Sarna, S., Crites-Battie, M., Koskinen, S., Gill, K., Paananen, H. & Gibbons, L., "The Long Term Effects of Physical Loading and Exercise Lifestyles on Back-Related Symptoms, Disability, and Spinal Pathology Among Men," *Spine* 20 (1995): 669–709.

Wilder, D.G., Pope, M.H. & Frymoyer, J.W., "The Biomechanics of Lumbar Disc Herniation and the Effect of Overload and Instability," *J Spinal Disord* 1 (1988): 16–32.

Chapter 5

Adams, M.A., Dolan, P. & Hutton, W.C., "Diurnal Variations in the Stresses on the Lumbar Spine," *Spine* 12 (1987): 130–37.

Bucci, L., *Nutrients Applied to Injury Rehabilitation and Sports Medicine.* Boca Raton: CRC Press, 1995.

Buckwalter, J.A., "Spine Update: Aging and Degeneration of the Human Intervertebral Disc," *Spine* 20 (1995): 1307–14.

Grabiner, B., Liljeqvist, M. & Hansson, T., "Primary Prevention of Back Symptoms and Absence from Work," *Spine* 18 (1993): 587–94.

Hanna, T., *Somatics.* Menlo Park, Ca.: Addison-Wesley Publishing Co., 1988.

Harman, E., "The Biomechanics of Resistance Exercise," In *Essentials of Strength Training and Conditioning* Ed. T. R. Baechle. Champaign, Il.: Human Kinetics, 1994.

Horrigan, J., "Twisting and the Spine," *Ironman Magazine* (June 1991): 80–82.

Magnusson, M.L., Pope, M.H. & Hansson, T., "Does Hyperextension Have an Unloading Effect on the Intervertebral Disc?" *Scand J Rehab Med* 27 (1995): 5–9.

McGill, S.M. & Norman, R.W., "Low Back Biomechanics in Industry: The Prevention of Injury Through Safer Lifting," In *M. Grabiner, Current Issues in Biomechanics* Champaign, Il.: Human Kinetics Publishers, 1992.

Nachemson, A., "The Possible Importance of the Psoas Muscle for Stabilization of the Lumbar Spine," *Acta Orthop Scand* 39 (1968): 47–57.

Stokes, I.A.F., "Axis for Dynamic Measurement of Flexion and Extension Torques about the Lumbar Spine: A Computer Simulation," *Physical Therapy* 67 (1987):1230–33.

Stone, M.H., Chandler, T.J., Conley, M.S., et al., "Training to Muscular Failure: Is It Necessary?" *Strength and Conditioning* (1996): 18: 44–48.

Timm, K.E., "A Randomized-Control Study of Active and Passive Treatments for Chronic Low Back Pain Following L5 Laminectomy," *J Orthop Sports Phys Ther* 20 (1994): 276–86.

Waddell, G., et al., "Chronic Low-Back Pain, Psychologic Distress, and Illness Behavior," *Spine* 9 (1984): 209–13.

Weitz, B., "Minimizing Weight Training Injuries in Bodybuilders and Athletes," *Topics in Clinical Chiropractic* 4 (1997): 46-56.

Ben Weitz, D.C., C.C.S.P., C.S.C.S.

Dr. Ben Weitz is president and director of Weitz Sports Chiropractic and Rehabilitation Center in Santa Monica, CA. Dr. Weitz is a certified chiropractic sports physician as well as a sports and conditioning specialist. He has developed rehabilitative exercise programs for a variety of individuals—professional athletes, recreational athletes, and non-athletes alike.

In addition, Dr. Weitz has provided chiropractic care for numerous professional athletes, including bodybuilders, basketball players, football players, and golfers. He is an avid recreational athlete and has been in private practice for over 10 years.

Dr. Weitz has published articles in scientific journals and is a frequent contributor to various health and fitness magazines.

SOME OF OUR OTHER COURSES:

LEGENDARY ABS GOLD EDITION

After more than 15 years, **Legendary Abs** is still the premiere way to cut up your abs! **Legendary Abs Gold Edition** now gives you the same scorching ab workout as in previous editions—including all the synergistic routines and 10 progressive levels—plus more. We've added over 60% to the book to bring you a comprehensive ab training program for every training goal. You'll get • The complete text from Beyond Legendary Abs, our best-selling performance guide to the **Legendary Abs** routines • New exercises and routines for athletic performance • The new **Legendary Abs** High-Low Nutritional Plan for fat loss...and more! Male or female, athletic or not: whether you're looking for better muscle tone or cut-to-shreds definition, **Legendary Abs Gold Edition** is the fastest, most powerful program you can use! 160 pages.

SECRETS OF ADVANCED BODYBUILDERS

What Legendary Abs does for abdominal conditioning, **Secrets of Advanced Bodybuilders** does for your whole workout! **Secrets** explains how to apply the Synergism Principle to training back, chest, delts, biceps, triceps, quads, and hamstrings. It unlocks the secrets of the Optimum Workout and shows you how to develop the best routines for you—with your particular goals, strengths, and body structure.

Get the ultimate program. Plus, learn...A new back exercise that will pile on the mass and increase power without putting harmful stress on your lower back • A technique for making Leg Extensions 200% more intense by targeting both inner and outer quads • The shift in position that cranks pull-up and pull-down exercises to three times normal intensity • A body weight triceps exercise that will be "a growing experience" even for someone who's been training for years • A body weight lat exercise that will mass up your back faster than you would have believed possible • A special shoulder set that's more effective than most entire delt routines —also— The best way to integrate your other athletic endeavors—running, cycling, stretching, mountain climbing, martial arts, etc.—into your routine to create the optimum overall program • Techniques for maximizing the effectiveness of all exercises you do, not just those in the course...and much, much more! Stop working harder than you need to to get the results you want. Put the **Secrets of Advanced Bodybuilders** to work for you today! 158 pp. Over 300 illustrations.

MIND GAINS

Health For Life brings you a new, effective way to master the psychological tools of peak performance. Based on the techniques which led Eastern Bloc athletes to gold medal after gold medal, combined with the latest in Western sports psychology, **Mind Gains** is your ticket to the last frontier of physical performance.

You'll learn: How to cope with performance anxiety • How to stay motivated to succeed despite injuries, boredom, and other obstacles • How low self-esteem can sabotage your performance, and what you can do about it• How to achieve what psychologists call optimal arousal, a state in which time seems to slow and perfect technique execution occurs with ease • How to tell negative inner voices to shut up.

From proper goal setting to mental imagery rehearsals, you'll discover a wealth of new resources to increase your performance, gains, and personal satisfaction. Get the mental edge with **Mind Gains**! 150 pp., illustrated.

TRANSFIGURE I: FOR THE ULTIMATE BUTTOCKS AND THIGHS

Transfigure I is a revolutionary, high-gear system of buttock and thigh conditioning, keyed to a woman's specific aesthetic goals and based on sound biomechanical principles. Forget doing hundreds of ineffective leg exercises. Get set for the fastest results you've ever experienced, with routines that allow you to take control of your body and create the lean, shapely form you want! **Transfigure I** includes separate routines involving body weight exercise, light resistance exercise—even competition bodybuilding work. Whether you're working for general firmness and tone, or strength and high definition, **Transfigure I** is your formula for the ultimate lower body, in just 9 minutes! 126 pp. Over 200 photographs.

TRANSFIGURE II: FOR THE ULTIMATE UPPER BODY

Part two of our body-sculpting program for women, **Transfigure II** adds the finishing touches to the ultimate physique. It concentrates on two areas that make the biggest difference in the shape and definition of the upper body: the backs of the upper arms and the chest. It also promotes attractive, balanced development of the shoulders, back and biceps. From light-resistance exercises all the way to competition bodybuilding work...you select the intensity that matches your experience and goals. For all-around firmness, tone and shapely definition. 130 pp. Over 100 photographs.

SYNERSHAPE: A SCIENTIFIC WEIGHT LOSS GUIDE

We're surrounded by weight loss myths. Crash diets. Spot reducing. Exotic herbs. Still, most plans fail, and most people who lose weight gain it back again. Is there really an honest, effective solution? Yes! **SynerShape** represents the next generation in awareness of how the body gains and metabolizes fat. It synthesizes the most recent findings on nutrition, exercise, and psychology into a TOTAL program, offering you the tools you need to shape the body you want. **SynerShape** works. Let it work for you! 24 pp. illustrated manual.

THE PSYCHOLOGY OF WEIGHT LOSS

This special program-on-tape picks up where **SynerShape** leaves off. Noted psychologist Carol Landesman explores eating problems and solutions based on the latest research into human behavior and metabolism. Then, through a series of exercises, she helps you begin to heal the emotional conflicts behind your weight problem. **The Psychology of Weight Loss** is a unique program that brings the power of the therapy process into the privacy of your home. A 90-minute guided introspection. On audio cassette.

MAX 0_2: THE COMPLETE GUIDE TO SYNERGISTIC AEROBIC TRAINING

Maximize your aerobic capacity faster and with less work than ever before! **Max 0_2** represents an exciting new breakthrough in aerobic training. It offers a completely new perspective on the combined effect of VO_2 max and lactate threshold—and on the vital role this effect plays in optimum aerobic conditioning.

Learn: How the F.I.T. principle (Frequency, Intensity, and Time) can help you experience the same progress in your cardiovascular training as in other parts of your workout • How to build aerobics into any conditioning program (Bodybuilders: here's the secret to dropping bodyfat without losing muscle mass!) • Benefits and myths of cross-training • How to avoid injuries that can be caused by high-intensity aerobic work • Losing weight • Endurance events • and much, much more! Over 200 pp., illustrated.

THE 7-MINUTE ROTATOR CUFF SOLUTION

Almost everyone who works out experiences some kind of rotator cuff injury during a lifetime of training. Any of these injuries could spell the end of a workout career, but most can be prevented. **The 7-Minute Rotator Cuff Solution** is a quick, simple program to help prevent (or help you recover from) rotator cuff injuries. It explains in detail how the shoulder works, what can go wrong and why, and exactly what to do (and not to do) to stop shoulder problems before they happen. Plus: a simple 7-minute exercise program that can eliminate shoulder pain and restore normal shoulder function in just a few weeks. 144 pp., illustrated.

THE HUMAN FUEL HANDBOOK

Health For Life's guide to peak performance nutrition, written especially for the dedicated athlete. Nutrient by nutrient, you'll discover how protein, carbohydrate, fat, minerals and vitamins function in your body...and why much of what you've heard about these substances is wrong. You'll get the real story on energy production, sports drinks, free-form amino acids, B-15, ginseng, Omega-3, steroid replacements, and much more! Over 300 pages.

SYNERSTRETCH: FOR TOTAL BODY FLEXIBILITY...FAST!

Two programs in one. Both deliver lower- and upper-body flexibility in less than 8 minutes a day! **SynerStretch A** is for you if you need to maintain your flexibility. Originally designed for martial artists, who depend on extreme flexibility, **SynerStretch A** will also help bodybuilders, dancers, and other athletes stay flexible in less than 5 minutes per workout. A great way to end a training session of any kind! **SynerStretch B** is for you if you need to increase your flexibility. Not only does it take less than 8 minutes, but because it makes use of a new, relatively unknown technique (Isometric Agonist Contraction/Relaxation), it eliminates most of the pain usually associated with stretching. It works! When you order **SynerStretch**, you get both programs in one manual. Get loose, and stay loose with **SynerStretch**. 28 pp., illustrated manual. Also available on video.

POWER FOREARMS!

Here at last is a program that specifically targets the hard-to-develop forearm muscles. Like all Health For Life programs, **Power ForeArms!** is based on the Synergism principle and yields maximum results in minimum time. Designed for serious bodybuilders and martial artists, **Power ForeArms!** will help you build strong, solid, massive forearms in just 7 to 12 minutes, twice a week. Give **Power ForeArms!** a try. 32 pp., illustrated manual. Also available on video.

For pricing and order information,
or to receive a FREE copy of the Health For Life Catalog

Call 1-800-874-5339 or write to us at...

Health For Life
8033 Sunset Blvd., Suite 483
Los Angeles, CA 90046-5622